Logic for Lawyers
A Guide to Clear Legal Thinking

Logic for Lawyers
A Guide to Clear Legal Thinking

By Ruggero J. Aldisert
Senior United States Circuit Judge
The United States Court of Appeals
for the Third Circuit

Clark Boardman Company, Ltd.
New York, New York

For Agatha DeLacio Aldisert,
my caring and loving wife.

Copyright 1989 Clark Boardman Company, Ltd.

Library of Congress Cataloging-in-Publication Data

Aldisert, Ruggero J.
    Logic for lawyers: a guide to clear legal thinking.
      p. cm.
    Bibliography: p.
    Includes index.
    ISBN 0-87632-636-X
    1. Law—Methodology. 2. Law—Philosophy. 3.
Judicial process—
    United States. 4. Logic. I. Title.
    K213.A42 1989   340'.1 dc20 89-31818
                                  CIP

About the Author

Ruggero J. Aldisert, Senior United States Circuit Judge, is the former Chief Judge of the United States Court of Appeals for the Third Circuit. Prior to his appointment to the federal appellate bench in 1968, Judge Aldisert had extensive experience in Pittsburgh as a trial lawyer and as a Pennsylvania Common Pleas Court Judge. Since taking senior status in 1987, Judge Aldisert has continued to sit frequently with the Third Circuit, and by designation with other federal courts of appeal.

Judge Aldisert is a prominent author and teacher. His book, *The Judicial Process,* is widely used in law schools and is the standard text for continuing education programs for the appellate judiciary. A well-known contributor to legal periodicals, he has written on a variety of topics. Some of his works have been translated for publication in European legal journals.

Judge Aldisert served for twenty years as an adjunct professor at the University of Pittsburgh Law School and is a highly respected leader of seminars for newly selected United States circuit judges and state supreme court justices. He has lectured extensively at law schools and before bar, judicial, and academic groups both here and in Europe. He lives in Santa Barbara, California with his wife, Agatha. The Aldiserts have three grown children.

Foreword

This is a book about legal reasoning or legal logic. While not challenging Justice Holmes' classic statement that "The life of the law has not been logic; it has been experience," it offers telling arguments that legal reasoning or legal logic may play an equal or even more significant role in the life of the law.

The book is written particularly for judges, lawyers, and law students. It may seem strange that it is apparently the first book to address that subject purposely directed to judges, lawyers, and law students. Judge Aldisert does not suggest the need for any mandatory rules governing a particular form of opinion writing by judges or advocacy by lawyers. His emphasis is upon the need to develop guidelines, and he offers some. He brings to his proposals thirty years of judicial experience as a federal and state judge and twenty years experience as a law teacher. I am sure that he welcomes debate as to the soundness of the elements of his proposed guidelines—his aim is to advance understanding by bench and bar of the significance of legal reasoning in opinion writing and in advocacy. He believes his message is of special importance to beginning law students whom he cautions "from your first day in law school, that day of profound bewilderment, continuing through your career as a lawyer or judge . . . you are enveloped by that misty, murky phenomenon we call legal reasoning. . . . It is taught through a ritual of fire, charitably called the Socratic Method. The bane of all law students, the method is especially wrenching during the first year. It is a confusing experience because most students, frankly, do not know what the professor is driving at. . . . Let's face it, the system causes frustration, insecurity, embarrassment and many unpleasant hours." He strongly believes that legal reasoning is a subject in critical need of explanation during the abrupt transition in the reasoning process required of a college graduate upon entering law school. But he also believes his message can be of great assistance to judges and practicing lawyers.

Judge Aldisert deals comprehensively and thoroughly with every aspect of legal reasoning. He explains in his broad strokes the basics of logic and its application to legal thinking in order to have us understand the mental processes we use in "thinking like a lawyer." His axiom is "that for the law to be respected it must embody reason, and that no legal argument can be accepted unless based on the canons of legal thinking." He introduces us to the differences between deductive and inductive reasoning, and the Socratic Method; he also discusses at length reasoning and the common-law tradition, elements of legal thinking, fallacies to avoid, and much else. He particularly urges that we recognize the importance of legal reasoning by analogy, for, he insists, the "importance of legal reasoning by analogy cannot be overstated. It is the heart of the study of law; it lies at the heart of the Socratic Method."

A distinguished authority has cogently observed that:

> For centuries mankind has discussed the nature of the law. In one way or another, it touches every citizen of every nation. The contact may be pleasant or unpleasant, tangible or intangible, direct or indirect, but it is nonetheless a constant force in the lives of people everywhere on the globe. It is essential that we have some understanding of its nature and the human beings who interpret and administer it. [1]

This book is a major contribution to appreciation of that truth. All judges, lawyers, and law students will profit greatly by reading it.

William J. Brennan, Jr.
Associate Justice
Supreme Court of the United States

Washington, D.C.
June, 1989

[1] Henry J. Abraham, *The Judicial Process* 4 (4th ed. 1980).

Preface

I'm still not sure what triggered my research into the elements of legal reasoning. Certainly, by the time I became a Pennsylvania trial judge in 1961, I had begun to structure a method to analyze briefs and oral arguments, and had defined and refined some ideas for writing opinions. Pennsylvania required trial judges to write an opinion in every case that was appealed, a practice still not required for federal judges some thirty years later.

As I read through the briefs, I sought to find the squeaky clean order that was drummed into us in undergraduate writing classes: theme, topic sentence for each point, and supporting data. But alas, a gigantic slip appeared between the college courses' lip and the brief writers' cup. In too many cases, the much desired logical order was elusive or nonexistent.

At about the same time, while teaching at the University of Pittsburgh's law school, I discovered that students did not fare much better than lawyers. In class they were adept at asserting conclusions, yet unable to explain step-by-step how they reached those conclusions.

When I became a federal appellate judge and realized that the Courts of Appeals' written opinions are the final word in 99 percent of all federal cases, my interest in legal reasoning intensified. At the same time, I was crushed to discover that appellate briefs were not the pristine models of logical order I had hoped for.

However, I did not begin a serious study of legal logic until the early seventies, when I led a seminar in judicial opinion writing at the Institute of Judicial Administration's Senior Judge Seminars at New York University. It was then that I realized that there was no, repeat no, book strictly devoted to legal reasoning for law students, lawyers, or judges. Even more unfortunate, logician's textbooks seemed mired in exotic formulae, symbolic logic, quantification theories, diagram techniques, and probability calculus, certainly not designed to captivate law students, let alone the typical lawyer or judge.

So, I trudged along, photocopying an article or a book excerpt here and there, collecting materials, and relating my academic research to ideas accumulated from my experience as a lawyer, trial judge, and appellate judge. I gradually developed some satisfactory presentations for the NYU seminars, my Pitt law school classes, and also for the Federal Judicial Center's seminars for new circuit judges, a project that I chaired for about five years. At last, I was able to distill my materials and collate what I believed served as a guide to legal reasoning. I should not have been surprised that my interest in learning the rudiments of legal logic was shared by the profession's two extremes—judges and law students. The judges sought to avoid having dissenters or commentators criticize their opinions as "flawed reasoning"; the students wanted some help in surviving the trauma caused by drenching exposures to the Socratic method.

After I stepped down from my administrative chores as the Third Circuit's Chief Judge, I found the time to prepare a formal lecture on legal logic. The lecture became too cumbersome, so I started a law review article, but that also became unmanageable. This book is the result.

Whom is it for? It's for students. It covers a subject in critical need of explanation during the abrupt transition in the reasoning process required of a college graduate upon entering law school. Law students of the first through third years will benefit from the book. So will undergraduates who plan to enter law school or take graduate courses which involve problem solving by the case method.

Certainly, the book should assist law professors as they strive to produce reasoned thinking in their students. The benefits in every course utilizing the Socratic method are obvious. Moreover, it should be important in all orientation to legal methods and legal writing courses.

The book's advantage to the practicing lawyer is self-evident. It is as much a checklist for clear legal thinking as it is a guide for the conduct of a case. Courtroom dynamics dictate that when a judge rules, there are winners and losers. When based solely on the facts and the law—matters beyond the control of the lawyers—a loss, though never pleasant, can be acceptable to both lawyer and client. But when the loss is based on a court's public declaration that a lawyer's argument flies in the face of reason, the result can never be acceptable. Even though principled and sound in logic, an argument can still be wrong, but an unprincipled and unsound argument can never be right. This book proceeds from the axiom that for the law to be respected, it must embody reason, and that no legal argument can be acceptable unless based on the canons of logical thinking. It is designed to be a lawyer's tool—to ensure soundness in one's own arguments and to expose structural or material flaws in those of adversaries.

The book should also prove extremely helpful to judges. It addresses the concerns expressed by Illinois Chief Justice Walter V. Schaefer "that an opinion which does not within its own confines exhibit an awareness of relevant considerations, whose premises are concealed, or whose logic is faulty is not likely to enjoy either a long life or the capacity to generate offspring." It will enable judges to examine precedents, briefs, and oral arguments more precisely and to write leaner and crisper opinions, those critically important "performative utterances" that promulgate case law and affect today's society so very much.

I am indebted to many. Through their writings, I have become acquainted over the years with our great logicians. I make generous reference to their works: Joseph G. Brennan, John C. Cooley, Irving M. Copi, James Edwin Creighton, Ralph M. Eaton, W. Jevons, Raymond J. McCall, William S. and Mabel Lewis Sahakian, L.S. Stebbing, and Paul E. Treusch. In my early days at the law, I became exposed to the wisdom of John Dewey, Professor of Philosophy at Columbia. I continue to read and reread him. David H. Fischer has proved that you can have a sense of humor and still be a great historian. I have learned much in the field of legal reasoning from Dean (and former Attorney General) Edward H. Levi of the University of Chicago and have studied the fine contributions of Steven J. Burton, Martin P. Golding, and Neil MacCormick.

I thank John D. Goetz for his devoted research assistance in the early stages of this project; Catherine Hill for her excellent contributions to the final draft; and Susan M. von Frausing-Borch for her skill in transforming a battered handwritten manuscript into a clean transcript.

And finally, I acknowledge a debt to Caitlin Scully for her profound talents in editing all drafts of the book.

Ruggero J. Aldisert
Senior United States Circuit Judge

Santa Barbara, California
June, 1989

Summary of Contents

Table of Contents

TABLE OF CONTENTS

LOGIC FOR LAWYERS

There is in fact a true law—namely, right reason—which is in accordance with nature, applies to all men, and is unchangeable and eternal.

—Cicero, *Republic,* III, 22.

CHAPTER 1

Introduction

From your first day in law school, that day of profound bewilderment, continuing through your career as lawyer or judge, and I suppose, until the last day that you serve as a United States Supreme Court Justice, you are enveloped in that misty, murky phenomenon we call legal reasoning. Law students, at least most of those who graduate, learn this process—learn it, that is, with varying degrees of comprehension. It is taught through a ritual of fire, charitably called the Socratic method. Professor Kingsfield's line in *The Paper Chase* properly intimidates the first year law student on the first day: "You come here with your skull full of mush and our job is to make you think like a lawyer."

Some never master "thinking like a lawyer" even though they graduate, pass the bar exam, and become financially successful attorneys. But even those who master the technique of legal reasoning are not always certain what it is. Sure, they learn how to do it, some of it. They pick up the idiosyncratic signals of a given professor and learn his or her playbook. Eventually, they learn how to go through the process, and occasionally, they learn why we do it. But many times students, and unfortunately, even lawyers and judges, do not know exactly what is being done. They learn the exercise, they go through the motions, but most are a little shy on theory.

I know this from much personal experience—almost thirty years as a state trial and federal appellate judge, planning and teaching seminars for state and federal appellate courts, and twenty years as an adjunct law professor with administrative responsibilities at a prominent law

1

school. Moreover, my views are shared by the few commentators who have written in this field. Professor Steven I. Burton observes that "it is remarkable how few books have been written to explain directly how lawyers reason. It is more remarkable how few such efforts are directed at beginning law students, who find it so frustrating to learn how to 'think like a lawyer.'" [1] Professor Jack L. Landau complains:

> The idea of teaching traditional logic to law students does not seem to be very popular. Not one current casebook on legal method, legal process, or the like contains a chapter on logic. Only one text on legal writing, by Brand and White, contains even a list of common informal fallacies. [2]

This book is a modest attempt to fill that void. It is directed to "the what" of legal reasoning, or, if you will, legal logic, a term I use interchangeably with "legal reasoning." My purpose here is to explain, in very broad strokes, the basics of logic and its application to legal thinking, to describe the mental processes we utilize in "thinking like a lawyer." The purpose, quite frankly, is to get you thinking about thinking.

I have sought to illustrate the components of legal logic with excerpts from published judicial opinions. I must confess in advance that many examples are drawn from my own opinions. This was not intentional. I would have much preferred to draw examples from a broader spectrum of cases. But, alas, it is the happenstance that not many judges place a label on the particular element of logic involved. Too often, judges—like lawyers, law professors, and law review writers—use the cop-out phrase "flawed reasoning." This trite phrase means nothing. It does not indicate whether the criticism is of the choice of a controlling legal precept, its interpretation, its application of the facts, or is a signal that a formal or material fallacy is present. I hope that in time this will change and that future briefs and opinions will be more specific.

[1] S. Burton, *An Introduction to Law and Legal Reasoning* 1 (1985).

[2] Landau, "Logic for Lawyers," 13 Pac. L.J. 59, 60 (1981) (footnotes omitted) (citing N. Brand & J. White, *Legal Writing: The Strategy of Persuasion* (1976)).

This book is not an introduction to legal theory or juris-prudence. It deals only with logic in the law. It will define and describe the components of inductive reasoning, its main ramparts of specific instances—inductive generaliza-tion and the method of analogy. It will trace the role of these components in creating legal rules and transforming a se-ries of rules into a broader legal precept, which we some-times call a legal principle. It will explain their relationship to the common law doctrine of precedent.

It will describe deductive reasoning and how the selec-tion of the major premise in the deductive syllogism is criti-cal, whether that premise comes to us from a statute or was developed as judge-made law. It will outline the rules of the syllogism and describe what happens when they are breached, that is, when fallacies of form creep up on the best of us. But adherence to formalities is not enough. We must also learn how to avoid material fallacies.

There is no academy award for knowing or adhering to formal or material correctness. We all may reason well without knowing a single rule of syllogism or, conversely, know all the details of logic and still be an inept lawyer or judge. The payoff in any given case is whether you win or lose. The payoff is not measured by style or grace as with a Natalia Makarova or a Mikhail Baryshnikov. Instead you get prizes for winning, whether it's the 100-yard dash, the quarter-mile, or, in some instances, as in some antitrust cases, the marathon.

I am aware of the criticisms suggesting that logic has no place in legal reasoning because logic is concerned with form and not truth, and because the same set of facts may yield any number of perfectly logical conclusions. But these are only superficial observations. No one is suggesting that briefs can be written, arguments made, and cases decided solely by reference to the canons of logic. Were this so, the legal profession would simply move to analysis by comput-er, because the computer is the paradigm of formal logic. Value judgments reflecting the views of advocates and judg-es form the critical decisional points in the law. Rules of logic do not make these decisions; they are simply means to implement them. When these judgments are made, the formal reasoning process sets in to test the validity of the

LOGIC FOR LAWYERS

propositions constituting the argument. Criticisms of fealty to logical order "are not designed in large measure to remove logic from legal reasoning but to remove *bad* logic from legal reasoning." [3]

My thesis is that we might all be better lawyers (and, of course, better students) if we understood the rules of logic instead of simply memorizing some of the steps. Judges, too, could judge more fairly, and therefore better, and publish more convincing opinions. It's great to play the piano without being able to read music, but unless you're an Irving Berlin, you're not going to reach your full potential by merely memorizing tunes that you've heard somewhere before.

A specific knowledge of the canons of reasoning enables one to discover more readily where the fallacy of a misleading argument lies. Without professing to guard us infallibly from error, logic familiarizes us with the rules and canons to which correct reasoning processes must conform, and with the hidden fallacies and pitfalls to which such processes are commonly exposed. Among the obvious benefits to be derived from a careful study of logic is a facility in studying law, in detecting error in the reasoning process, in learning how to avoid errors, and in thinking about difficult matters with clearness and consistency—a capacity much rarer, even among we members of the legal profession, than is commonly suspected. [4] The function of logical legal reasoning goes beyond the efficient application of legal precepts; it goes to the very formation of those precepts in the common law tradition.

We all know "the why" of logic in the law. Justice Felix Frankfurter said it best on his retirement after twenty-three years on the Supreme Court: "Fragile as reason is and limited as law is as the expression of the institutionalized medium of reason, that's all we have standing between us and the tyranny of mere will and the cruelty of unbridled, unprincipled, undisciplined feeling." [5] We also know the test for a good legal argument or brief. It comes from what I call the Harry Jones/Roscoe Pound test for a "good" decision: "[H]ow thoughtfully and disinterestedly the Court

[3] *Id.* at 63.
[4] *See* Comment, "Logic and Law," 3 Marq. L. Rev. 203, 204 (1919).
[5] As quoted in the New York Herald Tribune, August 30, 1962.

4

weighed the conflicting social interests involved in the case and how fair and durable its adjustment of the interest-conflicts promised to be." [6] You cannot advocate or pronounce a position that is "fair and durable" unless formal rules of thought go into the process. We cannot have decisions by judicial fiat alone. Nor, in our common-law system, can we have court decisions like a double special super-saver airline ticket; good for passage on this flight on this date only.

What I propose in these pages is to describe the formal logic processes used in the common-law tradition. I will explain the difference between reasons and reasoning. I will identify the twin processes of inductive and deductive reasoning, and how they are used and sometimes abused. I will discuss logical forms. I will show how categorical premises are identified or created either properly as universals or improperly as particulars; how this process becomes critical in solving problems; how fragile becomes the legitimacy of such premises when they are improperly fashioned by the fallacy of hasty generalization and the converse fallacy of accident; how major or minor premises sometimes become illicit; how in hypothetical propositions the conclusion sometimes becomes skewed by not properly affirming the antecedent and instead affirming the consequent; and how the end may sometimes be legitimate but the means most tainted. I will draw upon many cases to demonstrate either fealty to, or disrespect of, logical form.

But form is only part of the problem. I'll also take a look at those material fallacies that somehow sneak up on us. Certainly, I will address the familiar non sequitur, post hoc ergo propter hoc, and petitio principii (begging the question), but there are also other swamplands into which we are tempted—hasty generalizations and faults in analogy where positive resemblances are not strong enough or negative resemblances are ignored.

I make no pretense that this book purports to be a comprehensive survey of logic, or even to provide a comprehensive introduction to the subject. Here you will find none of

[6] Jones, "An Invitation to Jurisprudence," 74 Colum. L. Rev. 1023, 1029 (1974).

the "complicated symbolic perambulations" [7] so characteristic of the esoteric world of modern logicians. This book is merely a guide, a guide for students and practitioners of the law. It seeks to tread only limited terrain. It traverses only the high peaks of logical reasoning without endeavoring to describe the very slippery slopes of the peaks, or the valleys and crevices that form the wilderness of the logician's world. Only elementary concepts with illustrations from case law are necessary for our purposes. [8]

This book does not purport to be a logician's treatise on legal reasoning. Rather, it is a snapshot of the logic of the law taken by a student of the judicial process, with many years' experience—experience on both sides of the bench and on either side of the classroom lectern. My view is not intended to be comprehensive. It focuses only on certain features that may be helpful to those who study and practice law. Although much current teaching in logic classes is entirely too cumbersome for our purposes here, certain techniques—deduction, induction (with its concomitants, analogy and generalized induction), and avoidance of formal and material fallacies can be explained—explained without a formal logic study prerequisite. These techniques directly bear on the legal reasoning process. As one experienced in teaching both students and new appellate judges, I am convinced that these techniques can improve the quality of reasoning by developing important thinking skills. But before entering upon the specifics of logic in the law, we must start with the rudiments of our common-law tradition.

---

[7] Landau, *supra* note 2, at 61.
[8] Many good writings in introductory logic exist in the literature. *See, e.g.,* J. Brennan, *A Handbook of Logic* (1957); J. Cooley, *A Primer of Formal Logic* (1942); I. Copi, *Introduction to Logic* (7th ed. 1986); J. Creighton, *An Introductory Logic* (1898); R. Eaton, *General Logic, An Introductory Survey* (1931); W. Jevons, *Elementary Lessons in Logic: Deductive and Inductive* (1870); R. McCall, *Basic Logic* (2d ed. 1952); W. Sahakian & M. Sahakian, *Ideas of the Great Philosophers* (1966); L. Stebbing, *A Modern Introduction to Logic* (6th ed. 1948).

CHAPTER 2

Reasoning and the Common-Law Tradition

What is the common law, the basis of the Anglo-American system of justice? Familiarly, it is known for its jurisprudence, for a system of legal precepts that emerge from court decisions. In the common-law countries today, governing substantive law emanates, first, from statutes enacted by a legislative body and, in the case of the United States and its constituent states, from the text of the federal and state constitutions, and second, from rules of law distilled from judicial decisions in cases and controversies. The particular body of law emanating from court decisions is known as the common law. In this respect, common-law countries differ from the civil law countries of Europe and Latin America, where, in theory, the source of law is limited to codes and statutes.

"Common law" also refers to a specific judicial process, known as the common-law tradition. In our discussion of legal reasoning, we shall address common law in the sense of process and tradition.

Unity of law throughout a jurisdiction and flexibility to incorporate developing legal precepts characterize this tradition. But our tradition is more than unity and the capacity to assimilate. Also at work is gradualness. Holmes noted that the great growth of the common law came about incrementally. [1] The common law, like progress, "creeps from point to point, testing each step," [2] and is, most characteristically, a system built by gradual accretion from the resolu-

[1] Holmes, "The Path of the Law," 10 Harv. L. Rev. 457, 468 (1897).
[2] A. Whitehead, *Adventures of Ideas* 24 (1956).

7

tion of specific problems. The sources of decision are *rules* of law in the narrow sense—rules of specific cases, "precepts attaching a definite detailed legal consequence to a definite, detailed state of facts." [3] These precepts provide "fairly concrete guides for decision geared to narrow categories of behavior and prescribing narrow patterns of conduct." [4] The courts fashion *principles* from a number of rules of decision, in a process characterized by experimentation. Rules of case law are, at common law, treated not as final truths, "but as working hypotheses, continually retested in those great laboratories of the law, the courts of justice." [5]

The heart of the common-law tradition is adjudication of specific cases. [6] Case-by-case development allows experimentation because each rule is reevaluated in subsequent cases to determine if it did or does produce a fair result. If the rule operates unfairly, it can be modified. The modification does not occur at once, "for the attempt to do absolute justice in every single case would make the development and maintenance of general rules impossible; but if a rule continues to work injustice, it will eventually be reformulated." [7] The genius of the common law is that it proceeds empirically and gradually, testing the ground at every step, and refusing, or at any rate evincing an extreme reluctance, to embrace broad theoretical principles.

The common-law method has been described as one of "Byzantine beauty," a method of "reaching what instinctively seem[s] the right result in a series of cases, and only later (if at all) enunciating the principle that explains the

[3] Pound, "Hierarchy of Sources and Forms in Different Systems of Law," 7 Tul. L. Rev. 475, 482 (1933).

[4] Hughes, "Rules, Policy, and Decision Making," 77 Yale L.J. 411, 419 (1968).

[5] M. Smith, *Jurisprudence* 21 (1909).

[6] For a discussion of the role of rationality in adjudication, see Fuller, "The Forms and Limits of Adjudication," 92 Harv. L. Rev. 353, 365-72 (1978). According to Fuller, adjudication is a device that gives formal and institutional expression to reasoned argument in human affairs. It assumes a burden of rationality not borne by other social processes. A decision that is the product of reasoned argument must be prepared to meet the test of reason.

[7] M. Smith, *supra* note 5.

patterns—a sort of connect-the-dots exercise." [8] Adherence
to the rules of formal logic and legal reasoning are absolutes
in this exercise. "Connecting the dots" is but a shorthand
way of describing inductive reasoning. The "dots" represent
holdings of individual cases, each announcing a specific consequence for a specific set of facts. They are "connected" by
techniques of induction for the purpose of fashioning broader precepts. Those techniques, which we will study in depth,
include the use of enumeration of specific instances of like
situations, and the use of analogy, where resemblances are
meticulously compared.

Precepts that are broader than narrow rules are called
legal principles. These principles—precepts covering more
generalized factual scenarios—are assembled from publicly
stated reasons justifying rules formulated in previously decided cases. Formulation of a principle is a gradual process,
shaped from actual incidents in social, economic, and political experience. It is a process in which countervailing rights
are challenged, evaluated, synthesized, and adjudicated on
a case-by-case basis, in the context of an adversary proceeding before a fact-finder in a court of law. For every rule at
common law there is a publicly stated reason, the ratio decidendi. And for each principle that slowly emerges, there is
a solid base of individual rules from particular cases and
from the reasons given to support the decisions in those
cases.

Common-law reasoning should not be characterized as
merely inductive. It is more than a congeries of fact patterns converging to compel an induced conclusion. Rather,
the reasoning process is both inductive and deductive. It re-
sembles the ebb and flow of the tide. A principle is induced
from a line of specific, reasoned decisions and, once identified, becomes the major premise from which a conclusion
may be deduced in the case at hand. The problem of common-law adjudication, in John Dewey's formulation, is that

[8] Ely, "The Supreme Court, 1977 Term—Foreword: On Discovering
Fundamental Values," 92 Harv. L. Rev. 5, 32 (1978) (citing Amsterdam,
"Perspectives of the Fourth Amendment," 58 Minn. L. Rev. 349, 351-52
(1974)); see also Holmes, "Codes and the Arrangement of the Law," 5 Am.
L. Rev. 1 (1870), reprinted in, "Early Writings of O.W. Holmes, Jr.," 44
Harv. L. Rev. 725, 725 (1931).

of finding "statements of general principle and of particular fact that are worthy to serve as premises." [9] By means of a value judgment, the common-law judge chooses these principles as controlling legal precepts, and then structures the major premises that lead to conclusions in the case at hand. To do this, he uses "a logic relative to consequences rather than to antecedents." [10] Use of this logic in the common-law tradition facilitates the gradual development of legal principles.

Another important characteristic of the common-law tradition is that it is fashioned by lawyers and judges from actual events that have raised issues for decision. It emerges as a by-product of the major function of the courts—dispute settling, the adjustment of a specific conflict between or among the parties. Harlan Fiske Stone emphasized that a "[d]ecision [draws] its inspiration and its strength from the very facts which frame the issues for decision." [11] By contrast, legislative lawmaking is not a subordinate effort. To a legislator, the law is not a by-product; it is the primary endeavor. Statutes are enacted as general rules to control future conduct, not to settle a specific dispute from past experience.

The common-law decisional process starts with the finding of facts in a dispute by a fact-finder, be it a jury, judge, or administrative agency. Once the facts are ascertained, the court compares them with fact patterns from previous cases and decides if there is sufficient similarity to warrant applying the rule of an earlier case to the facts of the present one. The judicial process culminates in a narrow decision confined to the facts before the court. Any portion of a judicial opinion that concerns an issue beyond the precise facts of the case is obiter dictum.

The common law is judge-made. Harlan Fiske Stone called it "the law of the practitioner rather than the philosopher." [12] The judge deciding the individual case is the centerpiece of the common-law tradition. As Stone stat-

[9] Dewey, "Logical Method and Law," 10 Cornell L.Q. 17 (1924).
[10] Id.
[11] Stone, "The Common Law in the United States," 50 Harv. L. Rev. 4, 6 (1936).
[12] Id.

10

ed, "He, not the legislator or the scholar, creates the common law." [13]

The difference between the common law and the law of the European continent and Latin America, known as the civil law, can be understood by recognizing the distinctive hierarchical disciplines of the two systems. In the civil law countries, the legislative codes are the sole sources of decision; theoretically, in every case, recourse must be made to the language of the code. But in common-law countries, the concept of stare decisis governs. Stare decisis commands that lower courts follow decisions of higher courts in the same judicial hierarchy. The tradition also demands that the most recent higher court decision be followed, regardless of whether the original precept stems from statutory law or from case law. In the United States, unity of judicial action within a given jurisdiction is ensured by the rule that a court may not deviate from precedents established by its hierarchical superior.

Cardozo's 1921 observations in *The Nature of the Judicial Process* [14] described the fundamental characteristics of the common-law tradition. They remain true today and provide an excellent summary of what we have been discussing. First, the tradition seeks and generally produces uniformity of law throughout the jurisdiction. Second, it produces decisions enunciating a narrow rule of law covering a detailed and real fact situation. Third, principles develop gradually as the courts reconcile a series of narrow rules emanating from prior decisions. Fourth, the common-law tradition produces judge-made law for the practitioner, not for the philosopher or academician. Fifth, lower courts operating in the tradition are bound by decisions of hierarchically superior courts.

Common law is case law of the specific instance. It is law created by a process of reasoning, an exercise that combines legal philosophy, a constantly expanding body of case law, statutes comprising the jurisprudence of a given state or the federal government, and a profound respect for logical form and critical analysis.

[13] *Id.*
[14] B. Cardozo, *The Nature of the Judicial Process* (1921).

11

PRECEDENT

Precedent is the basic ingredient of the common-law tradition. It is a narrow rule that emerges from a specific fact situation. One court has defined a precedent as follows:

> The essence of the common-law doctrine of precedent or *stare decisis* is that the rule of the case creates a binding legal precept. The doctrine is so central to Anglo-American jurisprudence that it scarcely need be mentioned let alone discussed at length. A judicial precedent attaches a specific legal consequence to a detailed set of facts in an adjudged case or judicial decision, which is then considered as furnishing the rule for the determination of a subsequent case involving identical or similar material facts and arising in the same court or a lower court in the judicial hierarchy. [15]

A rule, then, is a normative legal precept containing both specific facts and a specific result. In contrast, a principle emerges from a line of decisions as a broad statement of reasons for those decisions. It is important to understand that a single court decision cannot give birth to an all-inclusive principle.

Formulation of a broad principle from a single case decision exemplifies the material fallacy of hasty generalization, as we will discuss later in detail. Dean Pound warned of the danger of hasty generalization:

> You cannot frame a principle with any assurance on the basis of a single case. It takes a long process of what Mr. Justice Miller used to call judicial inclusion and exclusion to justify you in being certain that you have hold of something so general, so universal, so capable of dealing with questions of that type that you can say here is an authoritative starting point for legal reasoning in all analogous cases.
>
> . . . A single decision as an analogy, as a starting point to develop a principle, is a very different thing from the decision on a particular state of facts which announces a rule. When the court has that same state of facts before it, unless there is some very controlling reason, it is expected to adhere to the former decision. But when it [goes] further and endeavors to formulate a principle, *stare decisis* does not

[15] Allegheny Gen. Hosp. v. NLRB, 608 F.2d 965, 969-70 (3d Cir. 1979).

mean that the first tentative gropings for the principle . . . by this process of judicial inclusion and exclusion, are of binding authority. [16]

Much difficulty results from a confusion between "principled decision making" and decision making that purports to prescribe law for circumstances far beyond the facts before the court. When a specific holding of a case is suddenly anointed with the chrism of "principle," it has a very real effect on the doctrine of stare decisis. There is always the danger that a commentator or a subsequent opinion writer, either in the same court or another, will elevate the decision's naked holding to the dignity of a legal "principle," and attribute to that single decision a precedential breadth never intended. Such an act may confuse the court's dispute-settling role with its responsibility for institutionalizing the law. The common-law tradition, as I said before, is preeminently a system built up by the gradual accretion of special instances. The accretion is not gradual if an improper dimension is given to a specific instance.

Every holding of every decision does not deserve the black-letter law treatment that some judges or commentators wish to give it. If case law is to develop properly in the common-law tradition, the effect of specific instances, the rules of law in the narrow, Poundian sense, must be given proper weight—but only proper weight. Describing a rule of law as a principle or a doctrine interferes with that proper weight. It puts a jural butcher's thumb on the scale. Thus, the expression, "it is settled that," in a treatise, brief, or court opinion, should indicate a line of decisions supporting the statement, not simply a single decision from a favorite jurist.

ROLE OF LOGIC

It is essential to understand the sophisticated nuances of logic in the law employed in the common-law tradition. Rules of logic are only a means to the end in the law. They are implements—techniques to encourage, if not guarantee,

---

[16] Pound, "Survey of Conference Problems," 14 U. Cin. L. Rev. 324, 330-31 (1940).

acceptable supporting reasons for the final decision in a case, a decision that constitutes a legal rule. Putting aside constitutional law, in our tradition, legal precepts spring from two sources: legislative statutes and court decisions. These precepts are currency of equal value, but there is an important distinction. The legislature may promulgate a statute without offering one word of explanation or reason for it, and the statute will be respected until it is repealed. The same is not true of case law. Case law stands or falls solely on the reasons articulated to justify it. There can be legislative fiat, but not judicial fiat. Reason justifies the legal rule emanating from a court decision. Where stops the reason, there stops the rule.

Certainly, Holmes was correct when he told us, "The life of law has not been logic: it has been experience." [17] Although formal logic is one of the important means to the ends of law, formal logic is not the end itself. Professor Harry W. Jones has said: "[T]he durability of a legal principle, its reliability as a source of guidance for the future, is determined far more by the principle's social utility, or lack of it, than by its verbal elegance or formal consistence with other legal precepts." [18] But the statements of Holmes and Jones must not be taken out of context. They were stated as appeals that the law adjust to changing social conditions—that we should not be bound by rigid legal precepts that were once justified by good reasons but are no longer viable in a changing society. The appeals did not go unheeded. From what was once a rigid jurisprudence of conceptions fixed in a kind of jural cement has emerged a relatively new phenomenon in the life of the American law.

As the last century came to a close, Roscoe Pound decried excessive rigidity in American decision-making processes. He described our system at the time as one of conceptual jurisprudence, a slavish adherence to elegantia juris, the symmetry of law, and suggested that it too closely resembled the rigid German Begriffsjurisprudenz, which Ru-

[17] O. Holmes, *The Common Law* 1 (1881).
[18] Jones, "An Invitation to Jurisprudence," 74 Colum. L. Rev. 1023, 1025 (1974).

dolph Von Jhering styled as a jurisprudence of concepts. [19] In his classic lecture, "The Causes of Popular Dissatisfaction with the Administration of Justice," [20] Pound sounded a call for the end of mechanical jurisprudence: "The most important and most constant cause of dissatisfaction with all law at all times is to be found in the necessarily mechanical operation of legal rules." [21] He attacked blind adherence to precedents—and to the rules and principles derived therefrom—as "mechanical jurisprudence" and "slot machine justice." Pound advocated "pragmatism as a philosophy of law." [22] Vigorously, he stated: "The nadir of mechanical jurisprudence is reached when conceptions are used, not as premises from which to reason, but as ultimate solutions. So used, they cease to be conceptions and become empty words." [23]

Pound was trumpeting a theme more softly played by Oliver Wendell Holmes a decade earlier—that the social consequences of a court's decision are legitimate considerations in decision making. [24] This is precisely what Professor Jones meant in 1974. [25]

If Roscoe Pound's 1908 warning against mechanical jurisprudence did not create a new American school of jurisprudence, at least it spawned widespread respectability for social utilitarianism. It added a new dimension to law's traditional objectives of consistency, certainty, and predictability—namely, a concern for society's welfare. A few years after Pound's warning, Cardozo delivered his classic 1921 Storrs lectures at Yale. He stated his theme: "The final cause of law is the welfare of society. The rule that misses its aim cannot permanently justify its existence." [26] A half-century later, in many legal disciplines, the once desired ob-

[19] R. Von Jhering, *Der Geist Des Rominischen Rechts* (1877).

[20] Address by Roscoe Pound to the American Bar Association, Aug. 29, 1906, *printed in* 40 Am. L. Rev. 729 (1906), *reprinted in* 8 Baylor L. Rev. 1 (1956).

[21] *Id.* at 731.

[22] *See generally* Pound, "Mechanical Jurisprudence," 8 Colum. L. Rev. 605, 609 (1908).

[23] *Id.* at 620-21.

[24] O. Holmes, *supra* note 17, at 468-74.

[25] Jones, *supra* note 18.

[26] B. Cardozo, *supra* note 14, at 66.

jective of elegantia juris in legal precepts, institutions, and procedures had become subordinated to the objective of social utility.

In 1974, Professor Jones eloquently stated the new spirit of legal purpose: "A legal rule or a legal institution is a *good* rule or institution when—that is, to the extent that—it contributes to the establishment and preservation of a social environment in which the quality of human life can be spirited, improving and unimpaired." [27]

Typical of judicial utterances that had disturbed Holmes, Pound, and Cardozo was one by the Maryland Court of Appeals in 1895: "Obviously a principle, if sound, ought to be applied wherever it logically leads, without reference to ulterior results." [28] In contrast, the same year that Cardozo delivered the Storrs lectures at Yale, he seized the opportunity to put his theory into practice by publicly rejecting blind conceptual jurisprudence in *Hynes v. New York Central Railway Co.* [29] A sixteen-year-old boy had been injured while using a crude springboard to dive into the Harlem River. The trial court had stated that if the youth had climbed on the springboard from the river before beginning his dive, the defendant landowner would have been held to the test of ordinary care, but because the boy had mounted from land owned by the defendant railroad company, the court held the defendant to the lower standard of care owed to a trespasser. Cardozo rejected this analysis, describing it as an "extension of a maxim or a definition with relentless disregard of consequences to 'a dryly logical extreme.' The approximate and relative become the definite and absolute." [30]

Cardozo's opinion in *Hynes* is a prototype, and his *The Nature of the Judicial Process* an apologia, for decision making based on sociologically oriented judicial concepts of public policy. The philosophical underpinnings of what Cardozo described as the sociological method of jurisprudence run counter to the widely held notion that public policy should

[27] Jones, *supra* note 18.

[28] Gluck v. Baltimore, 81 Md. 315, 325, 32 A. 515, 517 (1895).

[29] 231 N.Y. 229, 131 N.E. 898 (1921).

[30] *Id.* at 231, 131 N.E. at 900. Rupert Cross commented on this case in R. Cross, *Precedent in English Law* 187-88 (1968).

be formulated and promulgated only by the legislative branch of government. When judges utilize this organon, laymen and lawyers label them "activists," "liberals," "loose constructionists," and a host of other epithets, gentle and otherwise. The debate continues today and will probably continue well into the future.

But to recognize that formal logic is not an end in itself, does not mean that logical form and logical reasoning have ever been subordinated in the judicial process. Certainly, in all but a few areas of static law, mechanical jurisprudence is more historical than operational. Yet the common-law tradition demands respect for logical form in our reasoning. Without it we are denied justification for our court decisions. Adhering to logical form and avoiding fallacies, I repeat for emphasis, are only a means to the ends of justice. But they are nonetheless critical tools of argument, implements of persuasion. They form the imprimatur that gives legitimacy and respect to judicial decisions. They are the acid that washes away obfuscation and obscurity.

Professor Edward H. Levi has offered a thoughtful analysis of our subject. He has outlined a basic pattern of legal reasoning and suggested the following characteristics:

- The basic pattern is reasoning by example.
- It is reasoning from case to case.
- The process involves the doctrine of precedent in which a proposition descriptive of the first case is made into a rule of law and applied to a similar situation.
- The process involves three steps:

  — Similarity is seen between cases.
  — A rule of law is announced in the first case.
  — This rule of law is then made applicable to the second case. [31]

These characteristics describe only one phase of legal reasoning—the process of analogy, which we will study in depth later.

[31] Levi, "An Introduction to Legal Reasoning," 15 U. Chi. L. Rev. 501 (1948).

But there is more to logic in the law than analogy. Logic in the law involves the processes of induction and deduction. Indeed, legal reasoning has some resemblance to the logic of mathematics, but in the common law tradition, major premises are constantly undergoing change, or are susceptible to change, sometimes in minor detail, at other times as dramatic as a sea change. This is because judge-made law, in the sense of either creating precepts or interpreting statutes and regulations, is affected by the scenarios of particular cases, as well as by the social and philosophical considerations we have described. Professor Levi says that "this change in the rules is the indispensable dynamic quality of law. It occurs because the scope of a rule of law, and therefore its meaning, depends upon a determination of what facts will be considered similar to those present when the rule was first announced. The finding of similarity or difference is the key step in the legal process." [32]

Although the applicability of a rule of law to a given case does depend on the degree of analogy that can be drawn, the "dynamic quality" of law is affected by more than the presence of novel facts in new cases. Often, more than one rule suggests itself as precedent; more than one principle arguably applies. Here, value judgments play a major part in the development of the common law. [33]

CRITICAL IMPORTANCE OF VALUE JUDGMENTS

To understand the role of value judgments, we must first identify the types of conflicts facing the courts. Cardozo taught that there are three:

[32] *Id.* at 502.

[33] Professor Golding makes the same point in the preface to his excellent book: "Logic, of course, is not the only academic or intellectual discipline concerned with argument or reasoning. Although the perspective of the logician is indispensable for studying judicial arguments, the perspective of other fields—particularly the normative fields of moral philosophy and political theory—are of equal importance." M. Golding, *Legal Reasoning* v-vi (1984).

- Where the rule of law is clear and its application to the facts is equally clear.
- Where the rule of law is clear and the sole question is its application to the facts at bar.
- Where neither the rule is clear, nor, a fortiori, its application is clear.

Cardozo described the third category as the "serious business" of judges, "where a decision one way or another, will count for the future, will advance and retard, sometimes much, sometimes little, the development of the law." [34] If the controversy is in the third category, it is imperative to recognize with specificity where lies the conflict between the litigants. Here, too, I suggest three categories:

- Choice of the controlling legal precept. This involves choosing among competing precepts. The choice becomes the major premise of the deductive reasoning syllogism.
- Interpretation of the legal precept. Here there are no competing precepts. The parties agree on the controlling major premise. They differ only as to what it means.
- Application of the chosen legal precept, as interpreted, to the facts found or to be found by the fact finder. The facts found comprise the minor premise; here is where many sparks fly in the pleading or trial stages.

Early recognition of the specific conflict can immediately sharpen the issues. If it's a category-one case, the lawyer and the judge must also proceed into a consideration of categories two and three; in a category-two case, it is necessary to consider category three as well.

We emphasize this aspect of the judicial process here because, at this stage, formal rules of logic do not inform the choice for the judge. Judges constantly strive to seek an accommodation between competing sets of principles. There are times, however, when the scales seem evenly balanced, and it is difficult to determine exactly where the weight does lie. At these times, the jural philosophy of the individu-

[34] B. Cardozo, *supra* note 14, at 168-70.

al judge comes into play, consciously or otherwise, by means of a value judgment that places a greater weight on one competing principle than another. "Indeed, the most important attributes of a judge are his value system and his capacity for evaluative judgment," writes Professor Robert S. Summers. "Only through the mediating phenomena of reasons, especially substantive reasons, can a judge articulately bring his values to bear." [35]

Consider the observations of Professor Paul Freund:

> Much of law is designed to avoid the necessity for the judge to reach what Holmes called his "can't helps," his ultimate convictions or values. The force of precedent, the close applicability of statute law, the separation of powers, legal preemptions, statutes of limitations, rules of pleading and evidence, and above all the pragmatic assessments of fact that point to one result whichever ultimate values be assumed, all enable the judge in most cases to stop short of a resort to his personal standards. When these prove unavailing, as is more likely in the case of courts of last resort at the frontiers of the law, and most likely in a supreme constitutional court, the judge necessarily resorts to his own scheme of values. It may therefore be said that the most important thing about a judge is his philosophy; and if it be dangerous for him to have one, it is at all events less dangerous then the self-deception of having none. [36]

United States v. Standefer
610 F.2d 1076, 1107 (3d Cir. 1979)
(Aldisert, J. dissenting)

The issue before us constitutes a classic example of how one's jural philosophy may predetermine a decision. When confronted by a close case in criminal law, necessitating the expression of a value judgment, I cast my lot in favor of the individual and not the society that seeks to regulate his conduct. To me this is an *a priori* proposition distilled not only from the Constitution but from the philosophical foundation of Anglo-

[35] Summers, "Two Types of Substantive Reasons: The Core of a Theory of Common-Law Justification," 63 Cornell L. Rev. 707, 710 (1978).
[36] Freund, "Social Justice and the Law," in *Social Justice* 93, 110 (R. Brandt ed. 1962).

American common law. "Administration of a technical and often semantical criminal justice system is the price we pay for the balance struck in the Constitution between the federal government and the individual defendant." . . . The balance is struck because, in Dean Rostow's words, "[t]he root idea of the Constitution is that man can be free because the state is not."

The expression of this value judgment is not confined to the fashioning of a rule for a particular case. It begins with the choice of a controlling legal precept, continues through the interpretation of that choice, and persists finally in the application of the precept as interpreted to the facts at hand. Value judgments inhere throughout; it is not a mechanical process. Values do not form in a vacuum; their range depends always on factual limitations. Thus, judges' decisions are governed by their beliefs about facts as well as abstract rules; the act of deciding involves both the determination of material facts and the determination of what rules are to be applied to the facts. Jerome Frank observed, cynically perhaps, that a judge "unconsciously selects those facts which, in combination with the rules of law which he considers to be pertinent, will make 'logical' his decision."

From counsel's trial memorandum or brief, or from experience and independent research, the judge recognizes that a weighing process or assigning of priorities precedes his or her embarkation on a journey of legal reasoning. The judge thus begins by choosing from among competing legal precepts or competing analogies. Often there is no choice. Often the judge must formulate a rule of law because no rule or principle appears visible for the choosing. In either event, this formulation must be fortified by persuasive reasoning. Two guidelines aid both the choice or formulation and its ultimate acceptance: first, the judge should avoid arbitrary or aleatory choices; second, the judge has a duty of "reasoned elaboration in law-finding." Julius Stone says this is necessary so that the choice seems, to the entire legal profession, "if not right, then as right as possible. The *duty* of elaboration indicates that reasons cannot be *merely* ritualistic formulae or diversionary sleight of hand." [37]

Max Weber, the important European social theorist, suggested that the term "value judgment" refers "to practical evaluation of a phenomenon which is capable of being . . . worthy of either condemnation or approval." He distinguished between "logically determinable or empirically observable facts" and "the value judgments which are derived from practical standards, ethical standards or . . . views." [38] We draw the same distinction here. We judges each have our own preferences among a sea of legal standards, any one in principle respectable, and we make our selections. Sometimes we select extralegal standards, making a choice from ethical, moral, social, political, or economic concepts offered by diverse teachers or philosophers. Because a value judgment figures in the choice of competing precepts, interpretations and applications, how can a judge arrive at this decision without being arbitrary?

Roger J. Traynor reminded us that "one entrusted with decision, traditionally above base prejudices, must also rise above the vanity of stubborn preconceptions, sometimes euphemistically called the courage of one's convictions. He knows well enough that he must severely discount his own predilections, of however high grade he regards them, which is to say he must bring to his intellectual labors a cleansing doubt of his omniscience, indeed even of his perception." [39]

In the law, as well as in life itself, judging is the act of selecting and weighing facts and suggestions as they present themselves, as well as deciding whether the alleged facts are really facts and whether an idea suggested is a sound idea or merely a fancy. A good judge, dealing with relative values, can estimate, appraise, and evaluate with discernment. No hard-and-fast rules can be given for this operation of selecting and rejecting, or fixing upon signifi-

[37] Stone, "Man and Machine in the Search for Justice," 16 Stan. L. Rev. 515, 530, 536-37 (1964).

[38] Weber, "Value Judgments in Social Science," in *Weber Selections* 69 (W. Runciman, ed. 1987).

[39] Traynor, "Reasoning in a Circle of Law," 56 Va. L. Rev. 739, 751 (1970).

cant evidentiary facts. It all comes down to the good judgment, and the good sense, of the one judging. To be a good judge is to perceive the relevant indicative or signifying values of the various features of a perplexing situation. It is to know what to eliminate as irrelevant and what to retain as relevant. In ordinary matters, we call this power knack, tact, or cleverness. In the law, as in other important affairs, we call it insight or discernment.

What we should expect from our judges, at a minimum, is a willingness to consider alternative solutions to a problem. A "result-oriented" judge, in the sense condemned, is one who consistently resists considering arguments contrary to an initial impression or preexisting inclination. We cannot expect judicial minds to be untainted by their first impressions of a case. What we can expect is that the initial impression will be fluid enough to yield to later impressions. We can also expect that judges will be intellectually interested in an outcome based on sound reason. What we can demand is that judges employ logically sound techniques of intellectual inquiry and reflection when making value judgments, and then explain both their premises and their conclusions to us in clear language evidencing impeccable logical form.

A PAUSE TO RECAPITULATE: AN INTERMEZZO

Let us now attempt to synthesize what has gone before. We have explained the distinction between rules and principles; we have described the role of value judgments and precedent; and we have briefly introduced concepts of formal logic. These seemingly diverse subjects are critically interrelated. Now we can put that relationship into proper perspective. A rule of law (1) is viewed in combination with other rules by a process of inductive reasoning, (2) to form a broader legal precept, a principle, which constitutes the major premise for a process of deductive reasoning in the next case, (3) leading to the conclusion of the deductive syllogism, forms the decision in the case, (4) which in turn takes the form of a new legal rule. Such is the common-law tradition of adjudication.

We have also warned that although reasoned exposition traditionally takes the form of a logical syllogism, there is much more to the common-law process than dry logical progression. We have recognized that judges do not always use formal logic to choose or formulate legal premises. In making such a choice, courts do not necessarily appeal to any rational or objective criteria; essentially they exercise a value judgment and should be recognized outright as doing so.

Moreover, because courts have the power to alter the content of rules, no immutability attaches to their major premises. The desirability of elegantia juris, with its concomitants of stability and reckonability, is often subordinate to the desirability of rule revision in the light of claims, demands, or expectations asserted in the public interest. Once a controlling rule or principle has been selected or modified, however, it must be applied in a manner that follows the canons of logic, with respect for formal correctness. The process requires fealty to logical order, to the formal consistency of concepts with one another. At this stage, our concern is with the relations between propositions rather than the content of the propositions themselves. Thus, the reasoning process dictates formal correctness, rather than material desirability. It is to the concept of formal correctness that we now turn.

CHAPTER 3

Elements of Legal Thinking

REFLECTIVE THINKING

The study of logic is the study of the methods and principles used to distinguish correct reasoning from incorrect reasoning. The case method study of law is the study of the logical methods and principles utilized in the decision-making process. This study method is all-important because law school is designed to teach you how to solve complex problems, and even if you never practice law a day in your life, upon graduation you will be equipped for a host of positions in the private sector and public service where there is a constant demand for skilled problem solvers. The case method of study is an intense exposure designed to develop and hone skills of analysis. It is the best educational system for demonstrating principles of clear reflective thinking as well as the pitfalls of incorrect thinking.

This does not mean that you can reason correctly only if you have studied logic. That an all-pro wide receiver may be highly gifted does not mean that he has studied the physics of a football's travel through the air or the physiology involved in running, jumping, leaping, and catching. He just does it. He does it because he is possessed of what is called native ability. Similarly, many individuals have natural logical instincts or have been sufficiently exposed to logical precepts, formally or informally, at home or in school. Taught today by the Socratic method, the study of logic in the law is similar to the study, concentration, and drills that are required to develop coordination in an athletic team. But there is a difference. The study of logic is an individual endeavor.

I defend the thesis that the person who has studied logic—law student, lawyer, or judge—and is familiar with the principles of logical thinking, is more likely to reason correctly than one who has not thought about the general concepts involved in reasoning. Logical thought in the law does not embrace all types of thinking. It does not include everything that passes through our heads. As Copi explains, "All reasoning is thinking, but not all thinking is reasoning." [1] When you say, "I think I'll go swimming," you are engaging in a mental process, but it is not a process of reasoning. When you say, "I think that the Steelers will win today," your thinking may be based on reasoning if you first studied the teams' records, checked the disability list, or heard the weather report, but it can also mean, "I have a hunch the Steelers will win. I feel it in my bones."

Judge Joseph C. Hutcheson, Jr., of the Fifth Circuit, was the judiciary's expert on "hunching":

> I knew, of course, that some judges did follow "hunches,"— "guesses" I indignantly called them. . . . [I]n my youthful, scornful way, I recognized four kinds of judgments; first the cogitative, of and by reflection and logomachy; second, aleatory, of and by the dice; third, intuitive, of and by feeling or "hunching;" and fourth, asinine, of and by an ass; and in the same youthful, scornful way I regarded the last three as only variants of each other, the results of processes all alien to good judges. [2]

> . . . I, after canvassing all the available material at my command, and duly cogitating upon it, give my imagination play, and brooding over the cause, wait for the feeling, the hunch—that intuitive flash of understanding which makes the jump-spark connection between question and decision, and at the point where the path is darkest for the judicial feet, sheds its light along the way. [3]

Reasoning is a progression of thought based upon the logical relation between truths. It is unlike daydreaming,

[1] I. Copi, *Introduction to Logic* 4 (7th ed. 1986).
[2] Hutcheson, "The Judgment Intuitive: The Function of the 'Hunch' in Judicial Decisions," 14 Cornell L.Q. 274, 275-76 (1929).
[3] *Id.* at 278.

which is the development of a chain of images from a train of thought, commonly derived from what we call idle reverie, woolgathering, or free association. The professor drones on in a dull lecture. You see that he wears a red tie. This reminds you of the red dress worn by Sally Mae, a friend, who recalls to mind Jim, her brother, who is a Marine Corps pilot, and this reminds you of Ollie North, which in turn reminds you of a paper shredder, which in turn makes you think of spaghetti. Then suddenly, the professor calls upon you and you immediately think: "Where am I?"

Logical thought is reflective thinking. It consists of solving a problem by pondering a given set of facts so as to perceive their connection. For the purposes of our inquiry, reflective thinking may be understood as an "operation in which present facts suggest other facts (or truths) in such a way as to induce belief in what is suggested on the ground of real relation in the things themselves, a relation between what suggests and what is suggested." [4] What we call clear legal thinking is the application of reflective thinking to problem solving in the law. We must not establish our conclusions by intense personal desire, keenly felt emotional belief, folklore, superstition, or dogmatic, unquestioning acceptance. Rather, we must state grounds for our conclusion. A conclusion cannot stand on its own direct account, but only on account of something else which stands as "witness, evidence, voucher or warrant." We have to see an objective connection leading from that which we know to that which we don't know. We have to see a "link in actual things, that makes one thing the ground, warrant, evidence, for believing in something else." [5] Reflective thinking, therefore, is moving from the known to the unknown by an objective logical connection. The ability to think reflectively depends upon the power of seeing those logical connections. The ability to study law depends upon the power of seeing logical connections in the cases, of recognizing similarities and dissimilarities.

Simple formulas are always treacherous, but I believe that our common-law tradition comes down to a recognition of a simple basic concept: If *p*, then *q;* here is *p;* therefore,

[4] J. Dewey, *How We Think* 12 (2d ed. 1933) (emphasis omitted).
[5] *Id.*

here is *q*. Thus, the perennial question: Are the facts *p* or not-*p*? Of course, there is much more to it than this, and we will learn it, but I offer this simplistic formula now only to indicate that reflective thinking goes to the heart of logic in the law and that this mode of thinking centers on determining connections.

Logical reasoning may be tested by objective criteria. We will set forth these standards so that you may test your own reasoning. These criteria also, of course, help you evaluate the reasoning of others. It is the purpose of logic to discover and make available those criteria that can be used to test arguments for correctness.

The logician is concerned primarily with the correctness of the complicated process of reasoning. The logician asks: "Does the problem get solved? Does the conclusion reached follow from the premises, used or assumed? Do the premises provide good reason for accepting the conclusion?" If the problem gets solved, if the premise provides adequate grounds for affirming the conclusion, if asserting the premises to be true warrants asserting the conclusion to be true also, then the reasoning is correct. Otherwise, it is incorrect. The law student soon learns that these are the questions presented by the Socratic method. Lawyers learn that their adversaries ask the same questions in response to a brief. Indeed, lawyers ask these question of their adversaries' brief. Both sides learn that the judge will ask the same questions when the briefs are read and oral arguments are heard.

LANGUAGE OF LOGIC

The study of law involves the use of technical terms used by logicians. We can start with a *proposition,* a statement describing in the predicate something denoted by the subject. Logicians describe it as a sentence or statement that expresses truth or falsity. It varies according to the inclusivity of the subject to which the predicate refers, for example, as in "'All men are mortal." A proposition consists of *terms,* words, or a group of words, which express a concept or simple apprehension. A term is the simplest unit into which a proposition, and later a syllogism, can be logically resolved. When we discuss the elements of a syllogism, you will be introduced to *middle term, major term,* and *minor term.*

In the law, propositions come from many sources. We may draw them from constitutional texts or statutes or from case law. Others may come from a controlling fact, a fact that is either uncontested or has been found by a fact-finder.

An *inference* is a process in which one proposition (a conclusion) is arrived at and affirmed on the basis of one or more other propositions, which were accepted as the starting point of the process. Stebbing observes: "Inference . . . may be defined as a mental process in which a thinker passes from the apprehension of something given, the datum, to something, the conclusion, related in a certain way to the datum, and accepted only because the datum has been accepted." [6] It is a process where the thinker passes from one proposition to another that is connected with the former in some way. But for the passage to be valid, it must be made according to the laws of logic that permit a reasonable movement from one proposition to another. Inference, then is "any passing from knowledge to new knowledge." [7] The passage cannot be mere speculation, intuition, or guessing. The key to a logical inference is the reasonable probability that the conclusion flows from the evidentiary datum because of past experiences in human affairs. A nickel-plated revolver was used in the bank holdup by a ski-masked robber who got away with $10,000 in marked money. A nickel-plated revolver, a ski-mask, and $10,000 in marked money is found in the apartment of Dirty Dan, its sole occupant. The inference is permissible that our friend Dan was the bank robber.

A word, and just a word, is necessary to discuss the difference between *inference* and *implication.* These terms are obverse sides of the same coin. We *infer* a conclusion from the data; the data *imply* the conclusion. Professor Cooley explains: "When a series of statements is an instance of a valid form of inference, the conclusion will be said to *follow* from the premises, and the premises to *imply* the conclu-

---

[6] L. Stebbing, *A Modern Introduction to Logic* 211-12 (6th ed. 1948).
[7] J. Brennan, *A Handbook of Logic* 1 (1957).

LOGIC FOR LAWYERS

sion. If a set of premises implies a conclusion, then, whenever the premises are accepted as true, the conclusion must be accepted as true also. . . ." [8] As Brennan put it, "In ordinary discourse, [implication] may mean 'to give a hint,' and [inference], 'to take a hint.' Thus when my hostess yawns and looks at her watch, I *infer* from her behavior that she would like me to go home. Her yawn and look *imply* that this is her desire." [9]

Whether an inference is deductive or inductive depends upon the nature of the relationship between the given proposition and the inferred proposition. As we shall soon see, there are conclusions reached by reasoning from the general to the particular (deduction), and conclusions reached by reasoning from a number of particulars to the general (induction).

Continental Group v. Coppage
58 Md. 158, 472 A.2d 1014, 1016 (1984)

Before the Commission, the claimant's medical expert opined the causal connection was a "possibility." Based on that, the Commission denied the claim. On appeal, another physician testified with somewhat more certainty; his opinion, said the Court of Appeals . . . "was more than mere guess or expression of possibility." The circuit court reversed the Commission.

Although three questions were raised before the Court of Appeals, the Court viewed "the basic question" as whether the evidence on causation sufficed to permit submission of the case to the jury. In that context, the Court stated, . . . "It is undeniable that mere possibility of causal connection between a workman's accidental injury and his death is not of itself sufficient to make a submissible case. The connection between a workman's injury and his death must be more than a mere guess or conjecture in point of time and circumstance. . . . The evidence must make the claimant's theory of the cause of death at least reasonably probable,

[8] J. Cooley, *A Primer of Formal Logic* 13 (1942).
[9] J. Brennan, *supra* note 7, at 2-3.

30

and must justify the inference that the death resulted from the accident rather than from some other cause." As the expert's testimony at the judicial proceeding was "more than a mere guess or expression of possibility," the Court concluded that there was sufficient evidence to submit the issue to the jury.

Tose v. First Pennsylvania Bank, N.A.
648 F.2d 879, 895 (3d Cir. 1981)

The line between a reasonable inference that may permissibly be drawn by a jury from basic facts in evidence and an impermissible speculation is not drawn by judicial idiosyncracies. The line is drawn by the laws of logic. If there is an experience of logical probability that an ultimate fact will follow a stated narrative or historical fact, then the jury is given the opportunity to draw a conclusion because there is a reasonable probability that the conclusion flows from the proven facts.

Edward J. Sweeney & Sons, Inc. v. Texaco, Inc.
637 F.2d 105, 116 (3d Cir. 1980)

The court's role is especially crucial when, as here, the plaintiff's case, and therefore the defendant's liability, is based solely on circumstantial evidence. The illegal action must be inferred from the facts shown at trial. Inferred factual conclusions based on circumstantial evidence are permitted only when, and to the extent that, human experience indicates a probability that certain consequences can and do follow from the basic circumstantial facts. The inferences that the court permits the jury to educe in a courtroom do not differ significantly from inferences that rational beings reach daily in informally accepting a probability or arriving at a conclusion when presented with some hard, or basic evidence. A court permits the jury to draw inferences because of this shared experience in human endeavors. . . . Perhaps the only distinction between extracting factual conclusions from circumstantial evidence in daily life and in the courtroom is that a jury's act of drawing or not drawing an inference is preceded by a judge's instruction. The instruction serves to guide the jury through some process of ordered consideration. The court informs the jury that it must weigh the narrative or historical evidence presented, making credibility findings when appropriate, and then draw only those inferences that are reasonable in reaching a verdict.

When a trial court grants a directed verdict in a circumstantial evidence case, the court makes a legal determination that the narrative or historical matters in evidence allow no permissible inference of the ultimate fact urged by the opposing party. It decides that no reasonable person could reach the suggested conclusion on the basis of the hard evidence without resorting to guesswork or conjecture. To permit a jury to draw an inference of the ultimate fact under these circumstances is to substitute the experience of logical probability for what the courts describe as "mere speculation."

For inferences to be drawn, however, it is essential that there be basic facts in evidence to justify the described inferences.

EEOC v. Greyhound Lines, Inc.
635 F.2d 188, 194 (3d Cir. 1980)

A legitimate or permissible inference must be deduced as a logical consequence of facts presented in evidence. . . . There must be a logical and rational connection between the basic facts presented in evidence and the ultimate fact to be inferred. EEOC's evidence, relating to the incidence of PFB in black males, showed only that some black males are likely to grow beards because of this disease. It may be inferred from this that some black males would be eligible for public contact positions if they did not suffer from PFB. That is the only necessary or even permissible inference that can be drawn from this data. The evidence was insufficient to support the next inference, the ultimate fact essential to EEOC's case: that proportionately fewer blacks than whites were eligible for public contact positions and therefore that Greyhound's policy had a racially discriminatory impact. We cannot draw this inference because no evidence was introduced demonstrating that there is no skin condition or disease affecting white males—other than PFB—that makes shaving difficult or painful and requires them to grow beards. Without this evidence EEOC proved only that Ferguson was disadvantaged because he had PFB, not that he was disadvantaged because he was black.

The value of inferential reasoning has been described by John Stuart Mill:

> To draw inferences has been said to be the great business of life. Every one has daily, hourly, and momentary need of ascertaining facts which he has not directly observed; not from any general purpose of adding to his stock of knowledge, but because the facts themselves are of importance to his interests or to his occupations. The business of the magistrate, [of the lawyer] of the military commander, of the navigator, of the physician, of the agriculturist, is merely to judge of evidence and to act accordingly. . . . [A]s they do this well or ill, so they discharge well or ill the duties of their several callings. It is the only occupation in which the mind never ceases to be engaged. [10]

A belief, in general as well as legal logic, must refer to something beyond itself if we are to determine its value. A belief is simply an assertion about a fact or law that we accept—something that we affirm, or at least acquiesce in, even though it is a matter of which we have no sure knowledge or proof. But it is something of which we are sufficiently confident to act upon—something we now accept as true. Unsupported beliefs become demolished in the crucible of advocacy. I have seen many eager lawyers, young and old,

[10] J. S. Mill, *A System of Logic Ratiocinative and Inductive* 5 (8th ed. 1916).

33

crusading with maximum passion and boundless energy, strident believers in their clients' causes, hopelessly shot down because their propositions were totally bereft of support in the law or logic. To passionately feel or believe is one thing; to prevail in the court, quite another. Those who put passion in place of reason seldom survive conflicts in the courtroom. Similarly, we cannot base our major proposition on the basis that we think it self-evident (i.e., that we think that its truth is obvious). Propositions that have been accepted by many careful thinkers as self-evident have finally been found not to be indubitable. Columbus did prove that the world was not flat. Thus our major premise may not be based on emotion or instinct.

Scott v. Commanding Officer
431 F.2d 1132, 1141-42 (3d Cir. 1970)
(Aldisert, J., concurring)

Professor James included as "movement consequent upon cerebromental change" expressions of emotions and instinctive and impulsive performances. "An emotion," he said, "is a tendency to feel, an instinct is a tendency to act, characteristically, when in the presence of a certain object in the environment." Instinct to him was "the faculty of acting in such a way as to produce certain ends without foresight of the ends, and without previous education in the performance," and he declared that every instinct is an impulse. Bertrand Russell believed it possible for there to be a spontaneous belief. C. J. Adcock suggests that it is sometimes difficult to decide whether behavior based on emotionality results because "the immediate drive strength is overvalued and so difficult to control. The same result will obtain if the control function itself is too weak. It is very important to notice that while low ego control and high emotionality have similar effects they are functionally very different." And no discussion of a comparison between reason and uncontrolled action would be considered complete without a reference to Freud's analysis: "The ego represents what may be called reason and common sense, in contrast to the id, which contains the passions."

John Quincy Adams has been quoted as saying, "I told him it was law logic—an artificial system of reasoning, exclusively used in the courts of justice, but good for nothing anywhere else." [11] I disagree. But I am willing to concede that there are idiosyncratic aspects to legal logic not necessarily found in other disciplines. Unlike reflective reasoning in everyday life, the statement of belief in our major proposition in law must come from some authority. We cannot start with a proposition simply because we have always believed it (everybody knows this; it's common knowledge).

In the law, our major proposition—called the *major premise*—must usually have the hallmark of legal authority, constitutional text, statute, or case law. In this respect, legal logic differs from everyday logic, or reflective thinking in ordinary life. Here, too, although legal logic follows the laws of general logic present in mathematics, it differs from the logic of an exact science. For example, in law there are no absolute truths like those established in mathematics. Lacking absolute truths, logical propositions merely express that which is likely to be true or false. In the process of *induction,* reasoning from a group of particulars to a generalization, we don't purport that our concluding proposition is a truth. We represent only that it is more probable than not. In some cases, because the law develops with the times, and changes as community values change, the major premise may change with the times. The proposition "separate but equal" with respect to school segregation deemed appropriate in 1896, [12] was rejected as a fact in 1954, and was rejected as a proposition of law in subsequent cases. [13]

Professor Levi has explained the process:

> Therefore it appears that the kind of reasoning involved in the legal process is one in which the classification changes as the classification is made. The rules change as the rules are applied. More important, the rules arise out of a process which, while comparing fact situations, creates the rules and

[11] Murphy, "Law Logic," 77 Ethics 193, 193 (1966).
[12] Plessy v. Ferguson, 163 U.S. 537 (1896).
[13] *E.g.,* Brown v. Board of Education, 347 U.S. 483 (1954).

then applies them. But this kind of reasoning is open to the charge that it is classifying things as equal when they are somewhat different, justifying the classification by rules made up as the reasoning or classification proceeds. In a sense all reasoning is of this type, but there is an additional requirement which compels the legal process to be this way. Not only do new situations arise, but in addition peoples' wants change. The categories used in the legal process must be left ambiguous in order to permit the infusion of new ideas. And this is true even where legislation or a constitution is involved. The words used by the legislature or the constitutional convention must come to have new meanings. Furthermore, agreement on any other basis would be impossible. In this manner the laws come to express the ideas of the community and even when written in general terms, in statute or constitution, are molded for the specific case. [14]

In law, as in logic, the word "argument" takes on a special meaning. An *argument* is a group of propositions of which one is claimed to follow from the others, which are regarded as providing support or grounds for the truth of that one. [15] An argument is not a mere collection of propositions, but has a formal structure that one trained in the law must recognize. The *conclusion,* or "therefore" statement of an argument—the relief sought in a brief or the decision contained in a judge's opinion—is a proposition that is affirmed on the basis of the other propositions of the argument, which we call *premises.* These premises provide evidence or reasons for accepting the conclusion. Later, we will explain how the conclusion of one argument may then become the major premise of another argument.

We can now see that in law the purpose of logical thinking is to reach a conclusion. The process of reaching a conclusion through a series of propositions in argument form is called *reasoning.* It is reflective thinking. We reason from something we know (the statute or case law) to something that we did not know prior to our reasoning, the conclusion. *Reasons,* as distinguished from reasoning, are the considerations set forth in the terms and propositions in the premises, "which have weight in reaching the conclusion as to

[14] Levi, "An Introduction to Legal Reasoning," 15 U. Chi. L. Rev. 501, 503 (1948) (footnote omitted).
[15] I. Copi, *supra* note 1, at 14.

what is to be done, or which we employed to justify it when it is questioned . . ." [16]

Our conclusion can be true only when (1) the other propositions (premises) are true, and (2) these propositions imply the conclusion (in other words, the conclusion is inferred from these propositions).

Major Premise: All men are mortal.
Minor Premise: Socrates is a man.
Conclusion: Therefore, Socrates is mortal.

How do we test this reasoning? Our approach will outline certain techniques, easily applied methods for testing the correctness of any reasoning in the law. Our study here will go a step further than do other current guides to legal reasoning. We will define, explain, and give examples of the main tests for determining the correctness of an argument—its examination and analysis for *fallacies*. Fallacies are arguments that appear to be valid but are incorrect methods of reasoning.

Not all means of persuasion are based on reflective thinking or formal logic. As we shall learn in our study of fallacies, some forms of persuasion do not qualify. For example, rhetoric is a means of persuasion. Seekers of public office, columnists, television commentators, editorial writers, and advertising experts are masters of persuasion, who often appeal to emotions rather than to reason. Their aim is to induce belief, not to demonstrate a conclusion by pure logical means. These presentations may be works of art, but they do not always demonstrate the logic that distinguishes legal argument in all but one important area (as we will demonstrate in our study of fallacies): impassioned closing speeches to courtroom juries.

Moreover, not all good reasoning is stated in the order of formal correctness. Often, the conclusion is stated first: "Socrates is a mortal because all men are mortal and Socrates is a man." Or, in a Supreme Court case: "It could hardly be denied that a tax laid specifically on the exercise of those

[16] J. Dewey, *supra* note 4, at 17.

freedoms would be unconstitutional. Yet the license tax imposed by this ordinance is, in substance, just that." [17]

At times, the argument is compressed to a single sentence. Thus, in *Roe v. Wade,* Justice Blackmun declared:

> This right of privacy, whether it be founded in the Fourteenth Amendment's concept of personal liberty and restrictions upon state action, as we feel it is, or, as the District Court determined, in the Ninth Amendment's reservation of rights to the people, is broad enough to encompass a woman's decision whether or not to terminate her pregnancy. [18]

Implicit in this statement was the following syllogism:

Major Premise: The right of privacy is guaranteed by the fourteenth amendment and the ninth amendment.
Minor Premise: A woman's decision to terminate her pregnancy is protected by a right of privacy.
Conclusion: Therefore, a statute prohibiting termination of pregnancy violates the fourteenth and ninth amendments.

From this, we also learn that a premise may be omitted from an argument: "All men are mortal, therefore, Socrates is mortal;" or "Socrates is a man; therefore, he is mortal"; or "All men are mortal. Socrates is a man."

Thus, in examining the cases and studying the syllogisms, keep in mind:

- The conclusion may follow the premises.
- The conclusion may precede the premises.
- The conclusion may come in between the premises.
- The conclusion may be stated explicitly.
- The conclusion may be implied.

In these pages we explain that not all thinking is logical thinking, nor all reasoning good reasoning. We seek to teach the basics of well-constructed argument, to exhibit the characteristics of clearness, correctness, and relevance,

[17] Murdock v. Pennsylvania, 319 U.S. 105, 108 (1943).
[18] 410 U.S. 113, 153 (1973).

to provide consistency, absence of contradiction, demonstrativeness, and cogency.

Thus, in *United States v. Standefer,* I commented: " 'People do take judicial reasoning seriously,' Professor Charles A. Miller has observed, 'and they are not fools nor being fooled in doing so, at least no more than in other forms of communication or with respect to other strands that form the web of a political culture.' Legal reasoning cannot be artificial, esoteric, or understandable only to an elite legal priesthood; it must be capable of public comprehension." [19]

An argument that is correctly reasoned may be wrong, but an argument that is incorrectly reasoned cannot be right.

USE OF LOGIC [20]

To state that a decision is based on logic or is logical may be ambiguous. According to Richard A. Wasserstrom's formulation, "the canons of logic are essentially concerned with the conditions of formal correctness as opposed to material desirability . . . [a concern] with the relations between propositions rather than the content of the propositions themselves." Logic so described refers to an instrumental use, a structured, syllogistic form, or what Professor Dewey labels a "logic of rigid demonstration" or "formal consistency, consistency of concepts with one another." Logic, as an instrument, structures the exposition and is utilized with other jurisprudential tools—history, custom, or sociology— as a device to relate selected premises to a conclusion. However, Karl N. Llewellyn asks us to "observe the difference between logical argument and argumentative statement, between showing a given logical relation between two matters, and *persuading* someone else that it exists by *attributing* the relationship to them in your discussion or description." Analogy is yet another aspect of logic in the legal process. It provides for the extension of a precedent to differing sets of facts. Thus, it becomes important to understand

[19] United States v. Standefer, 610 F.2d 1076, 1105 (3d Cir. 1979) (Aldisert, J., concurring and dissenting) (quoting C. Miller, *The Supreme Court and the Uses of History* 12 (1969)).
[20] *Reprinted from* R. Aldisert, *The Judicial Process* 253 (1976).

separate meanings of "logic in the law." What is meant in
Holmes' classic statement, "The life of the law has not been
logic; it has been experience," must be distinguished from
what Cardozo described as the "line of logical progression;
. . . the rule of analogy or the method of philosophy."

. . . A LAGNIAPPE

Yes, Virginia, you can have some fun playing games
with legal reasoning. Here are the exercises. The object is
to use your present understanding of drawing preliminary
inferences from the stated facts, and reaching various sub-
conclusions as you work out the answers. It will help if you
draw up lists or crosscharts, or boxes. What are the answers? Only you will know because the game is to construct
logical arguments to prove that your answers are correct.

---

1. Six professors at the University of Pittsburgh
School of Law are named Mr. Able, Ms. Baker, Ms.
Charlie, Mr. Dogge, Mr. Easy, and Ms. Foxx. Not necessarily in any particular order they are graduates of the
following law schools: two from Wisconsin and one
each from Virginia, Pitt, Penn, and Harvard. They
teach the following subjects: administrative law, contracts, evidence, torts, crimes, and civil procedure.
Your assignment is to identify each professor with
the subject he or she teaches and the law school from
which each graduated.
The civil procedure class is taught by a Harvard
graduate who lives in the same apartment house as
does Mr. Easy, who does not teach evidence, torts, administrative law, or crimes.
Ms. Charlie, who teaches evidence, and the contracts professor recently attended a reunion of their
same law school class.
Because of seniority, Mr. Dogge earns more money
than Ms. Foxx does. Additionally, he earns more than
does Professor Able, who teaches administrative law.
Ms. Foxx has never attended a class reunion, does not
teach torts, and did not go to Harvard or to any law

school located in Pennsylvania. Neither Mr. Able nor the torts professor attended Harvard. Mr. Able did not go to Pitt, and the torts professor did not go to Penn.

---

2. Six members of the first year law school class are Ms. Mike, Mr. Nancy, Mr. Oliver, Ms. Peter, Ms. Queen, and Mr. Roger. They formed a study group.

The occupations of the six, not necessarily in the order of their names are: paralegal, airline pilot, housewife, bishop, television producer, and retired army colonel.

Two received A's; two B's; one a C, and one, a D.

Tell us the occupation of each member and the grade each received.

Ms. Mike is single, lives in Pasadena, and received a higher grade than the airline pilot did and the same grade as the housewife did.

Her next-door neighbor, a white-haired gentleman who is ten years older than Mr. Nancy, is a retired army colonel who also belongs to the study group. He received a grade higher than that of the paralegal, who is single and received a C.

The housewife has the longest commute; she lives in Long Beach with her oil executive husband.

Ms. Queen is the daughter of one member of the group and lives with him in the same city as does the television producer, and received a grade which was two letter grades lower than that of her neighbor, one letter grade lower than that of the bishop, and one letter grade above that of Mr. Roger.

The television producer had the same grade as the housewife, which was three letter grades higher than that of the airline pilot.

---

3. Six men recently had a twenty-fifth law school reunion: Jiggs, King, Love, Sugar, Victor, and Tare. Their present occupations, not necessarily in the order of their names, are a federal judge, an assistant secretary of state, a professor, a banker, a New York City

corporate counsel, and an insurance company vice president. Again, not necessarily in the order in which they are named, they live as follows: two in New York City; one each in San Francisco, California; Washington, D.C.; Phoenix, Arizona; and Chicago, Illinois.

Name the occupation and city of residence of each.

The judge is older than either his former roommate, the assistant secretary of state, or Jiggs. The judge's present wife is King's daughter; his former wife is now married to the New York corporate counsel, who lives in the same city as Jiggs does.

The judge lives farther west than do the banker and the insurance company vice president, each of whom lives farther west than Tare does. King uses a monthly pass on the Metropolitan subway system in the nation's capital.

Tare's annual income is $100,000, exactly twice that of the professor. Sugar has an annual income of $49,800; he is the judge's cousin and Victor's stepbrother.

The insurance company vice president lives in a hotter climate than that of any of his classmates.

Sugar lives east of Love but west of Victor who lives west of Tare, the professor, or the assistant secretary of state.

CHAPTER 4

Introduction to Deductive and Inductive Reasoning

The logic of the law is neither all deductive nor all inductive. It is a circular process. First, as cases are compared, i.e., resemblances and differences noted, a legal precept is created. Next there is a period when the precept becomes more or less fixed. A further stage takes place when the "new" precept becomes "old" and breaks down, or evolves, as new cases are decided. Inductive reasoning figures in the first stage—the creation of the precept; deductive reasoning is used in refining the created precept and in applying it to the facts before the court; inductive reasoning appears again at a later stage, when efforts are made in subsequent cases to break down the precept.

This being so, what form of reasoning do we discuss first? Here we have a chicken-or-the-egg question. As we have explained, the common law develops from specific narrow rules to broader precepts, a classic process of inductive reasoning. Yet, to understand induction, it is best to first learn deduction. Hence I put the deductive cart before the inductive horse with some introductory observations on deductive reasoning.

DEDUCTIVE REASONING

Deductive reasoning is a mental operation that a student, lawyer, or judge must employ every working day of his or her life. Formal deductive logic is an act of the mind in which, from the relation of two propositions to each other, we infer, i.e., understand and affirm, a third proposition. In deductive reasoning, the two propositions which imply the third proposition, the *conclusion,* are called *premises.* The broad proposition that forms the starting point of deduction is called the *major premise;* the second proposition is called the *minor premise.* They have these titles because the major premise represents the *all;* the minor premise, something or someone included in the all.

Logical argument is a means of determining the truth or falsity of a purported conclusion. We do this by following well-established canons of logical order in a deliberate and intentional fashion. In law we simply must think and reason logically. We must follow a thinking process that emancipates us from impulsively jumping to conclusions, or from argument supported only by strongly felt emotions or superstitions. That which John Dewey said for teachers in generations past is still vital and important today: reflective thought "converts action that is merely appetitive, blind, and impulsive into intelligent action." [1]

The classic means of deductive reasoning is the *syllogism.* Aristotle, who first formulated its theory, offered this definition: "A syllogism is discourse in which, certain things being stated, something other than what is stated follows of necessity from their being so." [2] He continued: "I mean by the last phrase that they produce the consequence, and by this, that no further term is required from without to make the consequence necessary." [3] From this definition we can say that a syllogism is a form of implication in which two propositions jointly imply a third. [4]

Special rules of the syllogism serve to inform exactly under what circumstances one proposition can be inferred from two other propositions. Consider the classic syllogism:

> All men are mortal.
> Socrates is a man.
> Therefore, Socrates is mortal.

This is a *categorical syllogism,* an argument having three propositions—two premises and a conclusion. A cate-

---

[1] J. Dewey, *How We Think* 17 (1933).

[2] L. Stebbing, *A Modern Introduction to Logic* 81 (6th ed. 1948) (quoting *Anal. Priora* at 24b).

[3] *Id.* (quoting *Anal. Priora* at 18).

[4] *Id.*

gorical syllogism contains exactly three terms or class names, each of which occurs in two of the three constituent propositions. A few definitions:

- The *major term* is the predicate term of the conclusion, and of the major premise.
- The *minor term* is the subject term of the conclusion, and of the minor premise.
- The *middle term* does not appear in the conclusion, but must appear in each of the two other propositions.
- The *major premise* is the premise containing the major term.
- The *minor premise* is the premise containing the minor term.

Because the first proposition contains the major, or larger, term, it is called the *major premise,* the larger precept laid down. Because the second contains the minor, or smaller, term, it is called the *minor premise,* the lesser statement laid down. Because it follows from the major and minor premises, the third proposition is called the *conclusion.* In the standard form categorical syllogism as used in the law, the major premise is stated first, the minor premise second, and finally the conclusion. Returning to our classic syllogism:

Major premise:	All men are mortal
Major term:	Mortal
Middle term:	All men
Minor premise:	Socrates is a man
Minor term:	Socrates
Middle term:	Man
Conclusion:	Therefore, Socrates is mortal
Minor term:	Socrates
Major term:	Mortal

Let us parse this syllogism identifying its parts:

Major premise: The subject, "all men" (the middle term); the predicate "are mortal" (the major term).

Minor premise: The subject, "Socrates" (the minor term); the predicate "is a man" (the middle term).

Conclusion: Therefore "Socrates" (the minor term) "is a man" (the major term).

Some helpful hints derive from the foregoing rules: the middle term ("all men") may always be known by the fact that it does not occur in the conclusion. The major term ("mortal") is always the predicate of the conclusion. The minor term ("Socrates") is always the subject of the conclusion.

A universal proposition (*all* offers in contract law) is described as containing a "distributed subject term." A particular proposition (*some* offers in contract law) has an "undistributed subject term." Thus, logicians say that whatever is predicated of a distributed term (*all men* are mortal), whether affirmatively or negatively, may be predicated in like manner of everything contained under it (*Socrates* is mortal). For purposes of law, we say that what is incorporated in a general proposition (conveyances of land must be in writing) is also true in a specific of that proposition (*this* conveyance of land must be in writing). To put it more briefly, what pertains to the higher class pertains also to the lower one.

All logicians refer to six rules for categorical syllogisms. [5] They vary in language only slightly. For our purposes, I will use the formulations of Professor Copi:

Rule 1: A valid categorical syllogism must contain exactly three terms, each of which is used in the same sense throughout the argument.

Rule 2: In a valid categorical syllogism, the middle term must be distributed in at least one premise.

Rule 3: In a valid categorical syllogism, no term can be distributed in the conclusion which is not distributed in the premise.

[5] *See* I. Copi, *Introduction to Logic* 217-222 (7th ed. 1986); W. Jevons, *Elementary Lessons in Logic: Deductive and Inductive* 127-29 (1870); L. Stebbing, *supra* note 2, at 87-88; J. Creighton, *An Introductory Logic* 139 (1898); R. Eaton, *General Logic, An Introductory Survey* 95-100 (1931); J. Cooley, *A Primer of Formal Logic* 306 (1942).

Rule 4: No categorical syllogism is valid which has two negative premises.

Rule 5: If either premise of a valid categorical syllogism is negative, the conclusion must be negative.

Rule 6: No valid categorical syllogism with a particular conclusion can have two universal premises.

As we shall see in Chapters 9 and 10, a departure from these rules results in a fallacy of form, or formal fallacy. Unfortunately, such fallacies occur frequently in oral arguments, written briefs, and judges' opinions.

For a syllogism to be effective, however, more is necessary than proper logical form. The major premise must be correct. If, under analysis, the major premise falls, so does the conclusion.

For example, the following syllogism is logically correct, but the major premise is nonsense:

All federal judges have green blood.
Judge Aldisert is a federal judge.
Therefore, Judge Aldisert has green blood.

INDUCTIVE REASONING

Deductive reasoning and adherence to the Socrates-is-a-man type of syllogism is only one of the major components of the common law logic tradition. Inductive reasoning is equally important. In legal logic, it is very often used to fashion either the major or the minor premise of the deductive syllogism.

Often, in legal analysis, a statute or specific constitutional provision unquestionably qualifies as the controlling major premise. It is the law of the case, with which the facts (minor term) will be compared, so as to reach a decision (conclusion). Where no clear rule is present, however, it is necessary to draw upon the collective experience of the judiciary, to use Lord Diplock's felicitous phrase, to fashion a proper major premise from existing legal rules, and specific holdings of other cases. This is done by inductive reasoning. Deductive reasoning moves by inference from the more general, to the less general, to the particular. Inductive reasoning moves from the particular to the general, or from the particular to the particular.

In law, as in general logic, there is a fundamental difference between the two types of reasoning:

- In deduction, the connection between a given piece of information and another piece of information concluded from it is a *necessary* connection.
- In a valid deductive argument, if the premises are true, the conclusion *must* be true.
- In induction, the connection between given pieces of information and another piece inferred from them is *not* a logically necessary connection.
- In a valid inductive argument, the conclusion is not necessarily an absolute truth; by induction, we reach a conclusion that is *more probably* true than not.

For an introductory look at the process of induction, let's start with the all-men-are-mortal major premise. The premise, in general form, resulted from the process of *enumeration;* it was created by enumeration of billions of particulars to create a general statement. It is an example of *inductive generalization.*

Adam is a man and Adam is a mortal.
Moses is a man and Moses is a mortal.
Tiberius is a man and Tiberius is a mortal.

George Washington is a man and George Washington is a mortal.
John Marshall is a man and John Marshall is a mortal.

Pope John Paul II is a man and Pope John Paul II is a mortal.

Therefore, all men are mortal.

It should be clear that the truth of the conclusion drawn from this inductive process is not guaranteed by the form of the argument, not even when all the premises are true, and no matter how numerous they are. We always run the risk of the fallacy of hasty generalization, about which we will learn more later. We can say, however, that the creation of a major premise in law by the technique of *inductive enumeration,* although not guaranteed to produce an absolute truth, does produce a proposition more likely true than not. This premise is then, of course, always subject to modification as new cases are decided. Formulating a generalization, i.e., enumerating a series of tight holdings of cases to create a generalized legal precept, is at best a logic of probabilities. We accept the result, not because it is an absolute truth, like a proposition in mathematics, but because it gives our results a certain hue of credibility. The process is designed to yield workable and tested premises, rather than truths.

Closely akin to reasoning by generalization is reasoning by *analogy,* which is the basis of the Socratic method of teaching law. I have found it convenient to classify analogy as a type of inductive reasoning. Not all logicians agree, many suggest that there is a difference between argument by enumeration and argument by analogy. [6] Here, I examine both processes under the heading of inductive reasoning because each process begins with an examination of particular instances. Moreover, as we shall see later, in legal analysis the strength of analogy is sometimes measured by an enumeration of relevant resemblances.

For our purposes, the specific room to which analogies should be assigned in the house of logic is not as important as understanding the criteria to be applied to analogies. Pursuant to the method of analogy, the courts do not fashion a major premise from an enumeration of holdings, but proceed from certain relevant resemblances between cases to an inferred further resemblance. The relation between enumeration and analogy is close. Both are forms of probable reasoning. The force of an argument by analogy depends upon the strength of the positive and negative resemblances. Lawyers and courts are often vulnerable to attacks on their reasoning by analogy. A proper analogy should

[6] *See, e.g.,* J. Brennan, *A Handbook of Logic* 154 (1957) (noting that logicians distinguish between "arguments based on the number of instances examined (induction by *simple enumeration*) and arguments based on *analogy"*). *But see* I. Copi, *supra* note 5, at 433 ("Because of the great similarity between argument by simple enumeration and argument by analogy, it should be clear that the same types of criteria apply to both.").

identify the number of respects in which the compared cases, or fact scenarios, resemble one another (let us call these similarities positive analogies) and the number of respects in which they differ (negative analogies). In analogy, unlike the method of enumeration, the number of resemblances is not significant. Instead, what is important is *relevancy*—whether the compared facts resemble, or differ from, one another in relevant respects. John S. Mill asked the question: "Why is a single instance, in some cases, sufficient for a complete induction, while in others myriads of concurring instances, without a single exception known or presumed, go such a very little way towards establishing an universal proposition? Whoever can answer this question knows more of the philosophy of logic than the wisest of the ancients, and has solved the problem of Induction." [7]

To refer again to the all-men-are-mortal syllogism, we can also use the process of analogy to conclude that Socrates is a man. We start with the given that Adam was a man and possessed relevant characteristics X, Y, and Z, all critical to a description of a man. Socrates possesses these same relevant characteristics. Therefore, by analogy, we determine he, too, is a man. Let's turn to more practical examples of the process of analogy:

> Able Chevrolet Company, located in Philadelphia, is liable for violating the antitrust laws by requiring a tie-in purchase of a refrigerator manufactured by Mrs. Able if you want to buy a Camaro.

It is not difficult to analogize that liability also would follow from these facts:

> Baker Pontiac Company requires a tie-in purchase of a refrigerator manufactured by Mrs. Baker if you want to buy a Firebird.

What about other circumstances? Must the resemblances be relevant? Absolutely. Consider the following:

[7] J. S. Mill, *A System of Logic Ratiocinative and Inductive* 206 (8th ed. 1916).

Villanova had a championship basketball team in 1984-85. Team members came from high schools A, B, C, D, E, and F.

Villanova has now recruited new players from high schools A, B, C, D, E, and F for the 1985-86 team.

Therefore, Villanova will have a championship basketball team in 1985-86.

Are the resemblances relevant? We must ask if the resemblance (players from the same high schools) is relevant, i.e., critical to the conclusion we seek to draw—a championship basketball team. An irrelevant similarity cannot provide the proper basis for an analogy.

An appreciation of these methods of reasoning will both sharpen your power of analysis, and facilitate your study of law. We have outlined here only an introduction to deductive and inductive reasoning. We will describe the methods in depth in the following chapters.

CHAPTER **5**

Deductive Reasoning

Now we are ready to take a closer look at deductive reasoning. Here we should utilize two viewpoints. In the reasoning *process* we naturally begin with the premises and arrive at a conclusion. In *analyzing* reasoning we reverse the process: we begin with the conclusion, for it is in the conclusion that we as brief writers, brief readers, oral advocates, and judges, examine the quality of the reasoning and evaluate the soundness of the arguments. Accordingly, it is essential to understand the *terms* of the syllogism:

Major term: The predicate of the major premise and also of the conclusion.

Minor term: The subject of the minor premise and also of the conclusion. It is called minor because it is less inclusive than the predicate subject of the major premise.

Middle term: The medium of comparison between the major and minor term. It appears in the premises, and *not* in the conclusion. In a categorical syllogism it appears as the subject of the major premise and as the predicate of the minor premise.

The syllogism traces its ancestry to mathematics. Euclid's first axiom lies at the heart of the modern legal syllogism: Things which are equal to the same thing are equal to each other. Three canons or fundamental principles of the syllogism build on Euclid:

Two terms agreeing with one and the same third term agree with each other.

Two terms, of which one agrees and the other does not agree with one and the same third term, do not agree with each other.

Two terms both disagreeing with one and the same third term may or may not agree with each other. [1]

To recapitulate, by definition the syllogism consists of (a) a proposition called the major premise, in which the major and middle terms are compared together; (b) a minor premise, which compares the minor and middle terms; and (c) a conclusion, which contains the major and minor terms only. So much for structure.

In ordinary writing and speaking, the formal arrangement is seldom observed, except perhaps in teaching children. Good girls get a star on their forehead; Susie is a good girl; Susie gets a star on her forehead. Normally, we would say that Susie got a star on her forehead because she was a good girl. We would omit the major premise completely because it would be generally understood.

The omitted premise is called an *enthymeme*. Many legal briefs and opinions contain enthymemes because either the major or the minor premise is obvious and is understood (or is believed to be obvious and understood). Most often the omitted premise is the major premise (all good girls get a star on their forehead). This is called an enthymeme of the first order. When the minor premise is omitted, it is called an enthymeme of the second order (all good girls get stars; Susie gets a star). Note the enthymemes in this Iowa case.

Lubin v. Iowa City
257 Iowa 383, 131 N.W.2d 765, 770 (1964)

Whether we say the invasion of plaintiffs' property by water escaping from defendant's broken watermain constitutes a trespass or nuisance or results from an extra-hazardous activity as defined in the Restatement

[1] W. Jevons, *Elementary Lessons in Logic: Deductive and Inductive* 121-22 (1870).

of Torts, Section 520, or is an application of the doctrine of *Rylands v. Fletcher,* or that the practice of leaving pipes in place until they break is negligence per se, we believe the facts in this case disclose a situation in which liability should be imposed upon by the city without a showing of negligent conduct.

It is neither just nor reasonable that the city engaged in a proprietary activity can deliberately and intentionally plan to leave a watermain underground beyond inspection and maintenance until a break occurs and escape liability. A city or corporation so operating knows that eventually a break will occur, water will escape and in all probability flow onto the premises of another with resulting damage. We do not ordinarily think of watermains as being extra-hazardous but when such a practice is followed, they become "inherently dangerous and likely to damage the neighbor's property." . . . The risks from such a method of operation should be borne by the water supplier who is in a position to spread the cost among the consumers who are in fact the true beneficiaries of this practice and of the resulting savings in inspection and maintenance costs. When the expected and inevitable occurs, they should bear the loss and not the unfortunate individual whose property is damaged without fault of his own.

Enthymemes will only lead to a correct conclusion if the assumed and stated premises are also correct. Indeed, in all syllogisms, the accuracy of the conclusion depends upon the accuracy of the component premises. Let's look at the syllogisms in *MacPherson v. Buick Motor Co.* [2]

Judge Cardozo

Major premise: Any manufacturer who negligently constructs an article that may be inherently dangerous to life and limb when so constructed, is liable in damages for the injuries resulting.

[2] 217 N.Y. 382, 111 N.E. 1050 (1960).

55

Minor premise: A manufacturer who constructs an automobile so that the spokes on a wheel are defective is such a manufacturer.

Conclusion: Therefore, a manufacturer who constructs an automobile so that the spokes on a wheel are defective is liable in damages for the injuries resulting.

Chief Judge Bartlett

Major premise: The vendor of a carriage is not liable in an action for negligence to anyone save his immediate vendee.

Minor premise: This plaintiff was not the immediate vendee of the vendor defendant.

Conclusion: Therefore, defendant vendor is not liable in an action for negligence to this plaintiff.

Fault may not be found in the logic contained in either opinion. Although the results differ, the reasoning is not flawed. The results differ because the major premise of each opinion differs.

In each of the *MacPherson* syllogisms, the major premise is a broad legal concept that qualifies as a universal proposition. By *universal,* we mean that the subject term applies to all members of its class without restriction (*"any* manufacturer who . . . is liable"). Had the assertion applied only to a restricted, or partial class it would be called a *particular* proposition. The subject of a universal proposition is said to be *distributed.* In our example, we speak of *"any* manufacturer" or *"the* vendor." In each case, the assertion concerns all manufacturers and vendors in the stated class without restriction. Hence, the subject is distributed. Had the proposition stated *"some* manufacturers, who . . . are liable," the subject would have been particular. We would not know which of such manufacturers would be liable. The subject of a particular proposition is said to be *undistributed.* There are buzz words to help distinguish a universal proposition (or a distributed term) from a particular proposition (or a undistributed term). Those suggesting a universal include "every," "all," "each," "the," "always," "everywhere," "in every instance," "no," "never," "nowhere," "under no circumstances." Those suggesting a particular include "some," "certain," "a," "one," "this," "that," "sometimes," "not everywhere," "sometimes not," "occasionally," "once," "somewhere." The predicate term of a proposition is, likewise, either distributed or undistributed. Determining whether the predicate is distributed or undistributed is easy; understanding why it is so is not so easy. If the proposition is an *affirmative* statement ("All manufacturers . . . are liable"), then the predicate (liability) is undistributed. If the proposition is a *negative* statement ("The vendor . . . is not liable"), then predicate (liability) is distributed.

Consider Judge Cardozo's major premise: "Any manufacturer who negligently constructs an article . . . is liable. . . ." The subject, any manufacturer, is distributed—it tells us that the proposition will apply to all manufacturers who fit the given definition. Because the proposition is affirmative, we know that the predicate (liability) is undistributed. That means that the proposition tells us something about a limited group of liable persons—the group that coincides with the subject group of manufacturers. This group of liable persons is undistributed. It is limited because there are other liable persons not coincident with the subject group.

Now look at Judge Barlett's major premise: "The vendor of a carriage . . . is not liable. . . ." The subject, carriage vendors, is distributed—it refers to all carriage vendors. In this negative proposition, the predicate is distributed, because the proposition tells us something about all liable persons—that they never coincide with the subject group of carriage vendors.

In each of the examples above, the subject is distributed. But it could be undistributed and the same rules would apply. Let's look at another example: "Some manufacturers are liable." Here, the subject is undistributed. The proposition refers to only a limited group of manufacturers. Because the proposition is affirmative, the predicate (liability) must be undistributed. As in Judge Cardozo's major premise, the proposition is only concerned with a limited group of liable persons—the group that coincides with the subject group of manufacturers. In this case, both groups are limited, so both terms are undistributed. The proposition does not tell us about all manufacturers, or about all liable persons.

An undistributed subject can also appear in a negative proposition: "Some vendors are not liable." The subject here, as in the preceding example, is undistributed because it limits the group of vendors to whom the proposition will apply. The proposition is negative, so the predicate (liability) is distributed. It is distributed because it tells us something about all liable persons—none of them will ever coincide with the limited group of vendors in the subject class, because those vendors are liable.

To summarize, yet extend this discussion slightly beyond the perimeters of the *MacPherson* case:

1. The first inquiry is whether the subject or the predicate refers to the whole class, or part of the class.
2. If the reference is to the whole class, the subject or predicate is said to be distributed.
3. If the reference is to part of the class, the subject or the predicate is said to be undistributed.
4. The subject of a universal proposition is distributed because a universal proposition applies to the whole class.
5. The subject of a particular proposition is undistributed because the proposition applies to only part of the class.
6. The predicate of an affirmative proposition is undistributed. In "all men are mortal," the predicate mortal is not distributed because the proposition does not mean that only men are mortal.
7. The predicate of a negative proposition is distributed. "No federal judges are elected officials." By excluding all federal judges from the class of elected officials, we necessarily exclude all members of the class of elected officials from the class of federal judges.

The *MacPherson* majority opinion and the dissent both demonstrate deductive logic, a movement of the mind from an object as a whole to some point therein; a movement from the general to the particular; an inference from the all to anyone included in the all. Each takes the form of a syllogism.

Now that we understand the syllogism, we are ready to look at a case that demonstrates its usefulness in evaluating the logical validity of a proposed inference.

Leliefeld v. Johnson
104 Idaho 357, 659 P.2d 111, 118 (1983)

[*Issue:* Does evidence of repairs subsequent to an accident give rise to an inference of negligence?] Such a factor is the equal probability of an inference contrary to negligence being drawn from a subsequent remedial measure *viz.* a particulary prudent, circumspect, and fastidious individual doing something which the law would not dictate needed to be done.[4] See Adv. Comm. Note to Fed.R.Evid. 407 (("subsequent remedial measure) is not in fact an admission, since the conduct is equally consistent with injury by mere accident or through contributory negligence"); G. Lilly, *An Introduction to the Law of Evidence* § 48, at 150-51 (1978) ("An after-the-incident precautionary measure may reflect merely the exercise of extraordinary caution . . . and may not indicate the actor's belief that the condition in question was really hazardous"). It would be unfair to penalize such an individual by permitting his conduct to be introduced as evidence of his negligence because it is clear that his act could be that done by a supercautious man and not that required of a reasonable man. As Professor Lilly has written: "In negligence cases, liability attaches if the defendant acted unreasonably in view of the facts known (or which should have been known) to him before the incident in question. An after-incident remedial measure is usually taken on the basis of the additional facts revealed by the accident or injury. There is a risk that the trier, particularly a jury, might not keep this important distinction clearly in mind and might too easily infer prior knowledge from the subsequent remedial acts, which were generated by the knowledge learned from the incident itself." *Id.* at 152. *See also* 2 Wigmore, Evidence § 283, at 174-75 (Chadbourn rev. 1979).

[Note 4] In analyzing an example from Wigmore concerning subsequent repair of machinery involved in an accident, Professor James utilized a transmutation of a proposed direct inference into its deductive form to demonstrate its invalidity as suggested: "In the case of the repaired machinery we're told: 'People who make such repairs (after an accident) show a consciousness of negligence; *A* made such repairs; therefore, *A* was conscious of negligence.' Before this deductive proof can be evaluated, ambiguity must be eliminated from the major premise. By 'people' shall we understand 'some people' or 'all people'? If the argument is intended to read, 'Some people who make such repairs show consciousness of negligence; *A* made such repairs; therefore, *A* was conscious of negligence,' it contains an obvious logical fallacy. If intended to read, 'All people who make such repairs show consciousness of negligence; *A* made such repairs; therefore, *A* was conscious of negligence,' it is logically valid. However, few could be found to accept the premise that all persons who repair machinery after an accident show consciousness of guilt; that is, that no single case could be found of one who, confident of his care in the past, nevertheless made repairs to guard against repetition of an unforeseeable casualty or to preserve future fools against the consequence of their future folly. Here the result of transmuting a proposed direct inference into deductive form is discovery that it is invalid—at least in the terms suggested." James, *Relevancy, Probability and the Law,* 29 Cal. L. Rev. 689, 696-97 (1941) (footnotes omitted) (emphasis in the original).

Often a series of syllogisms are linked with conclusions of previous ones forming the premises of those which follow. Logicians call the first syllogism in such a series a prosyllogism; the syllogism that contains the conclusion, using the first syllogism as its premise, is called an episyllogism.

Inter-Tribal Council of Nevada, Inc. v. Hodel
856 F.2d 1344, 1349-50 (9th Cir. 1988)

For the plaintiff to prevail on the question of standing to seek a forfeiture under 25 U.S.C. § 293a, it must prove that it is the former beneficial owner of the Stewart School site. We have concluded, as did the district court, that the Council lacks standing because it has not proved that it is the former beneficial owner of the property.

The Council's best case scenario is drawn primarily, if not exclusively, from section 8 of the 1887 Nevada statute, which provides: "All lands purchased under the provisions of this Act shall be conveyed to said Indian School Commission *in trust for the benefit of such school.* . . ." 1887 Nev. Stat. ch. XII.

This provision forms the major premise of the Council's first syllogism. From this premise, the Council argues that it represents the majority, if not the entirety, of the Indian population of Nevada for whose benefit the school was established. From these two premises, the Council draws the conclusion that the land was conveyed in trust for the benefit of its member tribes, as contemplated in the 1887 Nevada statute.

The conclusion of this first syllogism then becomes a building block for the Council's second syllogism, which is based on 25 U.S.C. § 293a. The major premise here is that the Secretary of the Interior may not convey the property without the consent of the "former beneficial owner." The minor premise is that, as concluded above, the Council (in its representative capacity) is the former beneficial owner of the land. Therefore, the Council concludes, the Secretary may not convey the property without its consent.

The difficulty with the prosyllogism based on the 1887 Nevada statute, and the resulting episyllogism based on section 293a, is the Council's initial conclusion that the land was conveyed in trust for the benefit of the tribes it represents. The appellees argue that the tracts in question were never conveyed to the Indian School Commission in trust for anyone. Rather the tracts were conveyed directly to the federal government by the private owners in fee simple. Moreover, appellees assert, the Nevada statute's language does not support the suggestion that a trust was to be implied if the land was conveyed directly to the United States, instead of to the Commission. Furthermore, appellees contend, even if a trust had been implied, the Nevada statute did not contemplate a trust for the benefit of the Council, or a particular Nevada tribe, or the Nevada Indian population in general.

The Nevada statute explicitly described the limitation of any trust: "for the benefit of such school." It is not without significance that when Congress decided to close the Stewart Indian School, only twenty-seven students enrolled in the school came from Nevada. The remainder of the 400-student population came from other states, the majority from Arizona and California. This raises the question of whether Nevada Indians, whose children represented 6.75 percent of the school's population, could properly be considered the sole beneficiaries of any trust established for the benefit of the school. We think not.

A key premise of the Council's argument anchored in the Nevada statute, therefore, has no support in the statute itself. The land was not conveyed to the Indian School Commission in trust for anyone; it was conveyed to the federal government in fee simple. The only trust that was expressed or implied was (a) if the conveyance was to the Commission and (b) "for the benefit of such school," and not to any Indian tribe, band, or group. Accordingly, because the premise has no basis, the argument is not sound and its conclusion is flawed. This flawed conclusion may not then serve as the minor premise in the Council's critical contention that it is the former beneficial owner as contemplated by section 293a.

VALUE JUDGMENTS—CHOICE OF PREMISES

A "performative utterance" is an expression that is not only articulated but is also operative. [3] Because judicial decisions fit this description, we can say that a court's public performance in reaching a conclusion is at least as important as the conclusion. If we evaluate a decision in terms not of "right" or "wrong," nor of subjective agreement or disagreement with the result, but rather in terms of thoughtful and disinterested weighing of conflicting social interests, it becomes critical that the "performative utterance" include a societally acceptable explanation, set forth in logical form.

But in the formulation of major and minor premises in the law, there is more at work than rules of logic. The selection of a major premise, as we have emphasized before, is a *value judgment.* The advocate or the judge makes this value judgment. A choice is made. No unerring rules of logic dictate this important decision, which is the critical threshold, the prelude to the operation of the rules of logic.

In his classic essay, *The Nature of the Judicial Process,* Cardozo explained that sometimes the source of the law to be embodied in a value judgment, which we relate to selection of our *premises,* is obvious, as when the Constitution or a statute applies. In these situations, the judge simply obeys the constitutional or statutory rule. But when no constitutional or statutory mandate controls, the judge must "compare the case before him with the precedents, whether stored in his mind or hidden in the books." [4] If the comparison yields a perfect fit, if both the law and its application are clear, the task is simple. If the law is unclear, it is necessary to "extract from the precedents the underlying principle [and] then determine the path or direction along which the principle is to move and develop, if it is not to wither and die." [5]

Cardozo cautioned that decisions "do not unfold their principles for the asking. They yield up their kernel slowly

[3] J. Austin, *Philosophical Papers* 233-41 (1961).
[4] B. Cardozo, *The Nature of the Judicial Process* 19 (1921).
[5] *Id.* at 28

and painfully." [6] He discussed what he called the "organons" of the judicial process—the instruments by which we
fix the bounds and tendencies of that principle's development and growth. He also discussed the use of history and
custom, and what in 1921 was considered a revolutionary
technique of decision making—the method of sociology.

By describing the elements at work in the caldron, Cardozo was performing the valued task of a traditional common-law judicial analyst. That he ranks with Oliver Wendell Holmes, Jr., as one of our greatest common-law judges
is scarcely now debatable. But to the extent that he developed, persuasively and gracefully, a legitimation for result-
oriented jurisprudence, he became more a legal philosopher
than a common-law judge. He sought what *ought* to be the
law, in contrast to what *is*. For Cardozo, the preferred gap-
filler in addressing novel questions of law was the social
welfare, defined as "public policy, the good of the collective
body," or "the social gain that is wrought by adherence to
the standards of right conduct, which find expression in the
mores of the community." [7] To him "the power of social justice," among all organons of the decision making process,
was the force which was becoming the greatest directive
force of the law. [8]

Professor John Wisdom suggests that the process of selecting a controlling legal precept, which we relate to the
selection of the syllogism's premises, "becomes a matter of
weighing the cumulative effect of one group of severally inconclusive items against the cumulative effect of another
group of severally inconclusive items." [9] In exercising this
choice, courts do not necessarily appeal to any rational or
objective criteria. Essentially they exercise a value judgment and should be recognized flatly as doing so. Moreover,
because courts have the power to alter the content of rules,
no immutability attaches to their major or beginning premises. The desirability of elegantia juris, with its concomitants of stability and reckonability, often must be subordinated to the desirability of rule revision in the light of

[6] *Id.* at 29.
[7] *Id.* at 71-72.
[8] *Id.* at 65-66.
[9] J. Wisdom, *Philosophy and Psycho-Analysis* 157 (1953).

claims, demands, or desires asserted in the public interest in changing societal conditions.

Once the controlling rule or principle has been selected or modified, however, we must use canons of logic to reach a formally correct conclusion. Dewey described the process as "formal consistency, consistency of concepts with one another." [10] Logic is concerned with the relation between propositions, rather than with the content of the propositions themselves. Thus, the reasoning process dictates formal correctness, rather than material desirability.

Legal analysis is a three-step procedure: (1) selecting or choosing the legal precept, (2) interpreting that precept, and (3) applying it, as interpreted, to the case at hand. The procedure may be viewed also from the perspective of the relations between logical propositions. Thus, steps 1 and 2, selecting and interpreting the legal precept, refer to the major premise of a syllogism. Step 3, applying the selected and interpreted legal precept, might be analogized to the minor premise. If one accepts the value judgment inherent in the major premise, and if the minor premise is valid, then, theoretically, one must accept the conclusion. But we know that it is not always that neat, for the process often fails. One may accept a conclusion as a valid legal norm and use it as a precedent, although one disagrees with the beginning premise which "logically" led to the conclusion.

As we have emphasized before, to truly understand the syllogism, we must remember that the rules of formal logic deal only with its "validity" or "soundness" in terms of the six rules of the syllogism. There is a distinction between the *validity* of a syllogism and the *truth* of its contents. Assume we uttered this nonsense:

All middle terms are major terms.

Minor term is a part of middle term.

Therefore, all minor terms are major terms.

Can we say that it is valid? invalid?

[10] J. Dewey, *How We Think* 20 (1933).

The formally correct but ridiculous syllogism we referred to earlier bears repeating here to emphasize that proper content must be poured into the syllogism's terms:

All federal judges have green blood.

Judge Aldisert is a federal judge.

Therefore, Judge Aldisert has green blood.

The bottom line: The validity of a syllogism and the soundness of the argument's structure deal only with relations between the premises. Validity deals only with form. It has absolutely nothing to do with content. [11] Arguments, therefore, may be logically valid, yet absolutely nonsensical. Assuming valid form, the essence of argument must always be a search for the truth or falsity of the premises. Where inductive reasoning is used to determine the major premise, the search is a search for a determination that the premise is more likely true than not. Once this determination is made in constructing the premise, however, it is *not* the case that the conclusion *probably* will follow; the conclusion *must* follow.

Remember, in deductive logic, the conclusion *must* follow from the premises. Watch out for *GIGO:* garbage in, garbage out.

Hogan v. Florida
427 So. 2d 202, 203 (Fla. 1983)

Appellant was convicted of attempting sexual battery and kidnapping, and sentenced in two consecutive thirty-year terms in prison. Initially appellant contends that the trial court erred in requiring him to be tried by a six-person jury instead of a jury of twelve. His argument is that sexual battery committed by one over eighteen years upon a victim eleven years or younger is a capital felony. Section 913.10, Florida Statutes (1981), and Florida Rule of Criminal Procedure 3.270 are identical and provide that: "Twelve persons shall constitute a jury to try all capital cases." Therefore,

[11] *See* M. Golding, *Legal Reasoning* 39 (1984).

since he was being tried for a capital crime, appellant was entitled to the benefits of a twelve-person jury.

The argument is logical, but fallacious, because the major premise is invalid. Although the statute cited does provide that the sexual battery of a victim eleven years or younger by one over eighteen years is a capital felony, case law demonstrates that is no longer correct. As the Supreme Court of Florida said: "A capital offense is one that is punishable by death." In Florida, murder in the first degree is the only existing capital offense.

United States v. Menke
468 F.2d 20, 25 (3d Cir. 1972)

[The district court] distinguished the case at bar from *Berne:* "In both *Berne* and *Harris* consent was found, but in neither was the accused under arrest." From this major premise, the court proceeded to characterize the agents' questioning about the location of the marijuana as having "the same effect as a demand or order. The defendant's conduct, then, particularly absent knowledge of his right to refuse the search, cannot be construed to constitute consent."

Regrettably, the district court erred in its major premise; it misread the facts in *Berne*. In the second fourth amendment issue in that case, when the defendant informed the police there was a hunting knife in the car, the accused had already been "arrested and taken to police headquarters . . . there is not doubt that the defendant was 'in custody' at the time of the second seizure, having been arrested and taken to the station." Thus, because the *Berne* fourth amendment doctrine clearly applies to one in custody, the attempted distinction by the district court was improper. What was said in *Berne* has impressive significance here: "Having been warned that anything he said could be used against him, it is inconceivable that his election to . . . deliver [the evidence] up to the police was anything less than a free and voluntary abandonment of his security in this otherwise constitutionally protected area."

Hatcher v. Jackson
853 F.2d 212, 214 (3d Cir. 1988)

We come now to the critical issue of whether the district court correctly determined that the state courts deprived petitioner of due process of law. Petitioner defends the district court's order on the ground that the state deprived him of federal due process by failing to accord him the benefit of state-established guarantees.

Petitioner's argument is syllogistic. New Jersey law requires that a jury verdict in a criminal case be unanimous. N.J. Ct. R. 8-9. When there is doubt about a juror's vote, the New Jersey cases interpreting Rule 1:8-10 indicate that the trial judge should seek clarification. The judge did not question the juror about her poll answer. Citing *Vitek v. Jones,* 445 U.S. 480 (1980), petitioner concludes that the state court thereby deprived him of his state-guaranteed unanimous verdict and, in consequence, violated his federally guaranteed due process rights.

Essentially, the parties are in disagreement as to the minor premise in petitioner's syllogism: whether the state courts violated state law by not requiring clarification of the juror's vote under the circumstances. . . .

In construing Rule 1:8-10, the New Jersey courts have indicated that the trial judge seek clarification when a juror's vote is unclear. In this way it may be assured that the verdict is unanimous. However, the New Jersey trial judge determined that the particular juror's vote was unequivocal despite her subsequent emotional breakdown. The Appellate Division read the record the same way. The district court, nevertheless, concluded that the juror's response was confusing, ambiguous and not directly responsive to the question, thus requiring further inquiry. . . .

Lamon v. McDonnell Douglas Corp.
19 Wash. App. 515, 576 P.2d 426, 437 (1978)
(Anderson, J., dissenting)

[Airline stewardess brought a products liability case based on a strict tort liability theory against aircraft manufacturer for injuries sustained when she stepped into an open emergency hatch of a DC-10 airplane. Her expert witness stated the hatch was unreasonably dangerous. The Superior Court entered summary judgment for the manufacturer, and the stewardess appealed. The Court of Appeals held that the testimony of plaintiff's expert witness created a substantial fact issue as to whether design of the escape hatch was defect-free, thereby precluding summary judgment.]

In its final analysis, the fallacy of letting an expert witness' unsupported opinion create a fact issue in a case is perhaps better answered by logic than by legal precedent. Illustrative of this is a story told of Abraham Lincoln during his trial lawyer days. Lincoln is said to have cross-examined a witness as follows:

"How many legs does a horse have?"

"Four," said the witness.

"Right," said Abe.

"Now, if you call the tail a leg, how many legs does a horse have?"

"Five," answered the witness.

"Nope," said Abe, "callin' a tail a leg don't make it a leg."

So it is here that merely calling a product unreasonably dangerous does not, without more, make it so.

Legal reasoning is subject to more scrutiny than any other aspect of the judicial process. Forming the very fiber of argument and persuasion, it is the heart of both the written brief and the court's opinion, the essence of the process of justification. It constitutes the foundation of the case system by which law students are trained. Formal criticism of the "reasoning" of courts seems, at times, to form the *raison d'être* for law review publications. Yet there is little analysis of reasoning qua reasoning. Often an alleged attack on the "reasoning" of the court is really a disagreement with the value judgment implicit in the court's major premise—a disagreement with the court's selection and interpretation of the applicable legal precept. This disagreement with the selection of legal precepts, "the authoritative starting points for judicial reasoning" in Dean Pound's formulation, is, in reality, a quarrel with the validity of the legal norm or, in many cases, a philosophical difference with the values reflected in the choice.

Criticism of court opinions would be more professional, briefs more clear, points of friction between litigants earlier identified and accommodated, if resort to the cosmos of "reasoning" were minimized, and attention directed instead to the precise components of that cosmos. It is not too much to ask whether one disagrees with the choice of the "authoritative starting point" and, if so, why; or whether one's quarrel is with the formal correctness of the syllogism used and, if so, where. The facts in the minor premise might not be subsumed in the major, or the conclusion might lack elements common to the major and minor premises. As Professor Levi explains, there might be a "logical fallacy . . . the fallacy of the undistributed middle or [in hypothetical syllogisms] the fallacy of assuming the antecedent is true because the consequent has been affirmed." We will describe these particular fallacies in our discussion of fallacies of form.

To truly analyze the reasoning in a legal argument, we must strip away extraneous detail and verbiage. We must reduce the argument to the components of the syllogism. Do not look for spare, laconic briefs or judicial opinions setting forth only the bare bones of a syllogism. Very few do. We lawyers and judges write and talk too much. We fill our arguments with declarative sentences that are not the necessary propositions of our argument; that is, they are not the necessary premises of the syllogism. Rather, they are inserted to assist the reader to understand what the premises and the conclusion are all about. Indeed, the bare bones of the syllogism may be considered shorthand words of art designed for experts. Thus, a fifty-page brief in the United

States Court of Appeals is soon reduced to a fifteen-minute oral presentation that features a lively colloquy between the bench and bar. In the judges' conference following argument, a decision is often reached by mere recitation of the naked syllogism. This is because judges are experienced in the subject matter. They are able to identify the basic structure of the argument because they are familiar with most, if not all, of the reasons supporting the propositions. Fortunately, or unfortunately, when the statement of reasons appears in print, however, judicial opinions are filled with countless pages giving reasons for (1) selecting the major premise, (2) interpreting the major premise, (3) interpreting the minor premise, (4) applying the premises to the facts found by the fact finder, and (5) stating the conclusion. Thus, it is necessary always to identify the precise structure of the argument by stripping away explanatory materials. It is important not to confuse these materials with the critical framework of the argument.

We are now ready to examine excerpts from some leading United States Supreme Court cases. Read them not for their substantive content, but for their syllogisms. Identify the major and minor premises. In what order do the premises appear? Does the conclusion appear first? Look out for enthymemes and multiple syllogisms and decide if the court leaped to conclusions or followed logical order.

Marbury v. Madison
5 U.S. (1 Cranch) 137, 177-78 (1803)

[In the Judiciary Act, Congress had authorized the Supreme Court "to issue writs of mandamus, in cases warranted by the principles and usages of law, to any courts appointed or persons holding office, under the authority of the United States." The ultimate question in this case was whether the Court had the power to issue mandamus directed to Secretary of State, James Madison, because he was "such a person holding office." The court concluded that it had no jurisdiction to issue the writ and declared the statute giving the Court jurisdiction to be repugnant under Article III, section 2 of the Constitution. Chief Justice Marshall reasoned:]

Certainly, all those who have framed written constitutions contemplate them as forming the fundamental and paramount law of the nation, and consequently, the theory of every such government must be, that an act of the legislature, repugnant to the constitution, is void. This theory is essentially attached to a written constitution, and is, consequently, to be considered, by this court, as one of the fundamental principles of our society. It is not, therefore, to be lost sight of, in the further consideration of this subject.
. . . .

It is, emphatically, the province and duty of the judicial department, to say what the law is. Those who apply the rule to particular cases, must of necessity expound and interpret that rule. If two laws conflict with each other, the courts must decide on the operation of each. So, if a law be in opposition to the constitution; if both the law and the constitution apply to a particular case, so that the court must decide that case, conformable to the law, disregarding the constitution; or conformable to the constitution, disregarding the law; the court must determine which of these conflicting rules governs the case: that is of the very essence of judicial duty. If then, the courts are to regard the constitution, and the constitution is superior to any ordinary act of the legislature, the constitution, and not such ordinary act, must govern the case to which they both apply.

McCulloch v. Maryland
17 U.S. (4 Wheat.) 316, 435-36 (1819)

[This case required interpreting the supremacy clause. Speaking through John Marshall, the Court held that the state could not tax the operations of a branch of the bank of the United States.]

It has also been insisted, that, as the power of taxation in the general and state governments is acknowledged to be concurrent, every argument which would sustain the right of the general government to tax banks chartered by the states, will equally sustain the right of the states to tax banks chartered by the general government. But the two cases are not on the same reason. The people of all the states have created the general government and have conferred upon it the general power of taxation. The people of all the states, and the states themselves, are represented in congress, and, by their representatives, exercise this power. When they tax the chartered institutions of the states, they tax their constituents; and these taxes must be uniform. But when a state taxes the operations of the government of the United States, it acts upon institutions created, not by their own constituents, but by people over whom they claim no control. It acts upon the measures of a government created by others as well as themselves, for the benefit of others in common with themselves. The difference is that which always exists, and always must exist, between the action of the whole on a part, and the action of a part on the whole—between the laws of a government declared to be supreme, and those of a government which, when in opposition to those laws, is not supreme.

Dred Scott v. Sandford
60 U.S. (19 How.) 393, 403, 408, 416, 426,
454, 572, 576, 582 (1856)

Mr. Chief Justice Taney delivered the opinion of the Court:

The question is simply this: can a negro whose ancestors were imported into this country and sold as slaves, become a member of the political community formed and brought into existence by the Constitution of the United States, and as such become entitled to all the rights, and privileges, and immunities, guaranteed by that instrument to the citizen. One of these rights is the privilege of suing in a court of the United States in the cases specified in the Constitution.

. . . .

The opinion thus entertained and acted upon in England was naturally impressed upon the colonies they founded on this side of the Atlantic. And, accordingly, a negro of the African race was regarded by them as an article of property, and held, and bought and sold as such, in every one of the thirteen Colonies which united in the Declaration of Independence, and afterwards formed the Constitution of the United States. The slaves were more or less numerous in the different Colonies, as slave labor was found more or less profitable. But no one seems to have doubted the correctness of the prevailing opinion of the time.

The legislation of the different Colonies furnishes positive and indisputable proof of this fact. . . .

The legislation of the States therefore shows, in a manner not to be mistaken, the inferior and subject condition of that race at the time the Constitution was adopted, and long afterwards, throughout the thirteen states by which that instrument was framed; and it is hardly consistent with the respect due to these states to suppose that they regarded at that time, as fellow citizens and members of the sovereignty, a class of beings whom they had thus stigmatized; whom, as we are bound, out of respect to the state sovereignties, to assume they had deemed it just and necessary thus to stigmatize, and upon whom they had impressed such deep and enduring marks of inferiority and degradation; or that when they met in convention to form the Constitution, they looked upon them as a portion of their constituents, or designed to include them in the provisions so carefully inserted for the security and protection of the liberties and rights of their citizens. . . .

What the construction was at that time, we think can hardly admit of doubt. We have the language of the Declaration of Independence and of the Articles of Confederation, in addition to the plain words of the Constitution itself; we have the legislation of the different states, before, about the time, and since the Constitution was adopted; we have the legislation of Congress, from the time of its adoption to a recent period; and we have the constant and uniform action of the Executive Department, all concurring together, and leading to the same result. And if anything in relation to the construction of the Constitution can be regarded as settled, it is that which we not give to the word "citizen" and the word "people."

Upon the whole, therefore, it is the judgment of this court, that it appears by the record before us that the plaintiff in error is not a citizen of Missouri, in the sense in which that word is used in the Constitution; and that the Circuit Court of the United States, for that reason, had no jurisdiction in the case, and could give no judgment in it. . . .

Mr. Justice Curtis, dissenting.

To determine whether any free persons, descended from Africans held in slavery, were citizens of the United States under the Confederation, and consequently at the time of the adoption of the Constitution of the United States, it is only necessary to know whether any such persons were citizens of either of the States under the Confederation, at the time of the adoption of the Constitution.

Of this there can be no doubt. At the time of the ratification of the Articles of Confederation, all free native-born inhabitants of the States of New Hampshire, Massachusetts, New York, New Jersey, and North Carolina, though descended from African slaves, were not only citizens of those states, but such of them as had the other necessary qualifications possessed the franchise of electors, on equal terms with other citizens.

. . . .

I can find nothing in the Constitution which, *proprio vigore,* deprives of their citizenship any class of persons who were citizens of the United States at the time of its adoption, or who should be native-born citizens of any state after its adoption; nor any power enabling Congress to disfranchise persons born on the soil of any state, who is a citizen of that state by force of its Constitution or laws, is also a citizen of the United States.

. . . .

It has been often asserted that the Constitution was made exclusively by and for the white race. It has already been shown that in five of the thirteen original

75

states, colored persons then possessed the elective franchise, and were among those by whom the Constitution was ordained and established. If so, it is not true, in point of fact, that the Constitution was of those persons who were qualified by its laws to act thereon, in behalf of themselves and all other citizens of that state. In some of the states, as we have seen, colored persons were among those qualified by law to act on this subject. These colored persons were not only included in the body of "the people of the United States," by whom the Constitution was ordained and established, but in at least five of the states they had the power to act, and doubtless did act, by their suffrages, upon the question of its adoption. It would be strange, if we were to find in that instrument anything which deprived of their citizenship any part of the people of the United States who were among those by whom it was established.

Youngstown Sheet & Tube Co. v. Sawyer
343 U.S. 579, 582-83, 585-87 (1952)

We are asked to decide whether the President was acting within his constitutional power when he issued an order directing the Secretary of Commerce to take possession of and operate most of the Nation's steel mills. The mill owners argue that the President's order amounts to lawmaking, a legislative function which the Constitution has expressly confided to the Congress and not to the President. The Government's position is that the order was made on findings of the President that his action was necessary to avert a national catastrophe which would inevitably result from a stoppage of steel production, and that in meeting this grave emergency the President was acting within the aggregate of his constitutional powers as the Nation's Chief Executive and the Commander in Chief of the Armed Forces of the United States.

. . . On April 4, 1952, the Union gave notice of a nation-wide strike called to begin at 12:01 a.m. April 9. The indispensability of steel as a component of substantially all weapons and other war materials led the

President to believe that the proposed work stoppage would immediately jeopardize our national defense and that governmental siezure of the steel mills was necessary in order to assure the continued availability of steel.

. . . .

The President's power, if any, to issue the order must stem either from an act of Congress or from the Constitution itself. There is no statute that expressly authorizes the President to take possession of property as he did here. Nor is there any act of Congress to which our attention has been directed from which such a power can fairly be implied. Indeed, we do not understand the Government to rely on statutory authorization for this seizure.

. . . .

The contention is that presidential power should be implied from the aggregate of his powers under the Constitution. Particular reliance is placed on provisions in Article II which say "The executive power shall be vested in a President"; that "he shall take Care that the Laws be faithfully executed"; and that "he shall be Commander-in-Chief of the Army and Navy of the United States."

The order cannot properly be sustained as an exercise of the President's military power as Commander-in-Chief of the Armed Forces. The Government attempts to do so by citing a number of cases upholding broad powers in military commanders engaged in day-to-day fighting in a theater of war. Such cases need not concern us here. Even though "theater of war" be an expanding concept, we cannot with faithfulness to our constitutional system hold that the Commander-in-Chief of the Armed Forces has the ultimate power as such to take possession of private property in order to keep labor disputes from stopping production. This is a job for the Nation's lawmakers, not for its military authorities.

Nor can the seizure order be sustained because of the several constitutional provisions that grant executive power to the President. In the framework of our

Constitution, the President's power to see that the laws are faithfully executed refutes the idea that he is to be a lawmaker. The Constitution limits his functions in the lawmaking process to the recommending of laws he thinks wise and the vetoing of laws he thinks bad. And the Constitution is neither silent nor equivocal about who shall make laws which the President is to execute.

Brown v. Board of Education
347 U.S. 483, 492-95 (1954)

[T]here are findings below that the Negro and white schools involved have been equalized, or are being equalized, with respect to buildings, curricula, qualifications and salaries of teachers, and other "tangible" factors. Our decision, therefore, cannot turn on merely a comparison of these tangible factors in the Negro and white schools involved in each of the cases. We must look instead to the effect of segregation itself on public education.

In approaching this problem, we cannot turn the clock back to 1868 when the Amendment was adopted, or even to 1896 when *Plessy v. Ferguson* was written. We must consider public education in the light of its full development and its present place in American life throughout the Nation. Only in this way can it be determined if segregation in public schools deprives these plaintiffs of the equal protection of the laws.

. . . .

We come then to the question presented: Does segregation of children in public schools solely on the basis of race, even though the physical facilities and other "tangible" factors may be equal, deprive the children of the minority group of equal education opportunities? We believe that it does.

. . . .

. . . To separate [children in grade and high schools] from others of similar age and qualifications solely because of their race generates a feeling of inferiority as to their status in the community that may affect their hearts and minds in a way unlikely ever to be undone. The effect of this separation on their educational opportunities was well stated by a finding in the Kansas case by a court which nevertheless felt compelled to rule against the Negro plaintiffs: "Segregation of white and colored children in public schools has a detrimental effect upon the colored children. The impact is greater when it has the sanction of law; for the policy of separating the races is usually interpreted as denoting the inferiority of the Negro group. A sense of inferiority affects the motivation of a child to learn. Segregation with the sanction of law, therefore, has a tendency to [retard] the educational and mental development of Negro children and to deprive them of some of the benefits they would receive in a racial[ly] integrated school system." Whatever may have been the extent of psychological knowledge at the time of *Plessy v. Ferguson,* this finding is amply supported by modern authority. [Famous footnote 11 setting forth titles of books and articles showing deleterious effects of segregation in education.] Any language in *Plessy v. Ferguson* contrary to this finding is rejected.

We conclude that in the field of public education the doctrine of "separate but equal" has no place. Separate educational facilities are inherently unequal. Therefore, we hold that the plaintiffs and others similarly situated from whom the actions have been brought are, by reason of the segregation complained of, deprived of the equal protection of the laws, guaranteed by the Fourteenth Amendment.

Griswold v. Connecticut
381 U.S. 479, 484-86 (1965)

Various guarantees create zones of privacy. The right of association contained in the penumbra of the First Amendment is one. . . . The Third Amendment in its prohibition against the quartering of soldiers "in any house" in time of peace without the consent of the owner is another facet of that privacy. The Fourth Amendment explicitly affirms the "right of the people to be secure in their persons, houses, papers, and effects, against unreasonable searches and seizures." The Fifth Amendment in its Self-Incrimination Clause enables the citizen to create a zone of privacy which government may not force him to surrender to his detriment. The Ninth Amendment provides: "The enumeration of the Constitution, of certain rights, shall not be construed to deny or disparage others retained by the people."

. . . .

The present case, then, concerns a relationship lying within the zone of privacy created by several fundamental constitutional guarantees. And it concerns a law, which, in forbidding the *use* of contraceptives rather than regulating their manufacture or sale, seeks to achieve its goals by means of having a maximum destructive impact upon that relationship. Such a law cannot stand in light of the familiar principle, so often applied by this Court, that a "governmental purpose to control or prevent activities constitutionally subject to state regulation may not be achieved by means which sweep unnecessarily broadly and thereby invade the area of protected freedoms." [citation omitted] Would we allow the police to search the sacred precincts of marital bedrooms for telltale signs of the use of contraceptives? The very idea is repulsive to the notions of privacy surrounding the marriage relationship.

Roe v. Wade
410 U.S. 113, 129, 152-53, 172-73 (1973)

The principal thrust of appellant's attack on the Texas statutes is that they improperly invade a right, said to be possessed by the pregnant woman, to choose to terminate her pregnancy. Appellant would discover this right in the concept of personal "liberty" embodied in the Fourteenth Amendment's Due Process Clause; or in personal, marital, familial, and sexual privacy said to be protected by the Bill of Rights or its penumbras . . . or among those rights reserved to the people by the Ninth Amendment. . . .

. . . .

The Constitution does not explicitly mention any right of privacy. In a line of decisions . . . the Court has recognized that a right of personal privacy, or a guarantee of certain areas or zones of privacy, does exist under the Constitution. In varying contexts, the Court or individual Justices have, indeed, found at least the roots of that right in the First Amendment . . . in the Fourth and Fifth Amendments . . . in the penumbras of the Bill of Rights . . . in the Ninth Amendment . . . or in the concept of liberty guaranteed by the first section of the Fourteenth Amendment. . . . These decisions make it clear that only personal rights that can be deemed "fundamental" or "implicit in the concept of ordered liberty," . . . are included in this guarantee of personal privacy [and thus require strict scrutiny rather than the less stringent test of examining whether the legislation has a rational relation to a valid state objective]. They also make it clear that the right has some extension to activities relating to marriage . . . procreation . . . contraception . . . family relationships . . . and child rearing and education. . . .

This right of privacy, whether it be founded in the Fourteenth Amendment's concept of personal liberty and restrictions upon state action, as we feel it is, or, as the District Court determined, in the Ninth Amendment's reservation of rights to the people, is broad enough to encompass a woman's decision whether or not to terminate her pregnancy.

. . . .

Rehnquist, J., dissenting.

. . . I have difficulty in concluding, as the Court does, that the right of "privacy" is involved in this case. Texas, by the statute here challenged, bars the performance of a medical abortion by a licensed physician on a plaintiff such as Roe. A transaction resulting in an operation such as this is not "private" in the ordinary usage of that word. Nor is the "privacy" that the Court finds here even a distant relative of the freedom from searches and seizures protected by the Fourth Amendment to the Constitution, which the Court has referred to as embodying a right to privacy.

If the Court means by the term "privacy" no more than that the claim of a person to be free from unwanted state regulation of consensual transactions may be a form of "liberty" protected by the Fourteenth Amendment, there is no doubt that similar claims have been upheld in our earlier decisions on the basis of that liberty. I agree with the statement of MR. JUSTICE STEWART in his concurring opinion that the "liberty," against deprivation of which without due process the Fourteenth Amendment protects, embraces more than the rights found in the Bill of Rights. But that liberty is not guaranteed absolutely against deprivation, only against deprivation without due process of law. The test traditionally applied in the area of social and economic legislation is whether or not a law such as that challenged has a rational relation to a valid state objective.... The Due Process Clause of the Fourteenth Amendment undoubtedly does place a limit, albeit a broad one, on legislative power to enact laws such as this. If the Texas statute were to prohibit an abortion even where the mother's life is in jeopardy, I have little doubt that such a statute would lack a rational relation to a valid state objective.... But the Court's sweeping invalidation of any restrictions on abortion during the first trimester is impossible to justify under that standard, and the conscious weighing of competing factors that the Court's opinion apparently substitutes for the established test is far more appropriate to a legislative judgment than to a judicial one.

Bowers v. Hardwick
478 U.S. 186, 190-91, 195-96 (1986)

This case does not require a judgment on whether laws against sodomy between consenting adults in general, or between homosexuals in particular, are wise or desirable. It raises no question about the right or propriety of state legislative decisions to repeal their laws that criminalize homosexual sodomy, or of state court decisions invalidating those laws on state constitutional grounds. The issue presented is whether the

Federal Constitution confers a fundamental right upon homosexuals to engage in sodomy and hence invalidates the laws of the many States that still make such conduct illegal and have done so for a very long time. The case also calls for some judgment about the limits of the Court's role in carrying out its constitutional mandate.

We first register our disagreement with the Court of Appeals and with respondent that the Court's prior cases have construed the Constitution to confer a right of privacy that extends to homosexual sodomy and for all intents and purposes have decided this case. The reach of this line of cases was . . . described as dealing with child rearing and education; . . . with family relationships; . . . with procreation; . . . with marriage; . . . with contraception; and . . . with abortion. [Certain] cases were interpreted as construing the Due Process Clause of the Fourteenth Amendment to confer a fundamental individual right to decide whether or not to beget or bear a child.

Accepting the decisions in these cases and the above description of them, we think it evident that none of the rights announced in those cases bears any resemblance to the claimed constitutional right of homosexuals to engage in acts of sodomy that is asserted in this case. No connection between family, marriage, or procreation on the one hand and homosexual activity on the other has been demonstrated, either by the Court of Appeals or by respondent. Moreover, any claim that these cases nevertheless stand for the proposition that any kind of private sexual conduct between consenting adults is constitutionally insulated from state proscription is unsupportable. Indeed, [we have] asserted that the privacy right, which the *Griswold* line of cases found to be one of the protections provided by the Due Process Clause, did not reach so far.

Precedent aside, however, respondent would have us announce, as the Court of Appeals did, a fundamental right to engage in homosexual sodomy. This we are quite unwilling to do. It is true that despite the language of the Due Process Clauses of the Fifth and Fourteenth Amendments, which appears to focus only on the processes by which life, liberty, or property is taken, the cases are legion in which those Clauses have been interpreted to have substantive content, subsuming rights that to a great extent are immune from federal or state regulation or proscription. Among such cases are those recognizing rights that have little or no textual support in the constitutional language. . . .

Striving to assure itself and the public that announcing rights not readily identifiable in the Constitution's text involves much more than the imposition of the Justices' own choice of values on the States and the Federal Government, the Court has sought to identify the nature of the rights qualifying for heightened judicial protection.

It is obvious to us that neither of these formulations would extend a fundamental right to homosexuals to engage in acts of consensual sodomy. Proscriptions against that conduct have ancient roots. . . . Sodomy was a criminal offense at common law and was forbidden by the laws of the original thirteen States when they ratified the Bill of Rights. In 1868, when the Fourteenth Amendment was ratified, all but 5 of the 37 States in the Union had criminal sodomy laws. In fact, until 1961, all 50 States outlawed sodomy, and today, 24 States and the District of Columbia continue to provide criminal penalties for sodomy performed in private and between consenting adults. . . . Against this background, to claim that a right to engage in such conduct is "deeply rooted in this Nation's history and tradition" or "implicit in the concept of ordered liberty" is, at best, facetious. . . .

. . . .

Respondent, however, asserts that the result should be different where the homosexual conduct occurs in the privacy of the home. He relies on *Stanley v. Georgia*, 394 U.S. 557 (1969), where the Court held that the First Amendment prevents conviction for possessing and reading obscene material in the privacy of his home: "If the First Amendment means anything, it means that a State has no business telling a man, sitting alone in his house, what books he may read or what films he may watch."

Stanley did protect conduct that would not have been protected outside the home, and it partially prevented the enforcement of state obscenity laws; but the decision was firmly grounded in the First Amendment. The right pressed upon us here has no similar support in the text of the Constitution, and it does not qualify for recognition under the prevailing principles for construing the Fourteenth Amendment. Its limits are also difficult to discern. Plainly enough, otherwise illegal conduct is not always immunized whenever it occurs in the home. Victimless crimes, such as the possession and use of illegal drugs do not escape the law where they are committed at home. *Stanley* itself recognized that its holding offered no protection for the possession in the home of drugs, firearms, or stolen goods. And if respondent's submission is limited to the voluntary sexual conduct between consenting adults, it would be difficult, except by fiat, to limit the claimed right to homosexual conduct while leaving exposed to prosecution adultery, incest, and other sexual crimes even though they are committed in the home. We are unwilling to start down that road.

CHAPTER **6**

Inductive Reasoning

If we can say that deductive reasoning moves from the general to the particular, we can also say that inductive reasoning moves either from the particular to the general, or from the particular to the particular. I recognize that all logicians do not agree with my characterization. For the purposes of legal reasoning, however, I think my analysis is proper because it is useful, and utility is the name of the game.

In mathematics, an induced generalization is a mathematical truth or certainty. In the law, there is no pretense that the product of inductive reasoning is a certainty. All that we represent is that the result is more probably true than not. If in mathematics we take a series of consecutive odd numbers beginning with 1, the sum of these numbers will be equal to the number of terms multiplied by itself. Thus, the sum of the numbers 1-3-5-7-9-11 is 36, or 6 times 6. We reach the generalization—that the sum will equal the number of terms multiplied by itself—only after experience in adding sets of particular numbers. This produces a generality that is certain.

Yet the absence of complete certainty does not diminish the importance of induction in the law. Inductive reasoning is as important as any element in the common-law tradition. It lies at the heart of the judicial process and is the most distinctive characteristic of that process. More than any other technique, it is responsible for a legal tradition that began in England at the beginning of the eleventh century and continues today. Because it is reasoning by example, it is the key to many things. It undergirds the doctrine of precedent, or stare decisis: like things must be treated alike. In the law, the circumstances or phenomena that constitute the particulars in inductive reasoning are the holdings in previous similar cases. These are our precedents. Recall the definition of precedent outlined in Chapter 2; "A judicial precedent attaches a specific legal consequence to a detailed set of facts in an adjudged case or judicial decision, which is then considered as furnishing the rule for the determination of a subsequent case involving identical or similar material facts. . . ." [1] In part, this indicates the hold which the legal process has over litigants. Professor Levi has emphasized this:

> [The litigants] have participated in the law making. They are bound by something they helped to make. Moreover, the examples or analogies urged by the parties bring into the law the common ideas of the society. The ideas have their day in court, and they will have their day again. This is what makes the hearing fair, rather than any idea that the judge is completely impartial, for of course he cannot be completely so. Moreover, the hearing in a sense compels at least vicarious participation by all the citizens, for the rule which is made, even though ambiguous, will be law as to them. [2]

In the law, the method of arriving at a general or, perhaps, a universal proposition (a principle or doctrine) from the particular facts of experience (legal rules or holdings of cases) is called "inductive generalization." This is reasoning from the particular to the general. We borrow this process from the certainty of laboratory science experiments. If nine particular pieces of blue litmus paper turned red when dipped in acid, we may draw a general conclusion about what happens to all blue litmus paper dipped in acid. We use the technique of enumeration to reach an *inductive generalization.* Unlike in science, however, in law we do not assert that our conclusion is true; only that it is more probably true than not. Inductive generalization is used in all aspects of the law: in study, in practice by lawyers, and by judges in both the decisional process and the process of justifica-

[1] Allegheny Gen. Hosp. v. NLRB, 608 F.2d 965, 969 (3d Cir. 1979).

[2] Levi, "An Introduction to Legal Reasoning," 15 U. Chi. L. Rev. 501, 504 (1948).

tion (the court's public statement of its reasoning—the opinion).

Closely related to induced generalization is the process of *analogy*. Analogy is reasoning from the particular to the particular, instead of from the particular to the general. If, from the experience of nine pieces of blue litmus paper, we conclude only that the tenth piece will turn red, we reach a particular, not a general conclusion.

The structure of these two types of inductive arguments—induced generalization and analogy—may be similar, but there is a basic difference, extremely important in the law, when the premises report a number of instances in which the circumstances occur together:

By inductive generalization we may infer that *every* instance of the one attribute will also be an instance of the other. [3]

By analogy we may infer that a different *particular* instance of one attribute will also exhibit the other attribute. [4]

Let us examine inductive generalization in the law:

A's oral conveyance of real estate is invalid.
B's oral conveyance of real estate is invalid.
C's oral conveyance of real estate is invalid. . . .
Z's oral conveyance of real estate is invalid.

Therefore, all oral conveyances of real estate are invalid.

All inference proceeds on the assumption that the new instances will exactly resemble the old one in all material circumstances. This is purely hypothetical, of course, and sometimes we discover we are mistaken. Thus, for years the Europeans proceeded along the following induction:

[3] I. Copi, *Introduction to Logic* 432 (7th ed. 1986) (emphasis added).
[4] *Id.*

A is a swan and it is white.
B is a swan and it is white.
C is a swan and it is white. . . .
Z is a swan and it is white.

Therefore, all swans are white.

But then Australia was discovered and it was learned that there are swans that are black.

Inductive generalization underlies the development of the common law. From many specific case holdings, we reach a generalized proposition. From many cases deciding that individual oral conveyances of real estate were invalid, we reached the conclusion that all such conveyances were invalid. We arrived at that point by what Lord Diplock described as "the cumulative experience of the judiciary." In generalization by enumeration, we can say that the larger the number of specific instances, the more certain is the resulting generalization. This is simply fealty to the concept of probability. We must beware of the converse fallacy of accident (also known as the fallacy of hasty generalization), a fallacious reasoning that seeks to establish a generalization by the enumeration of instances, without obtaining a representative number of instances. You and I call it "jumping to conclusions." It is a practice in which a conclusion is drawn before all the particular instances have been taken into consideration. Thus, "Lawyer A lost a case last year; he lost another six months ago, and another just yesterday. Lawyer A loses all his cases."

In 1988, the Supreme Court decided a narrow issue. The Veterans' Administration characterized primary alcoholism as "willful misconduct" for the purpose of a statute which grants veterans extensions of time in which to use educational benefits, if they are prevented from using their benefits by a physical or mental disorder that did not result from their own "willful misconduct." The Court held that this characterization did not violate section 304 of the Rehabilitation Act, which prohibits discrimination against handicapped individuals solely because of their handicap. This was an extremely narrow decision, and even though the Court said that "[t]his litigation does not require the Court to decide whether alcoholism is a disease whose course its victims cannot control," most press accounts and television reports of the case leaped to a hasty generalization that the Court had decided that alcoholism is a disease within the control of the individual. [5]

Analogy does not seek proof of an identity of one thing with another, but only a comparison of resemblances. Unlike the technique of enumeration, analogy does not depend upon the quantity of instances but upon the quality of resemblances between things. J. S. Mill reduced it to a formula: Two things resemble each other in one or more respects; a certain proposition is true of one; therefore it is true of the other. [6] In legal analogies, we may have two cases which resemble each other in a great many properties, and we infer that some additional property in one will be found in the other. Moreover, the process of analogy is used on a case-by-case basis. It is used to compare the resemblance of prior cases to the case at bar reaching a conclusion as to cases other than the one at bar.

If reaching a conclusion by enumeration has the benefit of experience, reaching a conclusion by analogy has the benefit of the high degree of similarity of the compared data. The degree of similarily is always the crucial inquiry in analogies. Clearly, you cannot conclude that a partial resemblance between two entities is equal to an entire and exact correspondence. Here the skill of the advocate will often be the determining factor. Plaintiff's lawyer may argue that the historical event or entity A—in law, a precedent—bears many resemblances to the case at bar, B. The opponent will argue that although the facts in A and B are similar in some respects, this does not mean that those similarities are material and therefore relevant, or that the cases are similar in other respects; he or she will argue that a false analogy is present.

What is one man's meat is another man's poison. What is one attorney's material and relevant fact in analogical comparisons is the other attorney's immaterial and irrelevant fact. Often the art of advocacy resolves itself into convincing the court which facts in previous cases are indeed positive analogies, and which are not. The judge is required

[5] Traynor v. Turnage, 108 S. Ct. 1372, 1383 (1988).

[6] *See* J. S. Mill, *A System of Logic Ratiocinactive and Inductive* 98-142 (8th ed. 1916).

to draw this distinction. The successful lawyer is one who is able to have the judge draw the distinction in the manner most favorable to the advocate.

But effective advocacy in determining positive/negative analogies must at all times be kept within the perimeters of objectivity. Students and lawyers must not fall in love with pet theories by opening their eyes only to instances that corroborate a favorite belief more readily than those that contradict it. In the process of analogy you must always have a full view of all that relates to the question. Do not be the type of person who sincerely believes that only your thoughts are reason. In the words of John Locke: "They converse but with one sort of man, they read but one set of books, they will not come in the hearing but of one set of motions. . . . They have a pretty traffic with known correspondents in some little creek . . . but will not venture out in the great ocean of knowledge." [7]

Thus, it should now be understood that points of unlikeness are as important as likeness in the cases examined. Comparison without contrast is not an ideal to be followed. In examining the cases, as does a scientist in a laboratory, the lawyer should not look for the rigid fixity of facts. Seldom are there perfectly identical experiences in human affairs. The lawyer must recognize also the problems of those facts, which when compared, prove to be the rare experience in human affairs. And in order to understand completely what is being compared, always be aware of subtleties and minuteness.

Whether using enumerated instances to reach a generalized conclusion to frame a broad legal precept, or selected instances to bring about a convenient analogy, it is well to keep in mind the object of bringing into consideration a multitude of cases. It is to facilitate the selection of the evidential or significant features upon which to base inference in some single case.

To do this effectively, you will be well served to: (1) jettison any pet beliefs or theories if the research is not supportive—do not be dogmatic; (2) not hesitate to confront the novel situation; and (3) remember that the study and prac-

---

[7] J. Dewey, *How We Think* 26 (1933) (citing J. Locke, *The Conduct of Understanding* Ch. 3 (1690)).

tice of law has no room for mental inertia and laziness. Be aware always that the analysis you have failed to pursue will often be performed by your adversary, and if not by him or her, by the judge or the chambers' law clerks.

We repeat again for emphasis that the conclusion reached by inductive reasoning is not considered a truth; rather, it is a proposition that is more probably true than not. We must also understand that often in inductive reasoning the two processes of enumeration and analogy are used simultaneously. From this it follows that, if the conclusion is reached by simultaneously using the twin processes, there is a greater probability that truth will lie in the conclusion. Jevons described this process: "The things usually resemble each other only in two or three properties, and we require to have more instances to assure us that what is true of these is probably true of all similar instances. The less, in short, the intention of the resemblance the greater must be the extension of our inquiries." [8]

Other commentators have made perceptive observations relating to inductive reasoning. Jeffrey G. Murphy observes:

> Most of us, in claiming analogies between various things, rely on perception. That is, we "just see" that Mary is mighty like a rose. And, if pressed to give reasons for making such a claim, we will direct our questioner to certain features of the case that he too can "just see." But there are no decision procedures for "just seeing." There is no logic of perception. However, the legal use of analogy is more like the scientific use than the ordinary use in the following sense: that the claim that X and Y are analogous is made with respect to some theoretical basis. The appeal is not (at least wholly) to perception. Rather the theoretical basis (in law, certain conventional rules of relevance established as precedents) gives us a decision procedure for determining whether or not cases X and Y are indeed analogous. [9]

Yet we must be very careful to make sure that "Mary is mighty like a rose." We must look at Mary with all her warts and blemishes. There must be open-mindedness,

[8] W. Jevons, *Elementary Lessons in Logic: Deductive and Inductive* 208 (1870).
[9] Murphy, "Law Logic," 77 Ethics 193, 197 (1966).

whole-heartedness, and responsibility. [10] From my own experiences as a lawyer, with juices running fast because of intense sympathy for my client's cause—yes, a cause, not a case—I know how strong the tendency is to be closed-minded. This is a mistake. The consummate advocate must look at things free from bias, partisanship, traits, and habits that close the mind and make it unwilling to consider new problems and entertain new ideas. In analyzing previous cases for resemblances and differences in the facts, give full attention to facts from whatever source they come; give full attention to alternative propositions. It is difficult, to be sure, to abandon a pet notion and recognize the possibility of error. But the true advocate realizes that self-conceit is not always the best attitude and that to do your job properly for your client you must be prepared to undergo troublesome hours to alter beliefs that are strongly held at the beginning of research, but that, upon analysis, find little or no support in the law.

To do this there must be whole-heartedness, the ability to work long hours to test both old and new theories. Remember, your responsibility is to advance your client's interest, even if it means dumping the client's original theories and embarking upon fresh consideration of new points of view and new ideas.

Analogies can be considered the most important aspect of the study and practice of law. It is the method by which putative precedents are subjected to the acid test of searching analysis. It is the method to determine whether factual differences contained in the case at bar and those of the case compared are material or irrelevant. This requires counsel to be intellectually responsible at all times, to consider the consequences of projected steps when they reasonably follow from any position taken or about to be taken. Intellectual responsibility means integrity; it means recognizing the true consequences of any proposition or belief. It is irresponsible to cling to a proposition without acknowledging those consequences that will logically flow from it. If it is necessary to "kill the baby," do it, then move to another theory. If you don't, your opponent will kill it for you.

[10] *See, e.g.,* J. Dewey, *supra* note 7, at 30-33.

Arthur L. Goodhart has written:

Having established the material and immaterial facts of the case as seen by the court, we can then proceed to state the principle of the case. It is to be found in the conclusion reached by the judge on the basis of the material facts and on the exclusion of the immaterial ones. In a certain case the court finds that A, B and C exist. It then excludes fact A as immaterial, and on facts B and C it reaches conclusion X. What is the *ratio decidendi* of this case? There are two principles: (1) In any future case in which the facts are A, B and C, the court must reach conclusion X, and (2) in any future case in which the facts are B and C the court must reach conclusion X. In the second case the absence of fact A does not affect the result, for fact A has been held to be immaterial. The court, therefore, creates a principle [makes a value judgment?] when it determines which are the material and which are the immaterial facts on which it bases its decision. [11]

The importance of legal reasoning by analogy cannot be overstated. It is the heart of the study of law; it lies at the heart of the Socratic method. It is important for professors to use the Socratic method, because the method of analogy goes to the fundamentals of the common law tradition. Cardozo has taught us that "[t]he common law does not work from pre-established truths of universal and inflexible validity to conclusions derived from them deductively. Its method is inductive and it draws its generalizations from particulars." [12]

One must always appraise an analogical argument very carefully. Several criteria may be used:

- The acceptability of the analogy will vary proportionally with the number of circumstances that have been analyzed.
- The acceptability will depend upon the number of positive resemblances (similarities) and negative resemblances (dissimilarities).
- The acceptability will be influenced by the relevance of the purported analogies. An argument based on a

[11] Goodhart, "Determining the Ratio Decidendi of a Case," 40 Yale L.J. 161, 179 (1930).

[12] B. Cardozo, *The Nature of the Judicial Process* 22-23 (1921).

single relevant analogy connected with a single instance will be more cogent than one which points out
a dozen irrelevant resemblances.

Here, the keystone is materiality or relevance. Professor
Wigmore gives us an example:

To show that a certain boiler was not dangerously likely to
explode at a certain pressure of steam, other instances of
nonexplosion of boilers at the same pressure would be relevant, provided the other boilers were substantially similar
in type, age, and other circumstances affecting strength. [13]

The use of analogy is graphically illustrated by Judge
Cardozo's opinion in *MacPherson v. Buick Motor Co.,* [14] discussed in Chapter 4 in the explanation of the syllogism.
Buick sold an automobile to a retail dealer who in turn sold
it to MacPherson. While MacPherson was in the car it suddenly collapsed and he was thrown out and injured. One of
the wheels was made of defective wood and the spokes crum-
bled into fragments. Buick had bought the wheel from another manufacturer. There was evidence, however, that its
defects could have been discovered by reasonable inspection
and that Buick had not inspected the wheel.

The question to be determined was whether Buick owed
a duty of care to anyone but its immediate purchaser, in this
case the dealer. Until *MacPherson* was decided, it was settled New York law that liability in negligence was limited
to the immediate purchaser, except where the manufacturer's negligence "put human life in imminent danger." The
leading case was *Thomas v. Winchester,* [15] in which a poison
was falsely labelled and sold to a druggist, who in turn sold
it to a customer.

The *Winchester* rule of "imminent danger" had been applied in a very limited fashion over the years. The defense
in *MacPherson* was that an automobile was at best an "inherently dangerous" instrument and that there is a difference between things "inherently dangerous" (no liability)
and things "imminently dangerous" (liability).

[13] J. Wigmore, *Wigmore's Code of the Rules of Evidence in Trials at Law*
118 (3d ed. 1942).
[14] 217 N.Y. 382, 111 N.E. 1050 (1916).
[15] 6 N.Y. 397 (1852).

Cardozo outlined a series of cases in an effort to determine which facts in the previous cases were similarities and which were dissimilarities relevant to establishing or denying liability on the part of a manufacturer, where the injury was sustained by one who was not the immediate purchaser.

Case 1. *Winchester:* Manufacturer falsely labelled poison.
Held: Manufacturer liable.

Case 2. Manufacturer's defect in a small balance wheel used in a circular saw. Wheel lasted five years before defect surfaced.
Held: Manufacturer not liable.

Case 3. Boiler exploded after testing by manufacturer and owner.
Held: Manufacturer not liable.

Case 4. Contractor built scaffold for painter. An employee of painter was injured when it collapsed.
Held: Contractor liable.

Case 5. Large coffee urn installed in a restaurant exploded and injured a customer.
Held: Manufacturer liable.

Case 6. Bottle of aerated water exploded.
Held: Manufacturer liable.

Case 7. Builder built a defective structure.
Held: Builder liable.

Case 8. Otis built a defective elevator.
Held: Manufacturer liable.

Case 9. Contractor furnished a defective rope.
Held: Contractor liable.

Case 10. Cadillac produced a defective car. The car was then in an accident.
Held: Manufacturer not liable.

Case 11. (Leading English case) Action by driver of mail coach against a contractor who had agreed with the postmaster general to provide and keep the vehicle in repair for the purpose of conveying the royal mail over a prescribed route. The coach broke down and the driver was injured.

Held: Contractor not liable.

Case 12. Dock owner put up a staging outside a ship. Servants of shipowner injured.
Held: Dock owner liable.

Case 13. Defendant sent out a defective truck laden with goods which he had sold. Buyer's servants injured.
Held: Seller liable.

Case 14. Defendant made contract to keep van in repair.
Held: Repairman not liable.

Case 15. A livery stable sent out a vicious horse. A guest of the customer was injured.
Held: Stable owner liable.

Case 16. Master bought a tool for a servants' use. The servant was injured by the defective tool.
Held: Master not liable.

In determining that there was liability in *MacPherson,* Judge Cardozo reasoned:

• A relevant resemblance that established liability in the cases was whether the defendant was a manufacturer.

• A relevant resemblance is that the automobile was designed to go 50 m.p.h. and that unless its wheels were sound and strong, injury was almost certain.

• A relevant difference in the older cases, especially Case 11, the leading English case, is the change in methods of locomotion. Precedents drawn from days of travel by stagecoach do not fit the conditions of travel today.

• The "inherent/imminent" distinction is inapplicable. "[T]he case does not turn upon these restricted niceties. If danger was to be expected as reasonably certain, there was a duty of negligence, and this whether you call the danger inherent or imminent."

Thus, Cases 1, 5, 6, and 8 all involved manufacturers and imposed liability. Cases 2, 3 and 10 involved a manufacturer and imposed no liability. Cases 4, 7, 9, 13, and 15 imposed liability but did not involve manufacturers. Cases 11, 14 and 16 denied liability but did not involve manufacturers.

MacPherson was a landmark decision that produced a major change in the law. Its success as an example of reasoning by analogy can be attributed to the large number of circumstances that were analyzed, the number of positive resemblances in the cited cases, and the admitted relevances of the purported analogies. *MacPherson* announced a legal rule by the method of analogy, but because of the number of enumerated resemblances it soon became known as enunciating a legal principle through the method of inductive generalization.

But reasoning by induction is more than a mere tool in the logical process. It permits the law to move with the times, as aptly illustrated by Cardozo's comparison of the automobile wheels to those of the stagecoach. It is the counter-agent of attempts to embalm legal precepts. It permits the elasticity necessary in order to hearken to the adage: "The law must be stable, but it must not stand still." In a given year, a concept may be introduced in an argument suggesting differences from or similarities to precedents, but fail to win the court's acceptance. Although rejected, the idea achieves a standing in society, or at least, in the legal community, because it has been offered in a public brief and discussed in the official reports of the court either in the majority opinion rejecting it, or in a concurring or dissenting opinion endorsing it. Later, in another case, the idea is suggested again. This time the court may interpret the previous case, perhaps suggesting slight differences in the facts, but this time deciding to adopt the once-rejected idea. In future cases, the idea may be given further definition and tied to other ideas. In this manner, ideas of the community and the social, behavioral, or political sciences now bear the imprimatur of the law. And the process continues. In time the "new idea," once so fresh and novel, itself becomes encrusted and, perhaps, undesirable because new social, economic, and political concepts have been accepted by society. New ideas are then suggested to the court in a given case. Again, there may be a rejection by the court, but as time goes on and new cases are presented, the new "new idea" comes to replace the old "new idea."

Munroe Smith emphasized the same point:

In their effort to give to the social sense of justice articulate expression in rules and in principles, the method of the law-finding experts has always been experimental. The rules and principles of case law have never been treated as final truths, but as working hypotheses, continually retested in those great laboratories of the law, the courts of justice. Every new case is an experiment; and if the accepted rule which seems applicable yields a result which is felt to be unjust, the rule is reconsidered. It may not be modified at once for the attempt to do absolute justice in every single case would make the development and maintenance of general rules impossible; but if a rule continues to work injustice, it will eventually be reformulated. The principles themselves are continually retested; for if the rules derived from a principle do not work well, the principle itself must ultimately be re-examined. [16]

New ideas may take an extensive period of time to germinate and reach acceptance. A classic example is the following concurring opinion of Justice Roger J. Traynor, of the California Supreme Court, suggesting the new concept of strict products liability. The opinion was written in 1944.

Escola v. Coca-Cola
24 Cal. 2d 453, 150 P.2d 436, 440-41 (1944)
(Traynor, J., concurring)

I concur in the judgment, but I believe the manufacturer's negligence should no longer be singled out as the basis of a plaintiff's right to recover in cases like the present one. In my opinion it should now be recognized that a manufacturer incurs an absolute liability when an article that he has placed on the market, knowing that it is to be used without inspection, proves to have a defect that causes injury to human beings. *MacPherson v. Buick Motor Co.,* 217 N.Y. 382, 111 N.E. 1050, L.R.A. 1916F, 696, Ann.Cas.1916C, 440 established the principle, recognized by this court, that irrespective of privity of contract, the manufacturer is responsible for an injury caused by such an article to any

[16] M. Smith, *Jurisprudence* 21 (1909).

person who comes in lawful contact with it. *Sheward v. Virtue*, 20 Cal.2d 410, 126 P.2d 345; *Kalash v. Los Angeles Ladder Co.*, 1 Cal.2d 229, 34 P.2d 481. In these cases the source of the manufacturer's liability was his negligence in the manufacturing process or in the inspection of component parts supplied by others. Even if there is no negligence, however, public policy demands that responsibility be fixed wherever it will most effectively reduce the hazards to life and health inherent in defective products that reach the market. It is evident that the manufacturer can anticipate some hazards and guard against the recurrence of others, as the public cannot. Those who suffer injury from defective products are unprepared to meet its consequences. The cost of an injury and the loss of time or health may be an overwhelming misfortune to the person injured, and a needless one, for the risk of injury can be insured by the manufacturer and distributed among the public as a cost of doing business. It is in the public interest to discourage the marketing of products having defects that are a menace to the public. If such products nevertheless find their way into the market it is in the public interest to place the responsibility for whatever injury they may cause upon the manufacturer, who, even if he is not negligent in the manufacture of the product, is responsible for its reaching the market. However intermittently such injuries may occur and however haphazardly they may strike, the risk of their occurrence is a constant risk and a general one. Against such a risk there should be general and constant protection and the manufacturer is best situated to afford such protection.

Notwithstanding the logic of his opinion, Justice Traynor had to wait eighteen years, from 1944 to 1962, to see his individual views accepted by the California Supreme Court in *Greenman v. Yuba Power Products, Inc.* [17] Justice Traynor persisted; his views survived; and he eventually wrote the opinion of the court adopting the concept of strict

[17] 59 Cal. 2d 57, 377 P.2d 897, 27 Cal. Rptr. 697 (1963).

products liability that he had introduced almost two decades before. In the law, it sometimes takes many years, as here, for new ideas to get substantial acceptance.

But it must be emphasized that the acceptance or rejection of a new idea is a question of law, and this is for the judge, not the jury. It is for the judge to delineate the scope of the rule of law. Often this depends on what facts in the later case will be considered similar to those present when the rule was first announced. The key step in the process of analogy is the finding of similarity or difference, or, if you will, positive resemblances and negative resemblances. In a given case, a judge may find as relevant the existence or absence of facts which prior judges thought unimportant. The judge attempts to see the law as a fairly consistent whole, and in our tradition, he or she must always confront the problem: when is it just to treat different cases as though they were the same? And conversely: when is it just to treat seemingly similar cases as different? This is the ever present challenge for the advocate and the judge alike.

The system works because reasons must be given to justify the determination of resemblances and differences in the relevant facts. The fairness and durability of a judicial decision will always be directly dependent upon how thoughtfully and disinterestedly the court has first identified and then weighed the conflicting social interests involved.

The system also works because there is a large measure of predictability or reckonability in the law. These qualities will be present to the extent that there are correlative logical processes by which conclusions are reached. After almost thirty years as a judge and over twenty years as a law professor, I can quickly recognize the illogical lawyer or student. This person wanders aimlessly. He or she shifts the topic without being aware of it, skips about at random, not only jumps to a conclusion (all of us have to do that at some point), but fails to retrace steps to see whether the conclusion to which he or she has jumped is supported by evidence. The illogical person makes contradictory, inconsistent statements without being sensitive to what he or she is doing.

The system works because good lawyers, and most judges, function as logical persons, that is, persons who carefully regulate processes of perception, comparison, suggestion, inference, and constant testing, to determine what consequence will flow from that being perceived, compared, suggested, inferred and tested. But this does not mean that an analysis, loud with good reason, and presented in logical order will command an inevitable result.

Clark v. Burns
118 Mass. 275, 277 (1875)

The liabilities of common carriers and innkeepers, though similar, are distinct. No one is subject to both liabilities at the same time, and with regard to the same property. The liability of an innkeeper extends only to goods put in his charge as keeper of a public house, and does not attach to a carrier who has no house and is engaged only in the business of transportation. The defendants, as owners of steamboats carrying passengers and goods for hire, were not innkeepers. They would be subject to the liability of common carriers for the baggage of passengers in their custody, and might perhaps be so liable for a watch of the passenger locked up in his trunk with other baggage. But a watch, worn by a passenger on his person by day, and kept by him within reach for use at night, whether retained upon his person, or placed under his pillow, or in a pocket of his clothing hanging near him, is not so intrusted to their custody and control as to make them liable for it as common carriers.

Whether the defendants' regulations as to keeping the doors of the state rooms unlocked, the want of precautions against theft, and the other facts agreed, were sufficient to show negligence on the part of the defendants, was, taking the most favorable view for the plaintiff a question of fact, upon which the decision of the court below was conclusive.

Adams v. New Jersey Steamboat Co.
151 N.Y. 163, 45 N.E. 369 (1896)

The principle upon which innkeepers are charged by the common law as insurer of the money or personal effects of their guests originated in public policy. It was deemed to be a sound and necessary rule that this class of persons should be subjected to a high degree of responsibility in cases where an extraordinary confidence is necessarily reposed in them, and where great temptation to fraud and danger of plunder exists by reason of the peculiar relations of the parties. . . . The relations that exist between a steamboat company and its passengers, who have procured staterooms for their comfort during the journey, differ in no essential respect from those that exist between the innkeeper and his guests.

The passenger procures and pays for his room for the same reasons that a guest at an inn does. There are the same opportunities for fraud and plunder on the part of the carrier that was originally supposed to furnish a temptation to the landlord to violate his duty to the guest.

A steamer carrying passengers upon the water, and furnishing them with rooms and entertainment is, for all practical purposes, a floating inn, and hence the duties which the proprietors owe to their charge ought to be the same. No good reason is apparent for relaxing the rigid rule of the common law which applies as between innkeeper and guest since the same considerations of public policy apply to both relations. . . .

. . . The two relations, if not identical, bear such close analogy to each other that the same rule of responsibility should govern. We are of the opinion, therefore, that the defendant was properly held liable in this case for the money stolen from the plaintiff, without any proof of negligence.

Hixson v. Arkansas
266 Ark. 773, 587 S.W.2d 70, 75-76 (1979)
(Newbern, J., dissenting)

[Defendant was convicted of unlawfully, feloniously, and knowingly obtaining an aggregate sum of money in excess of $2,500 by deception, with the purpose of depriving owners and members of churches of their funds by promising to deliver church directories to the churches. Defendant appealed.]

Assuming there was substantial evidence of deception here, however, I believe this record is devoid of evidence that the Appellant obtained property in excess of a value of $2,500.00 as a result of the offenses charged. As the majority opinion points out, the churches were to pay nothing for the directories. Those institutions were out the value of whatever their services (no pun intended) might have been worth, but there was no attempt whatever to produce evidence of the value of the efforts they expanded in getting their constituent families rounded up for the photography sessions. Nor was any attempt made by the State to show the difference between the value of what the church members received (the photographs) and what they were promised (the photographs plus the "free" directories).

The argument could be made that regardless of the fact that many if not most of the church members received photographs for their money, . . . all that was paid to Appellant for photographs and directories was obtained by deception. The logical extension of that argument, and its fallacy, is perhaps best demonstrated by these illustrations which bear degrees of analogy:

1. X promises A a one-carat diamond in exchange for $1,000.00. A gives X $1,000.00 but X then delivers to A a chunk of glass which is completely without value and which X intended all along to deliver to A instead of a diamond.

2. X promises A a one-carat diamond in exchange for $1,000.00. A gives X $1,000.00, but X then delivers to A a diamond weighing three-quarters of a carat which X intended all along to deliver to A, knowing of the deficiency. The lesser stone is worth $750.00.

3. X promises A a one-carat diamond in exchange for $1,000.00. A gives X $1,000.00, but X then delivers to A a diamond weighing one and one-quarter carats which X intended all along to deliver to A, knowing it to be larger than the one promised. The stone delivered is worth $1,200.00.

If no account is taken of the value received by *A*, then in each of these illustrations, *X* could be convicted of theft of property of a value in excess of $1,000.00. I simply cannot believe our statute contemplates that result in illustrations 2 and 3.

The record here shows many church members received accepted photographs in exchange for their money. The most that can be said for certain is that Appellant took those parts of their payments which could fairly be attributed to the value of the "bonus" directories. We have no idea what that value was. . . . [T]he record here is indeed "replete" with testimony as to other churches which had entered agreements with the Appellant. Even if that evidence was relevant to show a scheme or Appellant's intent, it was completely irrelevant to show the value of the property obtained in the theft alleged here.

As indicated earlier, Justice Traynor waited eighteen years to get his views accepted. Yet this may be considered an extremely short time on some important issues. Often community mores, at least as reflected by its majority views, are not susceptible to quick change. This is especially true in social and political issues where sometimes courts will hide behind selected instances of community views as sources for drawing analogies, and in the process, refuse to recognize the rightness or justness of important and sensitive concerns. The following "fable" is illustrative.

A FABLE FOR OUR TIME

Once upon a time in a galaxy far, far away, certain tribunals held forth to say what was just or what was unjust. The judges who did sit on the tribunals, those who wore beards and long robes, were said to be strong and brave. So brave were they that they feared not the beast of the forest nor man who walked tall and strong in the field and in the town. Yet they had one fear, and its name was woman. The judges feared the rolls of papyrus upon which was written the proclamation of civil righteousness, but most of all their chief fear was three small letters of the alphabet: E and R and A. And when the causes came to be heard before the tribunal, the judges consulted the moon and the stars, and the oracles who divined to discover in the entrails that which they called resemblances in life to serve as implements of decisions that they called analogies. And it was written:

Joyner v. Joyner
59 N.C. 322, 324-26 (5 Jones 331, 333-35) (1862)

It is said on the argument that the fact that a husband, on one occasion "struck his wife with a horse-whip, and on another occasion, with a switch, leaving several bruises on her person," is, of *itself,* a sufficient cause of divorce, and consequently the circumstances which attended the infliction of these injuries are immaterial, and need not be set forth. This presents the question in the case:

The wife must be subject to the husband. Every man must govern his household, and if by reason of an unruly temper, or an unbridled tongue, the wife persistently treats her husband with disrespect, and he submits to it, he not only loses all sense of self-respect, but loses the respect of the other members of his family, without which he cannot expect to govern them, and forfeits the respect of his neighbors. Such have been the incidents of the marriage relation from the beginning of the human race. Unto the woman it is said, "Thy desire shall be to thy husband, and he shall rule over thee," Genesis, chap. 3, v. 16. It follows that the law gives the husband power to use such a degree of force as is necessary to make the wife behave herself and know her place. Why is it that by the principles of the common law if a wife slanders or assaults and beats a neighbor the husband is made to pay for it? Or if the wife commits a criminal offense, less than felony, in the presence of her husband, she is not held responsible? Why is it that the wife cannot make a will disposing of her land? and cannot sell her land without a privy examination, "separate and apart from her husband," in order to see that she did not (*sic*) so voluntarily, and without compulsion on the part of her husband? It is for the reason that the law gives this power to the husband over the person of the wife, and has adopted proper safe-guards to prevent an abuse of it.

We will not pursue the discussion further. It is not an agreeable subject, and we are not inclined, unnecessarily, to draw upon ourselves the charge of a want of proper respect for the weaker sex. It is sufficient for our purpose to state that there may be circumstances, which will mitigate, excuse, and so far justify the husband in striking the wife "with a horse-whip on one occasion and with a switch on another, leaving several bruises on the person," so as not to give her a right to abandon him and claim to be divorced. For instance: suppose a husband comes home and his wife abuses him in the strongest terms—calls him a scoundrel, and repeatedly expresses a wish that he was dead and in torment! and being thus provoked in the *furor brevis,* he strikes her with the horse-whip, which he happens to have in his hands, but is afterwards willing to apologize, and expresses regret for having struck her: or suppose a man and his wife get into a discussion and have a difference of opinion as to a matter of fact, she becomes furious and gives way to her temper, so far as to tell him he *lies,* and upon being admonished not to repeat the word, nevertheless does so, and the husband taking up a switch, tells her if she repeat it again he will strike her, and after this notice she again repeats the insulting words, and he thereupon strikes her several blows; these are cases in which, in our opinion, the circumstances attending the act, and giving rise to it, so far justify the conduct of the husband as to take from the wife any ground of divorce for that cause, and authorize the Court to dismiss her petition with the admonition, "if you will amend your manners, you may expect better treatment," see Shelford on Divorce. So that there are circumstances under which a husband may strike his wife with a horse-whip, or may strike her several times with a switch, so hard as to leave marks on her person, and these acts do not furnish sufficient ground for a divorce. It follows that when such acts are alleged as the causes for a divorce, it is necessary in order to comply with the provisions of the statute, to state the circumstances attending the acts and which gave rise to them.

In re Goodell
39 Wisc. 232, 244 (1875)

So we find no statutory authority for the admission of females to the bar of any court of this state. And, with all the respect and sympathy for this lady which all men owe to all good women, we cannot regret that we do not. We cannot but think the common law wise in excluding women from the profession of the law. The profession enters largely into the well being of society; and, to be honorably filled and safely to society, exacts the devotion of life. The law of nature destines and qualifies the female sex for the bearing and nurture of the children of our race and for the custody of the homes of the world and their maintenance in love and honor. And all life-long callings of women, inconsistent with these radical and sacred duties of their sex, as is the profession of the law, are departures from the order of nature; and when voluntary, treason against it. The cruel chances of life sometimes baffle both sexes, and may leave women free from the peculiar duties of their sex. These may need employment, and should be welcome to any not derogatory to their sex and its proprieties, or inconsistent with the good order of society. But it is public policy to provide for the sex, not for its superfluous members; and not to tempt women from the proper duties of their sex by opening to them duties peculiar to ours. There are many employments in life not unfit for female character. The profession of the law is surely not one of these. The peculiar qualities of womanhood, its gentle graces, its quick sensibility, its tender susceptibility, its purity, its delicacy, its emotional impulses, its subordination of hard reason to sympathetic feeling, are surely not qualifications for forensic strife. Nature has tempered woman as little for the juridical conflicts of the court room, as for the physical conflicts of the battle field. Womanhood is moulded for gentler and better things. And it is not the saints of the world who chiefly give employment to our profession. It has essentially and habitually to do with all that is selfish and malicious, knavish and criminal, coarse and brutal, repulsive and obscene, in human life. It would be revolting to all female sense of the innocence and sanctity of their sex, shocking to man's reverence for womanhood and faith in woman, on which hinge all the better affections and humanities of life, that woman should be permitted to mix professionally in all the nastiness of the world which finds its way into courts of justice; all the unclean issues, all the collateral questions of sodomy, incest, rape, seduction, fornication, adultery, pregnancy, bastardy, legitimacy, prostitution, lascivious cohabitation, abortion, infanticide, obscene publications, libel and slander of sex, impotence, divorce: all the nameless catalogue of indecencies, *la chronique scandaleuse* of all the vices and all the infirmities of all society, with which the profession has to deal, and which go towards filling judicial reports which must be read for accurate knowledge of the law. This is bad enough for men. We hold in too high reverence the sex without which, as is truly and beautifully written, *le commencement de la vie est sans secours, le milieu sans plaisir, et le fin sans consolation,* voluntarily to commit it to such studies and such occupations. *Non tali auxilio nec defensoribus istis,* should juridical contests be upheld. Reverence for all womanhood would suffer in the public spectacle of woman so instructed and so engaged. This motion gives appropriate evidence of this truth. No modest woman could read without pain and self abasement, no woman could so overcome the instincts of sex as publicly to discuss, the case which we had occasion to cite *supra, King v. Wiseman.* And when counsel was arguing for this lady that the word, person, in sec. 32 ch. 119, necessarily includes females, her presence made it impossible to suggest to him as *reductio ad absurdum* of his position, that the same construction of the same word in sec. 1,

110

ch. 37, would subject woman to prosecution for paternity of a bastard, and in secs. 39, 40, ch. 164, to prosecution for rape. Discussions are habitually necessary in courts of justice, which are unfit for female ears. The habitual presence of women at these would tend to relax the public sense of decency and propriety. If, as counsel threatened, these things are to come, we will take no voluntary part in bringing them about.

By the Court—The motion is denied.

And five score years came to pass and the tribunals and the lawgivers and man who walked the field and town no longer had the fear in the heart that had made them tremble and shake as a quaking aspen. They no longer feared woman; woman who now, too, walked head high in the forest and in the field and in the town.

Eslinger v. Thomas
476 F.2d 225, 227 (4th Cir. 1973)

[T]he South Carolina Senate adopted Resolution S.525, establishing new classifications and duties of part-time employees formerly known as pages. Under this resolution, females may be employed as "clerical assistants" and "committee attendants," but not as "Senate pages." . . .

When we apply the [proper] test . . . we are compelled to conclude that S.525 denies equal protection. The "public image" of the South Carolina Senate and of its members is obviously a proper subject of state concern. Apparently, the South Carolina Senate felt that certain functions performed by pages on behalf of senators, e.g., running personal errands, driving senators about in their autos, packing their bags in hotel rooms, cashing personal checks for senators, etc., were "not suitable under existing circumstances for young ladies and may give rise to the appearance of impropriety." . . . In their brief, defendants argue that "[i]n placing this restriction upon female pages, the Senate is merely attempting to avoid placing one of its employees in a conceivably damaging position, protecting itself from appearing to the public that an innocent relationship is not so innocent, and maintaining as much public confidence while conducting the business of the people of South Carolina as possible."

We find this rationale unconvincing. It rests upon the implied premise, which we think false, that "[o]n the one hand, the female is viewed as a pure, delicate and vulnerable creature who must be protected from exposure to criminal influences; and on the other, as a brazen temptress, from whose seductive blandishments the innocent male must be protected. Every woman is either Eve or Little Eva—and either way, she loses." . . . We have only to look at our own female secretaries and female law clerks to conclude that an intimate business relationship, including traveling on circuit, between persons of different sex presents no "appearance of impropriety" in the current age, graduated as we are from Victorian attitudes. We note also that South Carolina has had female senators. While the record does not reflect their ages, the association of female senator with male page has not given rise to a sufficient "appearance of impropriety" to require legislative regulation which is the reverse of S.525. In short, present societal attitudes reject the notion that, in most forms of business endeavor, free association between the sexes is to be limited, regulated and restricted because of a difference in sex.

The 1973 *Eslinger* case shows how far we have come since the former reprehensible treatment of women by the highest courts of the states. The Wisconsin and North Carolina cases have been set forth as recorded examples of the plight of women as recent as the era of our great-grandparents. Those cases purport to draw analogies— improper, to be sure—from the set of mores allegedly present in nineteenth century communities. It is worthwhile to keep these cases in mind if for no other reason than as a reminder, or perhaps an impetus, to say, "Never again!"

CHAPTER 7

The Paradigmatic Common-Law Case

CASE OF DORSET YACHT COMPANY

This chapter discusses how the theoretical concepts of issue identification and the processes of inductive and deductive reasoning apply to a live case. To illustrate these concepts I will use the opinion of Lord Diplock in the House of Lords in *Dorset Yacht Co. v. Home Office.* [1] The case was one of first impression in the Court of Appeal and the House of Lords. Seven Borstal boys (British juvenile detention residents) were working on an island under the control and supervision of three officers from the Home Office. During the night, the boys left the island, boarded, cast adrift, and damaged the plaintiffs' yacht, which was moored offshore. The plaintiffs brought an action for damages against the Home Office which charged negligence. In particular, they alleged that the officers, knowing of the boys' criminal records and records of previous escapes from Borstal institutions, and knowing that crafts such as the plaintiffs' yacht were moored offshore, had failed to exercise effective control and supervision of the boys. The Home Office conceded that they were vicariously liable for the torts of their servants (the officers), but denied that they, or their servants or agents, owed the plaintiffs any duty of care with respect to the detention, supervision, or control, of the boys.

Lord Diplock stated the issue:

[1] 1970 App. Cas. 1004, 1057-1071 (Lord Diplock). All quotations in this chapter are excerpted from Lord Diplock's opinion in *Dorset Yacht Co. v. Home Office.*

113

Is any duty of care to prevent the escape of a Borstal trainee from custody owed by the Home Office to persons whose property would be likely to be damaged by the tortious acts of the Borstal trainee if he escaped?

Lord Diplock then explained that the first task of the court was to decide among several competing legal precepts. He noted that this was a case of first impression and that some subjective input, a value judgment, would go into the decision of choosing between the two legal precepts: denying or extending liability.

This is the first time that this specific question has been posed at a higher judicial level than that of a county court. Your Lordships in answering it will be performing [the] judicial function . . . of deciding whether the English law of civil wrongs should be extended to impose legal liability to make reparation for the loss caused to another by conduct of a kind which has not hitherto been recognised by the courts as entailing any such liability.

This function, which judges hesitate to acknowledge as lawmaking, plays at most a minor role in the decision of the great majority of cases, and little conscious thought has been given to analysing its methodology. Outstanding exceptions are to be found in the speeches of Lord Atkin in *Donoghue v. Stevenson* and of Lord Devlin in *Hedley Byrne & Co. Ltd. v. Heller & Partners Ltd.* It was because the former was the first authoritative attempt at such an analysis that it has had so seminal an effect upon the modern development of the law of negligence.

It will be apparent that I agree with the Master of the Rolls that what we are concerned with in this appeal "is . . . at bottom a matter of public policy which we as judges, must resolve." He cited in support Lord Pearce's dictum in *Hedley Byrne & Co. Ltd. v. Heller & Partners Ltd.* [1964] A.C. 465, 536: "How wide the sphere of the duty of care in negligence is to be laid depends ultimately upon the courts' assessment of the demands of society for protection from the carelessness of others."

The reference in this passage to "the courts" in the plural is significant, for as Lord Devlin in the Court of Appeals had put it: "As always in English law, the first step in such an inquiry is to see how far the authorities have gone, for new categories in the law do not spring into existence overnight."

114

In the next section, Lord Diplock combines the processes of enumeration and analogy to justify the court's use of public interest in a negligence case. He also describes how the process of inductive reasoning is used to arrive at the major premise.

The justification of the courts' role in giving the effect of law to the judges' conception of the public interest in the field of negligence is based upon the cumulative experience of the judiciary of the actual consequences of lack of care in particular instances. And the judicial development of the law of negligence rightly proceeds by seeking first to identify the relevant characteristics that are common to the kinds of conduct and relationships between the parties which are involved in the case for decision and the kinds of conduct and relationships which have been held in previous decisions of the courts to give rise to a duty of care.

The method adopted at this stage of the process is analytical and inductive. It starts with an analysis of the characteristics of the conduct and relationship involved in each of the decided cases. But the analyst must know what he is looking for, and this involves his approaching his analysis with some general conception of conduct and relationships which ought to give rise to a duty of care.

A generalization "based on the cumulative experience of the judiciary," is simply an elegant way of describing an enumeration of instances. Just as "seeking . . . to identify the relevant characteristics that are common [among cases]" is no more than analogy. You will also note that the process described in the second cited paragraph is a classic description of inductive reasoning.

As we read on, Lord Diplock will carefully craft the logical form that the preliminary conclusion will take. This is very important because the *conclusion* of the inductive reasoning process will become the *major premise* of the subsequent deductive reasoning process.

This analysis leads to a proposition which can be stated in the form: "In all the decisions that have been analysed a duty of care has been held to exist wherever the conduct and the relationship possessed each of the characteristics A, B, C, D, etc., and has not so far been found to exist when any of these characteristics were absent."

For the second stage, which is deductive and analytical, that proposition is converted to: "In all cases where the conduct and relationship possess each of the characteristics A, B, C, D, etc., a duty of care arises." The conduct and relationship involved in the case for decision is then analysed to ascertain whether they possess each of these characteristics. If they do the conclusion follows that a duty of care does arise in the case for decision.

Note well the presence of the elements we discussed in the anatomy of the Socrates-is-a-man syllogism. The subject (middle term) of the proposition is distributed because it encompasses all. ("In *all* cases where the conduct, etc.") The proposition is affirmative. The major premise is thus both categorical and distributed.

Lord Diplock goes on in the next excerpt to explain that because the present case is lacking at least one of the characteristics, A, B, C, or D, etc., a reasoned judgment must be made by the House of Lords, a judgment that goes beyond the formal logical structure of any argument. It is a judgment influenced by the judges' concept of public policy: Do we hold the line on liability here, or, do we redefine the characteristics in more general terms, so as to extend the law of liability beyond what has gone before?

To preserve the logical form, however, in the process of analogy, it is necessary to exclude those cases not relevant to the case at bar. This is extremely critical because (if you will pardon an Aldisert aphorism that has become a cliche to my students and colleagues): "We must separate that which is important from that which is merely interesting." You will note how the emphasis is now on *relevant* resemblances:

But since ex hypothesi the kind of case which we are now considering offers a choice whether or not to extend the kinds of conduct or relationships which give rise to a duty of care, the conduct or relationship which is involved in it will lack at least one of the characteristics A, B, C or D, etc. And the choice is exercised by making a policy decision as to whether or not a duty of care ought to exist if the characteristic which is lacking were absent or redefined in terms broad enough to include the case under consideration. The policy decision will be influenced by the same general conception of what ought to give rise to a duty of care as was used in approaching the analysis. The choice to extend is given effect to by redefining the characteristics in more general terms so as to exclude the necessity to conform to limitations imposed by the former definition which are considered to be inessential. The cases which are landmarks in the common law, such as *Lickbarrow v. Mason* (1787) 2 Term Rep. 63, *Rylands v. Fletcher* (1868) L.R. 3 H.L. 330, *Indermaur v. Dames* (1866) L.R. 1 C.P. 274, *Donoghue v. Stevenson* [1932] A.C. 562, to mention but a few, are instances of cases where the cumulative experience of judges has led to a restatement in wide general terms of characteristics of conduct and relationships which give rise to legal liability.

Inherent in this methodology, however, is a practical limitation which is imposed by the sheer volume of reported cases. The initial selection of previous cases to be analysed will itself eliminate from the analysis those in which the conduct or relationship involved possessed characteristics which are obviously absent in the case for decision.

Lord Diplock then restates the conclusion previously reached by inductive reasoning, which now becomes the major premise of the formulation of the deductive syllogism.

The proposition used in the deductive stage is not a true universal. It needs to be qualified so as to read: "In all cases where the conduct and relationship possess each of the characteristics A, B, C and D, etc., *but do not possess any of the characteristics Z, Y or X etc. which were present in the cases eliminated from the analysis,* a duty of care arises."

But this qualification, being irrelevant to the decision of the particular case, is generally left unexpressed.

A survey of cases then followed (about which more later). His research completed, Lord Diplock stated:

The result of the survey of previous authorities can be summarised in the words of Dixon J. in *Smith v. Leurs,* 70 C.L.R. 256, 262: "The general rule is that one man is under no duty of controlling another man to prevent his doing damage to a third. There are, however, special relations which are the source of a duty of this nature."

From the previous decisions of the English courts, in particular those in *Ellis v. Home Office* [1953] 2 All E.R. 149 and *D'Arcy v. Prison Commissioners,* "The Times," November 17,

1955, which I accept as correct, it is possible to arrive by induction at an established proposition of law as respects one of those special relations, viz.: "A is responsible for damage caused to the person or property of B by the tortious act of C (a person responsible in law for his own acts) where the relationship between A and C has the characteristics (1) that A has the legal right to detain C in penal custody and to control his acts while in custody; (2) that A is actually exercising his legal right of custody of C at the time of C's tortious act and (3) that A if he had taken reasonable care in the exercise of his right of custody could have prevented C from doing the tortious act which caused damage to the person or property of B; and where also the relationship between A and B has the characteristics (4) that at the time of C's tortious act A has the legal right to control the situation of B or his property as respects physical proximity to C and (5) that A can reasonably foresee that B is likely to sustain damage to his person or property if A does not take reasonable care to prevent C from doing tortious acts of the kind which he did."

Upon the facts which your Lordships are required to assume for the purposes of the present appeal the relationship between the defendant, A, and the Borstal trainee, C, did possess characteristics (1) and (3) but did not possess characteristic (2), while the relationship between the defendant, A, and the plaintiff, B, did possess characteristic (5) but did not possess characteristic (4).

What your Lordships have to decide as respects each of the relationships is whether the missing characteristic is essential to the existence of the duty or whether the facts assumed for the purposes of this appeal disclose some other characteristic which if substituted for that which is missing would produce a new proposition of law which *ought* to be true.

Lord Diplock then decided:

I should therefore hold that any duty of a Borstal officer to use reasonable care to prevent a Borstal trainee from escaping from his custody was owed only to persons whom he could reasonably foresee had property situate in the vicinity of the place of detention of the detainee which the detainee was likely to steal or to appropriate and damage in the course of eluding immediate pursuit and recapture.

The major premise thus being narrowed and restated through an analysis of the relevant cases, Lord Diplock proceeded to set out the framework for determining the major premise:

> If, therefore, it can be established at the trial of this action (1) that the Borstal officers in failing to take precautions to prevent the trainees from escaping were acting in breach of their instructions and not in bona fide exercise of a discretion delegated to them by the Home Office as to the degree of control to be adopted and (2) that it was reasonably foreseeable by the officers that if these particular trainees did escape they would be likely to appropriate a boat moored in the vicinity of Brownsea Island for the purpose of eluding immediate pursuit and to cause damage to it, the Borstal officers would be in breach of a duty of care owed to the plaintiff and the plaintiff would, in my view, have a cause of action against the Home Office as vicariously liable for the "negligence" of the Borstal officers.

The minor premise then becomes obvious:

> *Minor Term*   *Middle Term*
>
> The Borstal officers did or did not act as described in (1) and (2).

As does the conclusion:

> *Minor Term*   *Major Term*
>
> Therefore, the Borstal officers are or are not liable.

METHOD OF ANALOGY

It may be useful now to summarize the facts considered by Lord Diplock when he utilized the method of analogy. His inquiry was divided into two stages. The first was to decide if the plaintiffs' interpretation of the leading case of *Donoghue v. Stevenson* [2] was correct.

In *Donoghue,* Lord Atkin had warned, "it is of particular importance to guard against the danger of stating propositions of law in wider terms than is necessary." Lord Diplock pointed out that the plaintiff, Dorset Yacht Co., disregarded the warning by seeking "to treat as a universal not the specific proposition of law in *Donoghue v. Stevenson* which was about a manufacturer's liability for damage caused by his

[2] 1932 App. Cas. 562, 589.

dangerous products but the well-known aphorism used by Lord Atkin to describe a 'general conception of relations giving rise to a duty of care.' "

> You must take reasonable care to avoid acts or omissions which you can reasonably foresee would be likely to injure your neighbour. Who, then, in law is my neighbour? The answer seems to be—persons who are so closely and directly affected by my act that I ought reasonably to have them in contemplation as being so affected when I am directing my mind to the acts or omissions which are called in question.

Lord Diplock explained that this aphorism is to be "[u]sed as a guide to characteristics which will be found to exist in conduct and relationships which give rise to a legal duty of care," but "misused as a universal it is manifestly false." He went on to demonstrate that in English law, there are many instances in which no legal liability would be incurred where an act or omission by one party causes loss or damage to another, even though that loss or damage might have been anticipated. His examples included:

> You may cause loss to a tradesman by withdrawing your patronage even though the goods supplied are entirely satisfactory;

> You may damage your neighbour's land by intercepting the flow of percolating water to it even though the interception is of no advantage to yourself;

> You need not warn him of a risk of physical danger to which he is about to expose himself unless there is a special relationship between the two of you such as that of occupier of land and visitor;

> You may watch your neighbour's goods being ruined by a thunderstorm though the slightest effort on your part could protect them from the rain and you may do so with impunity unless there is some special relationship between you such as that of bailor and bailee.

Lord Diplock then noted that the propositions of law in *Donoghue* were not applied in *Hedley Byrne & Co., Ltd. v. Heller & Partners, Ltd.,* [3] which involved careless words rather than careless deeds. He proceeded to formulate the inquiry for stage two of his analysis:

[3] 1964 App. Cas. 465.

In the present appeal, too, the conduct of the defendant which is called in question differs from the kind of conduct discussed in *Donoghue v. Stevenson* in at least two special characteristics. First, the actual damage sustained by the plaintiff was the direct consequence of a tortious act done with conscious volition by a third party responsible in law for his own acts and this act was interposed between the act of the defendant complained of and the sustention of damage by the plaintiff. Secondly, there are two separate "neighbour relationships" of the defendant involved, a relationship with the plaintiff and a relationship with the third party. These are capable of giving rise to conflicting duties of care.

This appeal, therefore, also raises the lawyer's question: "Am I my brother's keeper?" A question which may also receive restricted reply.

I start, therefore, with an examination of the previous cases in which both or one of these special characteristics are present.

It bears mention that here Lord Diplock had to make a value judgment as to what facts are really relevant; that is to say, what are the relevant resemblances in the facts and the relevant differences.

Case 1, 2   (*Ellis v. Home Office* & *D'Arcy v. Prison Commissioners*) The legal custodian of a prisoner detained in a prison owed a duty of care to prevent that prisoner from injuring another. Difference from the case at bar: the prisoner was in actual custody of the defendant, giving the custodian a continuing power of physical control over the acts of the prisoner.

Lord Diplock: "But I do not think that, save as a deliberate policy decision, any proposition of law based on the decisions in these two cases would be wide enough to extend to a duty to take reasonable care to prevent the escape of a prisoner from actual physical custody and control owed to a person whose property is situated outside the prison premises and is damaged by the tortious act of the prisoner *after his escape.*"

Case 3   New York and California cases. Lord Diplock
           did not find them helpful because American
           law was developing differently from that in
           England.
Case 4   Damage to plaintiff by mental patient re-
           leased on a visit. Doctors were sued. Jury
           found for plaintiff.
Case 5   Four-year-old child ran out into the highway
           from a school maintained by defendant and
           caused an accident to a driver trying to avoid
           him. Defendant held liable for not taking rea-
           sonable care to keep the gate shut.
           Lord Diplock: Cases 4 and 5 do not control be-
           cause the acts were not committed by mature
           responsible human beings.

CONCLUSION

From the previous decisions, particularly Cases 1 and
2 above, Lord Diplock concluded it is possible to arrive by
induction at an established proposition of law describing
special relations which give rise to a duty in one man to control another to prevent his doing damage to a third. Because
the relationship in the Borstal boys case did not exactly
match that in the prior cases, Lord Diplock had to decide
whether the resemblances were sufficient and/or the differences significant. By examining several over-arching common law principles relating to the acts of public authorities,
Lord Diplock was able to show how the resemblances out-
weighed the differences.

So to hold would be a rational extension of the relationship
between the custodian and the person sustaining the damage which was accepted in *Ellis v. Home Office* (1953) 2 All
E.R. 149 and *D'Arcy v. Prison Commissioners*, "The Times,"
November 17, 1955, as giving rise to a duty of care on the
part of the custodian to exercise reasonable care in controlling his detainee. In those two cases the custodian had a legal
right to control the physical proximity of the person or property sustaining the damage to the detainee who caused it.
The extended relationship substitutes for the right to control
the knowledge which the custodian possessed or ought to
have possessed that physical proximity in fact existed.

CHAPTER 8

Socratic Method

We can now talk about the Socratic method of teaching law. The bane of all law students, the method is especially wrenching during the first year. It is a confusing experience because most students, frankly, do not know what the professor is driving at. The answer is simple: The professor is giving the student a double-barreled learning exercise—teaching the fundamentals of substantive law, but doing it in such a way that the student is exposed to daily drills in legal logic. Let's face it, the system causes frustration, insecurity, embarrassment, and many unpleasant hours.

This book has been designed to eliminate some of the bewilderment and help students understand the nature of the Socratic beast. And, lest lawyers might say at this point, "that stuff is all behind me—I need read no further," let me say now that the Socratic method is utilized every day by thinking lawyers to analyze written and oral arguments, by senior partners in discussing young associates' memoranda, and, especially, by judges in "hot courts" who use the method on lawyers. It is not an exaggeration to say that many lawyers appear as befuddled as first-year law students when judges use the Socratic method in open court to test the soundness of oral argument. Judges use the method for two purposes—one, to clarify arguments that appear muddled in the briefs or as offered in court, and, two, in multi-judge courts, as a sort of internal advocacy by which a judge may inform colleagues on the bench of his views on a case. The failure of many lawyers to be prepared for piercing questions has led me to state often, "Cases are not won in oral argument, they are only lost there."

The Socratic method may be defined as a dialectical method of teaching or discussion as used by Socrates. It involves the asking of questions that inevitably lead the answerer to a logical conclusion, intended and foreseen by the professor or judge. It is an art or practice of forcing opinions or ideas to be examined with an unrelenting logical process in order to test their soundness and validity.

The Socratic method follows a specific ritual in today's law schools. The centerpieces are previously assigned lead cases from casebooks covering a specific legal discipline, e.g., contracts, torts, crimes, property, constitutional law, civil procedure. These cases consist of excerpts from publicly recorded opinions of a court—usually an appellate court, but sometimes a trial court. Prior to class, the student is required to read each assigned case and be familiar with (a) the facts, (b) the issue posed for decision, (c) the conclusion, and (d) the reasons stated to support the conclusion (the ratio decidendi or rationale). Often, comments supplementing the leading case and references to other cases will be found. It is critical to read the case in advance and to outline (brief) its elements; otherwise, the student will be lost in the discussion. Often, the cases are selected by the professor for their excellent reasoning content; yet sometimes, for the exact opposite, as examples of poor reasoning.

Preparing for class is only a threshold endeavor. It is simply the beginning point of the lesson. The professor takes off from there and seeks to draw from the students whether the reasoning stated in the case is sound or unsound. The professor does this by posing questions, not only to the student called upon to recite, but to other students as well. The professor will be prepared to follow up each answer with further questions. The students soon understand that there is usually no quick "yes/no" answer in the law. The professor will introduce hypothetical fact situations that differ from those in the assigned case and inquire whether added or subtracted facts would make a difference in the result. This is done to sharpen the students' perception by requiring them to evaluate resemblances and differences in the fact patterns of the compared cases. Students are consistently tossed in an unrelenting sea change of analogy. They are required to understand and evaluate stated reasons in an effort to conclude whether the particular rationale supporting the case can legitimately support the same result in other fact patterns, and if so, why. An understanding of the principles of deduction and induction will significantly assist the student in this daily exercise. These principles will not supply a pat answer, but they form a guide to a reasoned response.

Aside from adhering to logical form, the student must be able to perceive the relative truth or falsity of asserted legal propositions to determine if there is any material fallacy of content (of which more later) in both the case and the hypothetical posed by the instructor. Knowledge of legal propositions comes from previous cases studied, for the case books are arranged to show the development of the relevant legal precepts. With an understanding of logic, the student should be able to grasp the sense of the questions if the student knows (a) the truth or falsity of the premises (reflected in legal precepts), (b) the rules of deduction and induction, and (c) how to spot the relevant and material resemblances and differences in fact situations put by the professor in the questions. Thus, the goal of the study of law is twofold: to learn the high points of substantive and procedural law, subject by subject, and at the same time to develop skills in legal logic.

SOCRATES' DIALOGUES

The Socratic method comes from the memorable dialogues of Socrates, the great Athenian philosopher and teacher who set the model used today. Plato has recorded Crito's visit to Socrates in his prison cell in 399 B.C. Socrates had been found guilty by the Athenian court and was scheduled to die on the day following the visit by Crito, his good friend. Crito explained to Socrates that Socrates was loved and respected by many Athenians and that Crito and his friends could manage Socrates' escape from the Athens prison to Thessaly. Socrates responded:

Soc.: Now you, Crito, are a disinterested person who are not going to die tomorrow—at least, there is no human probability of this, and you are therefore not liable to be deceived by the circumstances in which you are placed. Tell me then, whether I am right in saying that some opinions, and the opinions of some men only, are to be valued, and other opinions, and the opinions of other men, are not to be valued. I ask you whether I was right in maintaining this?

Cr.: Certainly.

Soc.: The good are to be regarded, and not the bad?

Cr.: Yes.

Soc.: And the opinions of the wise are good, and the opinions of the unwise are evil?

Cr.: Certainly.

Soc.: And what was said about another matter? Was the disciple in gymnastics supposed to attend to the praise and blame and opinion of every man, or of one man only—his physician or trainer, whoever that was?

Cr.: Of one man only.

Soc.: And he ought to fear the censure and welcome the praise of that one only, and not of the many?

Cr.: That is clear.

Soc.: And he ought to live and train, and eat and drink in the way which seems good to his single master who has understanding, rather than according to the opinion of all other men put together?

Cr.: True.

Soc.: And if he disobeys and disregards the opinion and approval of the one, and regards the opinion of the many who have no understanding, will he not suffer evil?

Cr.: Certainly he will.

. . .

Soc.: Then, my friend, we must not regard what the many say of us: but what he, the one man who has understanding of just and unjust, will say, and what the truth will say. And therefore you begin in error when you suggest that we should regard the opinion of the many about just and unjust, good and evil, honorable and dishonorable.—Well, some one will say, "but the many can kill us."

Cr.: Yes, Socrates; that will clearly be the answer.

Soc.: That is true: but still I find with surprise that the old argument is, as I conceive, unshaken as ever. And I should like to know whether I may say the same of another proposition—that not life, but a good life, is to be chiefly valued?

. . .

Cr.: I think that you are right, Socrates; how then shall we proceed?

Soc.: Let us consider the matter together, and do you either refute me if you can, and I will be convinced; or else cease, my dear friend, from repeating to me that I ought to escape against the wishes of the Athenians: for I am extremely desirous to be persuaded by you, but not against my own better judgment. And now please to consider my first position, and do your best to answer me.

Cr.: I will do my best.

Soc.: Are we to say that we are never intentionally to do wrong, or that in one way we ought and in another way we ought not to do wrong, or is doing wrong always evil and dishonorable, as I was just now saying, and as has been already acknowledged by us? Are all our former admissions which were made within a few days to be thrown away? And have we, at our age, been earnestly discoursing with one another all our life long only to discover that we are no better than children? Or are we to rest assured, in spite of the opinion of the many, and in spite of consequences whether better or worse, of the truth of what was then said, that injustice is always an evil and dishonor to him who acts unjustly? Shall we affirm that?

Cr.: Yes.

Soc.: Then we must do no wrong?

Cr.: Certainly not.

Soc.: Nor when injured injure in return, as the many imagine; for we must injure no one at all?

Cr.: Clearly not.

Soc.: Again, Crito, may we do evil?

Cr.: Surely not, Socrates.

Soc.: And what of doing evil in return for evil, which is the morality of the many—is that just or not?

Cr.: Not just.

Soc.: For doing evil to another is the same as injuring him?

Cr.: Very true.

Soc.: Then we ought not to retaliate or render evil for evil to any one, whatever evil we may have suffered from him. . . . Tell me, then, whether you agree with and assent to my first principle, that neither injury nor retaliation nor warding off evil by evil is ever right. And shall that be the premiss of our argument? Or do you decline and dissent from this? For this has been of old and is still my opinion; but, if you are of another opinion, let me hear what you have to say. If, however, you remain of the same mind as formerly, I will proceed to the next step.

Cr.: You may proceed, for I have not changed my mind.

Soc.: Then I will proceed to the next step, which may be put in the form of a question:—Ought a man to do what he admits to be right, or ought he to betray the right?

Cr.: He ought to do what he thinks right.

Soc.: But if this is true, what is the application? In leaving the prison against the will of the Athenians, do I wrong any? Or rather do I not wrong those whom I ought least to wrong? Do I not desert the principles which were acknowledged by us to be just? What do you say?

Cr.: I can not tell, Socrates; for I do not know.

Soc.: Then consider the matter in this way:—Imagine that I am about to play truant (you may call the proceeding by any name which you like), and the laws and the government come and interrogate me: "Tell us, Socrates," they say; "what are you about? Are you going by an act of yours to overturn us—the laws and the whole state, as far as in you lies? Do you imagine that a state can subsist and not be overthrown, in which the decisions of law have no power, but are set aside and overthrown by individuals?" What will be our answer, Crito, to these and the like words? Any one, and especially a clever rhetorician, will have a good deal to urge about the evil of setting aside the law which requires a sentence to be carried out; and we might reply, "Yes; but the state has injured us and given an unjust sentence." Suppose I say that?

Cr.: Very good, Socrates.

Soc.: "And was that our agreement with you?" the law would say; "or were you to abide by the sentence of the state?" And if I were to express astonishment at their saying this, the law would probably add: "Answer, Socrates, instead of opening your eyes: you are in the habit of asking and answering questions. Tell us what complaint you have to make against us which justifies you in attempting to destroy us and the state? In the first place did we not bring you into existence? Your father married your mother by our aid and begat you. Say whether you have any objection to urge against those of us who regulate marriage?" None, I should reply. "Or against those of us who regulate the system of nurture and education of children in which you were trained? Were not the laws, who have the charge of this, right in commanding your father to train you in music and gymnastic?" Right, I should reply. "Well then, since you were brought into the world and nurtured and educated by us, can you deny in the first place that you are our child and slave, as your fathers were before you? And if this is true you are not on equal terms with us; nor can you think that you have a right to do to us what we are doing to you. Would you have any right to strike or revile or do any other evil to a father or to your master, if you had one, when you have been struck or reviled by him, or received some other evil at his hands?—you would not say this? And because we think right to destroy you, do you think that you have any right to destroy us in return, and your country as far as in you lies? . . .

Cr.: I think that they do.

Soc.: Then the laws will say: "Consider, Socrates, if this is true, that in your present attempt you are going to do us wrong. For, after having brought you into the world, and nurtured and educated you, and given you and every other citizen a share in every good that we have to give, we further proclaim and give the right to every Athenian, that if he does not like us when he has come of age and has seen the ways of the city, and made our acquaintance, he may go where he pleases and take his goods with him; and none of us laws will forbid him or interfere with him. Any of you who does not like us and the city, and who wants to go to a colony or to any other city, may go where he likes, and take his goods with him. But he who has experience of the manner in which we order justice and administer the state, and still remains, has entered into an implied contract that he will do as we command him. And he who disobeys us is, as we maintain, thrice wrong; first, because in disobeying us he is disobeying his parents; secondly, because we are the authors of his education; thirdly, because he has made an agreement with us that he will duly obey our commands; and he neither obeys them nor convinces us that our commands are wrong; and we do not rudely impose them, but give them the alternative of obeying or convincing us;—that is what we offer, and he does neither. . . . And first of all answer this very question: Are we right in saying that you agreed to be governed accordingly to us in deed, and not in word only? Is that true or not? How shall we answer that, Crito? Must we not agree?

Cr.: There is no help, Socrates.

Soc.: Then will they not say: "You, Socrates, are breaking the covenants and agreements which you made with us at your leisure, not in any haste or under any compulsion or deception, but having had seventy years to think of them, during which time you were at liberty to leave the city, if we were not to your mind or if our covenants appeared to you to be unfair. You had your choice, and might have gone either to Lacedaemon or Crete, which you often praise for their good government, or to some other Hellenic or foreign state. Whereas you, above all other Athenians, seemed to be so fond of the state, or, in other words, of us her laws (for who would like a state that has no laws), that you never stirred out of her, the halt, the blind, the maimed were not more stationary in her than you were. And now you run away and forsake your agreements. Not so, Socrates, if you will take our advice; do not make yourself ridiculous by escaping out of the city. . . . Listen, then Socrates, to us who have brought you up. Think not of life and children first, and of justice afterwards, but of justice first, that you may be justified before the princes of the world below. For neither will you nor any that belong to you be happier or holier or juster in this life, or happier in another, if you do as Crito bids. Now you depart in innocence, a sufferer and not a doer of evil; a victim not of the laws, but of men. But if you go forth, returning evil for evil, and injury for injury, breaking the covenants and agreements which you have made with us, and wronging those whom you ought least to wrong, that is to say, yourself, your friends, your country, and us, we shall be angry with you while you live, and our brethren, the laws in the world below, will receive you as an enemy; for they will know that you have done your best to destroy us. Listen, then, to us and not to Crito."

This is the voice which I seem to hear murmuring in my ears, like the sound of the flute in the ears of the mystic; that voice, I say, is humming in my ears, and prevents me from hearing any other. And I know that anything more which you may say will be vain. Yet speak, if you have anything to say.

Cr.:   I have nothing to say, Socrates.

Soc.:   Then let me follow the intimations of the will of God. [1]

SOCRATIC DIALOGUE
LAW SCHOOL STYLE

A contracts to sell and *B* to buy twenty dressed hogs and twenty live hogs at stated prices for each quantity. *A* is to deliver the dressed hogs first and the live hogs fifteen days later. *B* is to pay for each delivery within thirty days after it is made. If either party breaches the agreement, the other party is released from an obligation to perform.

Socrates: Assume *A* delivers the dressed hogs, but fifteen days later refuses to deliver the live hogs. *A* demands payment for the dressed hogs thirty days after their delivery. Can *A* recover from *B* for the dressed hogs?

Student: Yes, because *B* now has twenty hogs and should pay for them.

Socrates: But *A* is in the wrong, isn't he? He won't deliver the live hogs. Why should he be able to recover for the dressed hogs? He's breached the agreement. Why should he get anything?

Student: Because he delivered the dressed hogs. He should pay *B* the value of the dressed hogs.

Socrates: But under the contract, if *A* breached, *B* doesn't have any obligation to perform.

Student: *A* didn't totally breach. He just breached the part about the live hogs.

Socrates: You're saying there's total breach, and there's partial breach—is that it?

Student: Yes, it looks that way.

Socrates: Then a person could just perform part of any contract, and not suffer in any way. Only perform what he wants to perform and expect to get paid anyway. Like painting half a house.

Student: But here it's as if there were two pieces of the contract. One for live hogs and one for dressed

[1] Plato, *The Republic and Other Works* 491-99 (B. Jowett trans.).

hogs. An agreed upon amount of money for an agreed upon amount of hogs of each kind. That's not like painting half a house.

Socrates: Assume *B* was to pay $5,000 for twenty dressed hogs and $5,000 for twenty live hogs. Now assume *A* delivered ten dressed hogs and ten live hogs. Can *A* recover $5,000 from *B*?

Student: No. It's not the same thing.

Socrates: Well, isn't *A* entitled to $2,500 for half the order of dressed hogs and $2,500 for half the order of live hogs. You just said we could parse out the contract. After all, it's $5,000 for twenty hogs. And money's money.

Student: But hogs aren't hogs. There's nothing in the contract about a grouping of ten hogs. Maybe *B* can't use only ten of either kind of hog. This kind of exchange wasn't agreed upon.

Socrates: But the other kind was?

Student: Yes, $5,000 for twenty of each kind. That was the agreed exchange.

Socrates: So how can we describe the agreed relationship between the $5,000 and twenty dressed hogs. They are agreed what?

Student: Equals.

Socrates: Equal? That's exactly the same. Can we be more precise?

Student: Equivalent. Agreed equivalents.

Socrates: Good. That's a legal concept. Now what if *A* did deliver the ten hogs of each kind. There's no agreed equivalent of ten hogs. But *B* now has twenty hogs. Is she obliged to pay? Where do we stand under the contract?

Student: *A* has really breached the contract this time. We don't know if each hog is worth $250 or if *B* was getting a special deal. We have no agreed equivalents. So, *B* has no obligation to pay.

Socrates: No obligation to pay? *A* is out twenty hogs and has gotten no payment. Does *A* have no rights under the contract?

Student: Probably not under the contract. But *B* still has a moral obligation to pay.

Socrates: Moral obligation? Should the law enforce moral obligations?

Student: I suppose not always. But here.

Socrates: Then, where? How do we decide?

Student: Well, *B* has received something that she didn't pay for.

Socrates: She's been enriched.

Student: Yes, but she hasn't paid for it. That's not fair.

Socrates: If she doesn't pay, she's been unjustly enriched. Could we put it that way?

Student: Yes.

Socrates: Now let's assume *A* has delivered nineteen dressed hogs to *B*. Must *B* pay?

Student: We can't parse out their value.

Socrates: Should we throw an entire contract out the window when one party has given 95 percent performance. Where would that leave us in the world of contract?

Student: We could make *B* pay the $5,000, but then *B* has overpaid.

Socrates: What could *B* do?

Student: Sue *A* for the twentieth hog.

Socrates: How could we justify enforcing contracts on this basis? Can we formulate a theory?

Student: Yes, we could say if someone has performed almost to the full extent of the contract, they have met their obligation enough to be entitled to their rights under the contract. But the other party will be entitled to damages for the missing degree of performance.

Socrates: Suppose in the law we were to call this substantial performance. As a matter of fact, we do call it substantial performance. Where would we draw the line? 95 percent? 90 percent? 80 percent performance? What if *A* were to deliver nineteen dressed hogs. Is that substantial performance?

Student: Yes. It's almost everything *B* wanted.

Socrates: What about thirteen hogs?

Student: Of course not. That's barely over half.

Socrates: How about sixteen hogs?

Student: Well . . .

It may not always appear so, but the good professor has a definite goal in using these searching methods of analysis and analogy.

The Socratic method is used in the study of law to reach conclusions through an analytical discussion led by a dialectition. This enables the student to grasp the major precepts of a given legal discipline, while gaining exposure to the process used to arrive at these precepts. The open dialogue serves as a repetitive laboratory demonstration of how solutions to legal problems must be logically justifiable and not reached by predetermined or ingrained belief, impression, hunch, instinct, or impulse.

For our purposes, at this point of our study, the Socratic method vividly demonstrates how the logical components of reflective thinking are applied to particular cases. Reflective thinking makes us look at links. It requires that we see a connection from the known to the unknown. We reach a conclusion in one set of facts by deciding what inferences may be drawn from other sets. We seek to determine whether legal consequences applicable to the facts of a decided case may or may not be applied to the facts before us. We experiment with inferences. We inquire as to the probability that certain consequences can and do follow from changing factual scenarios as tested by previous experience in human affairs.

Throughout the Socratic dialogue, without being conscious of labels, we employ aspects of inductive and deductive reasoning. To analyze different factual scenarios is to engage in inductive reasoning, a reasoning based on probabilities. The conclusion emerging from induction then serves as a premise—major or minor—in the deductive process that follows. If the premises are properly formulated, one conclusion must logically follow.

To be sure, our summary of the Socratic method is just that—a summary. All of the elements we have studied thus far appear at one time or another in the myriad versions of Socratic teaching that take place in each course, in each law school year, by each professor.

CHAPTER 9

Introduction to Fallacies

I love you
Therefore, I am a lover;
All the world loves a lover
You are all the world to me—
Consequently
You love me.

—J. G. Vivian [1]

In ordinary speech, the word "fallacy" is used in many ways. A perfectly proper use of the word is to designate any mistaken idea or false belief: "So long as Mike Ditka coaches, the Chicago Bears will be a winning team." "All lawyers are thieves; all doctors, quacks."

In ordinary usage then, "fallacy" can be used to describe a false or erroneous idea. But in the law, as in logic, the term has a more specific meaning; it refers to the logical form or content of a syllogism. Nevertheless, the terms "fallacy" or "fallacious" are often used by judges and lawyers to characterize a syllogism's major premise as false or erroneous.

Schiaffo v. Helstoski
492 F.2d 413, 435 (3d Cir. 1974)
(Aldisert, J., concurring and dissenting)

I flatly disagree with the suggestion that no governmental agency has the power to police the Congressional franking privilege. This is an essential predicate of the theory if the majority conclusion is to possess

---

[1] Quoted in J. Brennan, *A Handbook of Logic* 187 (1957).

threshhold support. Having asserted lack of enforcement power in any governmental agency, the argument then builds to the proposition that any enforcement of the franking statute can only emanate from the public, generally through the device of private attorney general suits like the instant case. Lacking a specific statute authorizing private suits, the majority finds one by implication, thereby satisfying the second prong of the "zone of interest test" of *Data Processing.*

I have little difficulty in discerning the fallacy in the basic premise that Congress failed to provide a governmental agency with statutory power to enforce the franking statutes. The United States Postal Service has this authority. To me this authority is so apparent as not to merit extended discussion.

It is the United States Postal Service which suffers from improper use of franking. It is the United States Postal Service whose revenues are depleted as a result of improper franking practices. It is the United States Postal Service which, with its predecessor, the office of the Postmaster General, has a history of no juniority to any department of the Executive. It is the United States Postal Service whose establishment is constitutionally mandated, Art. 1, § 8, and whose power to enforce postage regulations is explicit. . . .

The existence of these statutory provisions forms a dramatic refutation to the contention that a private remedy is required to be implied from the statute . . . because there is no other way to police the use of franking privileges other than by private suit.

California v. Gardner
56 Cal. App. 3d 91,
128 Cal. Rptr. 101, 105-06 (1976)

The crux of the contention is not that imprisonment is unjust, but that it is ineffective, or even counter-productive, when imposed upon one who, like defendant, (1) refuses to pursue his life without inflicting criminal injury upon others and (2) resents and rebels against punishment for his misconduct; he is therefore prepared to protest such punishment by committing vicious and unprovoked assaults upon innocent persons, for which he then defiantly asserts there should be no penalty.

A logical extension of this contention demonstrates its fallacy: No punishment or restraint can be effective as to such a person, for he will not be deterred. Since punishment is thus ineffectual, it is cruel and unusual. Society should therefore engage in no act of recrimination and the offender should be left undisturbed. Since a prison inmate has of course no monopolistic right to such inaction by society, the same "hands off" rule should apply to the misconduct of all incorrigible criminals, in or out of prison. Punishment of non-inmate miscreants then is also cruel and unusual, and hence unconstitutional. Therefore, no punishment should ever be imposed upon any criminals who resent punishment; society should just accept and tolerate their criminality. The *reductio ad absurdum* is complete.

As stated before, logicians and members of the legal profession generally use the term "fallacy" in a narrower sense, to describe a type of incorrect argument, rather than to label a statement as false or erroneous. It is used to describe a flaw in the purported relations between several statements. There are several types of fallacies. One type of fallacy occurs when we neglect the rules of logic and fall into erroneous reasoning, often from true factual premises. Other fallacies, generally called informal or material fallacies, meticulously follow logical form but suffer from improper content or emphasis. A fallacy then is not merely an error, but a way of falling into an error. The name comes from the Latin, *"fallax,"* which suggests a deliberate deception. But most fallacies are not intentional. Fallacies are dangerous, however, because they are false conclusions or interpretations resulting from processes of thinking that claim or appear to be valid, but fail to conform to the requirements of logic. [2] A fallacy can be defined as "any argument that seems conclusive to the normal mind but that proves, upon examination, not to establish the alleged conclusion," [3] or more succinctly, a form of argument that seems to be correct but which proves upon examination not to be so. They have been identified as such ever since Aristotle described these arguments: "That some reasoning are genuine, while others seem to be so but are not, is evident. This happens with arguments, as also elsewhere, through a certain likeness between the genuine and the sham." [4]

Although there is often agreement as to the existence of a fallacious argument, the method of labelling or characterizing them is up for grabs. Each logician seems to have his or her own method of classification. Common fallacies abound in all writings—speeches, commentaries, legislative debates, political oratory, television editorials, columns, articles, household and family discussions, and personal conversations. One commentator has indicated that over 120 different types of fallacies may be identified. [5] One logician, Augustus de Morgan, has said that "there *is* no such thing as a classification of the ways in which men may arrive at an error: it is much to be doubted whether there ever *can be*." [6] Our discussion here is limited to the violation of formal rules of inference. We do not represent that our categorization is at all complete, nor do we represent that the listed categories are mutually exclusive. Ours is a simple submission offered for the sole purpose that an understanding of these fallacies will be useful. The discussion divides into two subtopics:

    (a) Fallacies of logical form, or formal fallacies, and
    (b) Fallacies based on factual content, known as material or informal fallacies.

We will use this method of distinguishing the two groupings—formal   fallacies   and   material   fallacies—

[2] J. Creighton, *An Introductory Logic* 198 (1898).

[3] R. Eaton, *General Logic* 332 (1931).

[4] "De Sophisticis Elenchis," in *The Works of Aristotle* (W.D. Ross trans. 1928).

[5] Landau, "Logic for Lawyers," 13 Pacific L.J. 59, 89 (1981).

[6] A. de Morgan, *Formal Logic* 276 (1847).

acknowledging that the labels "runneth over," and what we and the reported cases may describe as a particular type, may very well properly bear another name. Labels and names aside, the importance is to avoid fallacious reasoning, whatever you call it.

I find the following definitions most useful to the legal profession: Formal fallacies occur when you do not follow the rules of the syllogism, set forth in Chapter 5. Formal fallacies can be discovered without any knowledge of the subject matter with which the argument is concerned. Factual or material fallacies involve the subject of the argument and cannot be set right except by those acquainted with the subject. They do not violate specific logical rules. They are said to exist not in the *form*, but in the *matter*, hence the label, material.

It is necessary to add a caveat at this time. We are analyzing logical processes in the law. This is not an attempt to discuss all fallacies in existence. Rather, we will concentrate on those fallacies that usually find expression in the law.

FORMAL FALLACIES

Formal fallacies arise when there is an error in the logic of the argument. My discussion will categorize the fallacies according to the type of syllogism asserted.

Fallacies in Categorical Syllogisms

In categorical arguments there are six possible fallacies:

1. Four terms instead of three.
2. Undistributed middle.
3. Illicit major term.
4. Illicit minor term.
5. Negative premises.
6. Particular premises.

Fallacies in Hypothetical Syllogisms

In hypothetical arguments there are two possible fallacies:

1.   Denying the antecedent.
2.   Affirming the consequent.

Fallacies in Disjunctive Syllogisms

In disjunctive arguments the fallacy consists of the imperfect disjunctive.

MATERIAL (INFORMAL) FALLACIES

Material fallacies can sneak up on us as do fallacies of form. Logicians, scientists, and other careful scholars are especially adept at detecting and avoiding these. Professors William and Mabel Sahakian describe them as "numerous, deceptive and elusive—so elusive that a person untrained in detecting them can easily be misled into accepting them as valid." [7] Logicians may differ as to their precise categorization because some do resemble, or relate to, a type of argument rather than a type of logic. For my purposes, I will follow, in major part, the classification set forth by the Sahakians.

Fallacies of Irrelevant Evidence

Fallacies of Irrelevant Evidence are arguments that miss the central point at issue and rely principally upon emotions, feelings, and ignorance, inter alia, to defend a thesis.

1.   Fallacy of irrelevance, often referred to as irrelevant conclusions or ignoratio elenchi.
2.   Fallacies of distraction.

[7] W. & M. Sahakian, *Ideas of the Great Philosophers* 11 (1966).

a. Argumentum ad misericordium, or the appeal to pity.
b. Argumentum ad verecundiam, or the appeal to prestige.
c. Argumentum ad hominem, or the appeal to personal ridicule.
d. Argumentum ad populum, or the appeal to the masses.
e. Argumentum ad antiquitam, or the appeal to age.
f. Argumentum ad terrorem, or the appeal to terror.

Miscellaneous Material Fallacies

1. Fallacy of accident, or dicto simpliciter.
2. Converse fallacy of accident, or the fallacy of selective instances or hasty generalizations.
3. False cause, or post hoc ergo propter hoc.
4. Conclusion that does not follow from the premise, or non sequitur.
5. Compound questions. The fallacy of multiple questions, or poisoning the wells.
6. Begging the question, petitio principii.
7. Tu Quoque, or you yourself do it so it must be right.

Linguistic Fallacies

1. Fallacy of equivocation.
2. Fallacy of amphibology.
3. Fallacy of composition.
4. Fallacy of division.
5. Fallacy of vicious abstraction.
6. Argumentum ad nauseum.

CHAPTER 10

Formal Fallacies

We have previously explained in Chapter 4 that a categorical syllogism is an argument having three propositions—two premises and a conclusion. The categorical syllogism is one of the major forms of argument in the law; it is so-called because its propositions are absolute and positive without qualifications or conditions. In this sense we can refer to them as simple syllogisms.

But we have in the law compound syllogisms as well. We refer to one as the hypothetical syllogism because it imposes a condition as necessary to the result. The other compound syllogism is the disjunctive syllogism, so-called because it contains alternative propositions.

FALLACIES IN CATEGORICAL SYLLOGISMS

Our inquiry into formal fallacies begins with the categorical syllogism. We have previously set forth the six rules of the categorical syllogism. We repeat them here to emphasize that they form guidelines upon which a deductive or inductive argument in proper logical form may be based. Conversely stated, to depart from any of these rules is to commit the logical fallacy of form; it is to commit what is known as a formal fallacy.

These then are the rules that you must follow to avoid the pitfalls of fallacy of form:

Rule 1: A valid categorical syllogism must contain exactly three terms, each of which is used in the same sense throughout the argument.

Rule 2: In a valid categorical syllogism, the middle term must be distributed in at least one premise.

Rule 3: In a valid categorical syllogism, no term can be distributed in the conclusion which is not distributed in the premise.

Rule 4: No categorical syllogism is valid which has two negative premises.

Rule 5: If either premise of a valid categorical syllogism is negative, the conclusion must be negative.

Rule 6: No valid categorical syllogism with a particular conclusion can have two universal premises.

In the discussion that follows, you will learn that the logicians have fashioned particular labels for violating these rules.

Fallacy of Four Terms
(Quaternio Terminorum)

This is a breach of the first rule of syllogisms which insists that a categorical syllogism must contain only three terms. By definition, such a syllogism (e.g., all men are mortal, etc.) consists of comparing two terms, the minor (Socrates) with the major (mortal) by means of a middle term (all men), to reach a conclusion. If there were four terms (e.g., all men are mortal, Socrates plays baseball) there would be no way to reach a conclusion. A fourth term (baseball) would not only be superfluous, but would destroy the comparison. When an argument has more than three terms, we call it a logical quadruped. When such an argument has, in effect, two middle terms, it lacks any basis of comparison for its minor and major terms, so that it is impossible to draw a legitimate conclusion. From the example: "Every ruminant is cloven-footed; every cow is multi-stomached," we can't move to a logical conclusion. The proper method is to use multiple syllogisms:

All A is C:	Every ruminant is cloven-footed.
B is A:	Every cow is a ruminant.
Therefore, B is C:	Therefore, every cow is cloven-footed.

All B is D:	Every cow is multi-stomached.
E is B:	This is a cow.
Therefore, E is D:	Therefore, this cow is multi-stomached.

United States v. Berrigan
482 F.2d 171, 183 (3d Cir. 1973)

Appellants' contention that the statute is over-broad is founded on the general rule that a statute is tainted if the conduct it prohibits includes protected activity as well as criminal conduct. "In every case the power to regulate must be so exercised as not, in attaining a permissible end, unduly to infringe the protected freedom." The minor premise proceeds that certain communications cannot constitutionally be excluded from prisons. [Cases have upheld] a prisoner's right to send and receive various types of correspondence and literature. Because prisoners enjoy the right to send and receive mail, appellants conclude that this statute is overbroad because it makes criminal certain acts protected by the First Amendment.

It hardly deserves extended discussion to observe that appellants' syllogism strains to a conclusion which is invalid and illict. [Note 16] Perhaps appellants' argument can best be described as a logical (or, more appropriately, illogical) quadruped because it excludes the additional minor premise that a prisoner's mail was denied him.

Fallacy of the Undistributed Middle

One who violates syllogism Rule 2 commits the fallacy of the undistributed middle. Rule 2 states that in a valid categorical syllogism, the middle term must be distributed in at least one of the premises.

Professor Copi has reminded us that the conclusion of any syllogism asserts a connection between two terms. This connection is justified only if those terms—the major and minor terms—can be connected with each other through or by means of the middle term. For the two terms that become part of the conclusion to be connected through a third, at least one of the two must be related to the *whole* of the class designated by the third or middle term. Otherwise each may be connected with a different part of the class and not necessarily connected with each other at all. [1]

It is critical, therefore, that the middle term encompass a larger universe than the minor term. Compared then to the minor term, which reflects only part of the class, the middle term is considered "distributed." If the middle term does not represent the larger portion of the class being considered, and represents or is equivalent to the portion represented by the minor term, we say that the middle term is "undistributed." When this occurs the connection to the conclusion cannot be justified; when this occurs we have the fallacy of the undistributed middle.

To put it in a formula, the fallacy occurs whenever it is argued that because x and y belong to the same class or possess a common property, they are identical. Some examples of the fallacy may help. Because business executives read the *Wall Street Journal,* a man who reads the *Journal* is a business executive. The ACLU supports the Democratic ticket; therefore, all those supporting the ticket adhere to ACLU causes.

Spencer v. Texas
385 U.S. 554, 569-60 (1967)
(Warren, C.J., dissenting)

[W]here the probative value of prior convictions evidence is thought to outweigh its prejudicial impact, the Court draws the legitimate conclusion that prior-convictions evidence is not so inherently prejudicial that its admission is invariably prohibited. It combines this premise with the concededly valid purpose of recidivist statutes to produce the following logic: since prior-

[1] I. Copi, *Introduction to Logic* 219 (7th ed. 1986).

crimes evidence may be admitted at the guilt phase of a trial where the admission serves a valid purpose and since the purpose of recidivist statutes is valid, prior crimes may be proven in the course of the guilt phase of a trial in order that the jury may also assess whether a defendant, if found guilty, should be sentenced to an enhanced punishment under recidivist statutes. I believe this syllogism is plausible only on the surface, because the Court's premises do not combine to justify its far-reaching result. I believe the Court has fallen into the logical fallacy sometimes known as the fallacy of the undistributed middle, because it has failed to examine the supposedly shared principle between admission of prior crimes related to guilt and admission in connection with recidivist statutes. That the admission in both situations may serve a valid purpose does not demonstrate that the former practice justifies the latter any more than the fact that men and dogs are animals means that men and dogs are the same in all respects.

Amusement Equipment, Inc. v. Mordelt 595 F. Supp. 125, 130-31 (E.D. La. 1984)

[T]here is nothing linking Mr. Mordelt's presence in New Orleans to the contract of sale. [FN.4] By attempting to link these two occurrences simply because of their connection to the New Orleans convention, Amusement Equipment commits the logical fallacy of the "undistributed middle." See I. Copi, *Introduction to Logic* 200 (4th ed. 1972). Consider the following syllogism which, like the argument of *Amusement Equipment,* contains the fallacy of the undistributed middle:

> All dogs are mammals.
> *All cats are mammals.*
> Therefore, all cats are dogs.

It is easy to see why this syllogism is invalid. Both dogs and cats are members of the larger class of mammals. This does not mean, however, that the class of dogs is identical to, or even overlaps with, the class of cats.

Yet the argument of Amusement Equipment takes precisely the same form. Amusement Equipment argues that:

The contract related to the trade show.
Mordelt's visit related to the trade show.
Therefore, the contract related to Mordelt's visit.

The syllogism is invalid. That both the contract and Mordelt's visit pertained to the trade show does not mean that the two were connected to each other. The contract related to the trade show in respects that Mordelt's visit did not. This is apparent from the fact that Mordelt visited New Orleans after the contract had been negotiated, executed, and allegedly breached.

Menora v. Illinois High School Assocs.
527 F. Supp 632, 636 (N.D. Ill. 1981)

IHSA's position has the inherent double vice of (1) equating the kind of affiliation that organizational membership represents with an identity of beliefs, and (2) then taking another impermissible leap by equating such presumed beliefs with judicial disqualification. In another era a similar "thought" process carried the pejorative label of "guilt by association."

Necessarily implicit in IHSA's affidavit and motion is the assumption that all Jews are alike, or all members of Jewish organizations are alike, or both. Such assumptions are just as wrong and just as demeaning as saying that all Blacks look alike or are alike, or all Orientals look alike or are alike. To put it in more formal terms, IHSA's affidavit and motion suffer from what logicians refer to as the fallacy of the undistributed middle.

Wein v. Carey
41 N.Y.2d 498, 362 N.E.2d 587, 590,
393 N.Y.S.2d 955 (1977)

Beyond the amounts of deficit anticipation notes running over from one fiscal year to another, the State in each of the last two fiscal years has experienced a deficit in the once balanced budget plans of revenues and expenditures. Either revenues have fallen short of the budget estimates or expenditures have exceeded those contained in the budget estimates, or both have occurred.

On the basis of these facts of the past and present, plaintiff urges that the State has failed in its constitutional obligation to provide for a balanced budget, and that therefore the recurring issuance of anticipation notes in successive years is in violation of the Constitution. . . .

His syllogism is simple but mistaken. It is, in effect, that a planned deficit is unconstitutional (which it is); that two successive annual deficits occurred (which is true); and, therefore, that there must have been a planned deficit (which results in a classic example of the fallacy of the undistributed middle term). On the basis of this disjointed syllogism, he argues, therefore, that the anticipation notes 1976-1977 were invalid, and, to make matters worse, by implication and necessary consequence from the relief he seeks, that the plan to issue more anticipation notes in 1977-1978 would be an ill-disguised "rollover" or unconstitutional refinancing of a planned deficit.

To support his flawed syllogism plaintiff quotes an inner quotation from the *Wein* case: "As was stated by the 1938 Subcommittee on Taxation and Finance of the Constitutional Convention Committee: 'The spirit of the clause implied that the State must not have two or more budgetary deficits in succession.' " The context in which the inner quotation appears makes clear that the reference is to two planned deficits in succession. In common sense it could not have meant otherwise. Note too that this is a quotation from a subcommittee of a committee for the planning of the convention, and not a dictum considered and voted by the convention.

The fact is that there may be an indefinite series of deficits honestly suffered. All that is necessary to produce the result are successive years of unpredictable shortfalls in revenues or rises in required spending beyond estimates. Depressed economic conditions can affect both sides of the balance. Catastrophies, emergencies, or, in smaller scale, significant needs may arise, which, if unanticipated, may upset the balance on one side or the other. Indeed, it is unattainable for any budget plan, perfectly and honestly balanced in advance, to remain in balance to the end of the fiscal year. There must, as a practical matter, in every year be either a deficit or a surplus. Nothing in the *Wein* case suggests otherwise.

Royer v. Florida
389 So. 2d 1007, 1015-16 (Fla. 1979)

Only two persons testified at the motion to suppress: the defendant Royer, and William Johnson, one of the two Dade County narcotics officers who effected the search of Royer's suitcases which revealed the cannabis. Since the state prevailed below, we must and do view the evidence in the light most favorable to its position. So considered, the record portrays a series of events which, while they fall generally within the "airport narcotics search" genre, must be considered in terms of their own particular and individual aspects.

Royer was first observed by Johnson and his partner, Magdalena, as he walked across the concourse of the Miami International Airport towards the National Airlines ticket counter, carrying two apparently heavily-laden suitcases. The officers were specifically assigned to interdict the transportation of narcotics through the airport. As Johnson stated, they based their initial decisions as to which travelers to approach upon a series of allegedly suspicious characteristics and circumstances, as contained in the now-familiar "drug courier profile," supplemented by the airport squad's own prior experiences. It may be fairly said as to all of the officers' bases of "suspicion" that, although they may indeed be characteristic of those who carry narcotics, they are at least equally, and usually far more frequently, consistent with complete innocence. The fallacy of the undistributed middle directly applies: all narcotics couriers act like parts of the profile, but most people who act like parts of the profile are not narcotics couriers. This point is well-illustrated by those aspects of Royer's behavior which attracted the attention of the officers. Johnson said that these were the facts that (a) the defendant was carrying American Tourister baggage of a type which "seemed to be standard brand for marijuana smuggling;" (b) he was "nervous in appearance, looking around at other persons as though he might be looking for possible police officers;" (c) he paid for the ticket to New York in cash (and therefore without the necessity of showing identification) from a roll of small-denomination bills; and (d) rather than filling out a full name, address, and phone number on the baggage tags furnished by National, he wrote only the words "Holdt" and "LaGuardia" on each of them.

Batty v. Arizona State Dental Board
57 Ariz. 239, 112 P.2d 870, 872-73 (1941)

The Supreme Court of Arizona quoted the California Supreme Court decision in *California v. State Bd. of Equalization*, 59 P.2d 119 (1936): "Concisely stated, our conclusion that we are without authority or jurisdiction to entertain this proceeding or to issue the writ here sought [to review an order revoking a license to practice dentistry] is based upon the established premises that a writ of certiorari, commonly refered to as a writ of review, will lie only to review the exercise of judicial functions and that the Legislature is without power, in the absence of constitutional provision authorizing the same, to confer judicial functions upon a statewide administrative agency of the character or the respondent.

. . .

"To hold that judicial power has been conferred upon the respondent board would be tantamount to holding such attempted grant unconstitutional to that extent. We think it was not intended by the Legislature to confer any judicial power on the respondent board and it necessarily follows that this proceeding for a writ of review lacks one of the elements essential to its proper determination." •

The rationale of the decision may be stated syllogistically as follows: (a) the legislature may not confer "judicial" powers upon any body created by law except the courts permitted by the Constitution; (b) a writ of certiorari may only be used to review the exercise of "judicial" powers; (c) therefore, it may not be used to review the action of any administrative body, since such body is not a court. With all due respect to the opinion of that court, we think it committed what is known as the fallacy of the undistributed middle in that the "judicial" power in the major premise is not co-extensive with the "judicial" power in the minor.

Fallacy of Illicit Process of the Major Term

When the major term in a syllogism is undistributed in the major premise, but distributed in the conclusion, the argument contains the fallacy of the illicit process of the major term, or more briefly, the illicit major. In this fallacy, the term is applied to *all* members of a class in the conclusion even though it was limited to *some* members of the class in the premise.

Courts may punish for contempt.
Legislatures are not courts.
Therefore, legislatures may not punish for contempt.

Larceny is a crime.
Driving under the influence is not larceny.
Therefore, driving under the influence is not a crime.

The major premise tells us that some crimes are larceny, but the conclusion goes further. It says that all crimes are outside the class of larceny.

State v. Zespy
723 P.2d 564 (Wyo. 1986)
(Urbigkit, J., concurring and dissenting)

In support of the trial court's decision to exclude the testimony of the nonexamining psychiatric witness, I will address the difference between rebuttal attack on the validity of procedures utilized by examining experts, described in their testimony, and a general attack on an entire field of academic inquiry.

It is not logical to contend, as did the witness (Coleman), and now the State of Wyoming in this bill of exceptions, that if the witness challenges the validity of specific processes he can also logically deny the validity of all processes without first demonstrating knowledge and expertise about every possible process or combination of processes that may or may not have been utilized by the examining expert witness on the subject of constitutionality and statutorily required absence of mental illness or deficiency.

Found in the syllogistic conclusion is one of the classic fallacies of logic.

The syllogism may be variously illustrated.

Either:

I am an expert about some evaluative processes.
Those processes are invalid.
All evaluative processes are invalid.

Or:

Some evaluative processes are invalid.
Other experts may use those processes.
The conclusions of those experts are invalid.

This appears to be the fallacy of an undistributed middle term and illicit process of a major or minor term. Chase, *Guides to Straight Thinking* 205 (1956).

The authorities evaluating logic as a reasoning process have also defined this negative argumentative approach as "scientific crank" logic—the attack of an entire area of expertise as a method to contradict the knowledge and testimony of the individual expert witness. See Salmon, *Logic,* p.68 (1963). Whatever Coleman may consider to be his limits to accomplish determinative evaluations within the field of psychiatry, the Wyoming legislature has determined that the knowledge and techniques of psychiatrists will be used to evaluate the mental illness or deficiency of a criminal defendant, and the United States Supreme Court requires the utilization of psychiatry to afford constitutional rights.

Fallacy of Illicit Process of the Minor Term

Illicit process of the minor term occurs when the minor term is undistributed in the minor premise, but distributed in the conclusion.

No holder in due course is a purchaser after maturity.
All holders in due course are transferees of title to a negotiable instrument.
Therefore, no transferees of title to a negotiable instrument are purchasers after maturity. [2]

The minor premise says something about only some who are transferees of title to a negotiable instrument (because all are obviously not holders in due course), therefore it is incorrect to conclude that all who are transferees of title to a negotiable instrument are not purchasers after maturity.

Fallacy of Negative Premises

To understand this fallacy, I first explain what it is not. The mere occurrence of a negative, "no" or "not," in a proposition does not render it a negative premise. Rule 4 (no cat-

[2] Example taken from Truesch, "The Syllogism," in *Readings in Jurisprudence* 539 (Hall ed. 1938).

egorical syllogism is valid which has two negative premises) is founded in the principle that inference can proceed only where there is *agreement*. Two differences or disagreements lead to no conclusion.

From the premises—Italians are not Iranians; Iranians are not Christians—we cannot conclude that Italians are Christians or that the Japanese are Christians, although they are not Iranians any more than Italians are Iranians.

If one premise is negative, the conclusion must be negative (Rule 5). Thus, to prove a negative conclusion, *one* of the premises must be negative. If *both* premises are negative, we cannot determine anything regarding their relation to one another. From the premises, James is not a lawyer; lawyers are not steelworkers, we cannot conclude that James is or is not a steelworker.

This type of reasoning is unacceptable because of the difficulty in sustaining a factual proposition merely by negative evidence. When an advocate determines that "there is no evidence that B is the case;" he or she is attempting to affirm or assume that non-B is the case. But all that is affirmed or assumed is that the advocate has found no *evidence* of non-B. The correct method of proceeding is to find affirmative evidence of non-B. This may be difficult, but it is absolutely necessary if logical order is to be preserved. To prove a negative is sometimes an impossible task. Not knowing that something exists is simply not knowing.

Alice's experience with the White Knight comes to mind:

"I see nobody on the road," said Alice.

"I only wish I had such eyes," the King remarked in a fretful tone. "To be able to see Nobody! And at that distance!" [3]

Bailey v. Maryland
16 Md. App. 83, 294 A.2d 123, 129 (1972)

Dr. Fahrney clearly testified on both direct and cross-examination that sperm cells, inside a vagina, lose their motility at some time no less than thirty min-

[3] *The Complete Works of Lewis Carroll* 223 (Modern Library ed. n.d.).

utes nor more than six hours after ejaculation. The examination was at 5:11 a.m. The only opinion as to the later limit beyond which ejaculation, with reasonable medical certainty, did not occur was, therefore, 4:41 a.m. The appellant argues that Dr. Fahrney really placed that later limit at a much earlier time, a time which would exculpate any of the Pagans.

The appellant asked Dr. Fahrney a question based upon a hypothetical opposite to the actual factual premise at bar. He asked the doctor to assume that the sperm cells he examined had been motile instead of non-motile. In that eventuality, would not the doctor have to agree, taking the range of thirty minutes to six hours for the loss of motility, that intercourse did not occur more than six hours earlier, to wit, not earlier than 11:11 p.m. Dr. Fahrney responded, "Yes." Then, by a clever but invalid exercise of logic, the appellant assiduously sought, before the trial court and before us, to identify the earlier limit of the motile hypothetical with the later limit of the non-motile actuality. He urges the deceptively persuasive but invalid proposition that if motility establishes that ejaculation did not occur before 11:11 p.m., then non-motility establishes that ejaculation did not occur after 11:11 p.m. He chooses to ignore that between 11:11 p.m. and 4:41 a.m. the two ranges overlap and that that area of overlap is consistent with both motility and non-motility. The trial judge did not buy the appellant's logic; nor do we.

[FN.4] The fallacy may be articulated in the formal terms of traditional Aristotelian logic. The appellant is taking the universal negative proposition, "No motile sperm are pre-11:11 (in terms of ejaculation)—No A is B—and attempting to infer the so-called contrapositive of that proposition, to wit, No non-motile sperm are post 11:11—(in purer terms, non-pre-11:11)—No non-A is non-B. By the laws of logic, however, the inference of the contrapositive is invalid where the starting proposition, as in the case at bar, is a universal negative.

Tri-Boro Bagel Co. v. Bakery Drivers Union Local 802
228 F. Supp. 720, 724-25 (E.D.N.Y. 1963)

The court rejects as false in logic and historically unrealistic plaintiff's argument. [FN.11] It is fallacious to reason from the negative. "No Court of the United States" is vested with power, to an affirmative that state courts must therefore be possessed of such authority. The technical name logicians assign to the paralogism is the fallacy of "false opposition" or "false disjunction." [citation omitted] The fallacy would be compounded were the multi-vocal term "without jurisdiction," constituting in its context no more than a loosely expressed equivalent for the forthright biblical imperative "Thou shalt not," to be construed in the unnecessarily restricted sense of denying to the federal court the authority even to receive a case for determination of an issue under federal law. [There are] multiple senses in which the word "jurisdiction" is used and understood. . . . "A fallacy takes place . . . when one asserts that certain premises necessitate a given conclusion and when this claim is false because of the absence of real connection, an absence *covered up by the use of the same word for two different things.*" [quoting Cohen & Nagel, *Introduction to Logic and the Scientific Method* 386 (1934)].

FALLACIES IN HYPOTHETICAL SYLLOGISMS

We have been concentrating on categorical syllogisms, so-called because they contain categorical propositions exclusively. But other kinds of propositions occur in other types of syllogisms. In law, we often encounter a compound proposition called the hypothetical syllogism. This does not directly assert the existence of a fact; instead, it contains a condition, "if," "unless," "granted," "supposing," etc. These hypotheticals are the little darlings of law professors; they go to the heart of the Socratic method.

The hypothetical syllogism contains two parts: the part that expresses the supposition or condition and follows "if" is known as the "antecedent" (if *A* is *B*); the clause following "then," stating the result, is the "consequent" (then *A* is *C*).

If the major premise is a hypothetical proposition, then in order to yield a correct conclusion, the minor premise must be in one of two forms. It must either:

— *affirm the antecedent,* or
— *deny the consequent.*

If the antecedent is affirmed, the consequent, freed of the condition and stated in categorical form, becomes the conclusion:

If this statute deprives plaintiff of his property without due process, this statute is unconstitutional.
This statute deprives plaintiff of his property without due process.
Therefore, this statute is unconstitutional.

But if the consequent is denied, then a categorical denial of the antecedent forms the conclusion:

If this statute deprives plaintiff of his property without due process, this statute is unconstitutional.
But this statute is not unconstitutional.
Therefore, this statute does not deprive plaintiff of his property without due process.

If the antecedent is denied or if the consequent is affirmed, no correct conclusion will follow. Suppose we argue:

If the testator was insane, his will is invalid.
But the testator was not insane.
Therefore his will is not invalid.

It is entirely consistent with the major premise to suppose that there are other invalidating circumstances (other possible antecedents) which will give the same consequent, e.g., undue influence over the testator in drafting his will. Thus, the denial of this particular circumstance (the insanity of the testator) does not warrant a denial of the consequent (that the will is invalid). Here the fallacy is denying the antecedent. Now suppose in arguing, the consequent is affirmed:

If the testator was insane, his will is invalid.
His will is invalid.
Therefore the testator was insane.

Here again the conclusion goes beyond the major premise by presupposing that the only condition under which a will can be invalid is that the testator was insane. Other conditions can invalidate a will, e.g., no signature, no witnesses. Thus, it is entirely in accord with the major premise to assume that the minor premise (*C* is *D*) resulted not from antecedent *A*, but from any number of other possible antecedents. This is the fallacy of affirming the consequent. [4]

United Telephone Co. of the Carolinas, Inc. v. FCC
559 F.2d 720, 725-26 (D.C. Cir. 1977)

The Commission properly characterized United's and Carolina's arguments as an attempt to attack the formula for dividing charges without alleging that the result of that formula is in fact unjust and unreasonable. United and Carolina insist that if the method of dividing charges is unjust and unreasonable, its result must also be unjust and unreasonable. . . . This exercise is sophistry miscasts the issue by reversing the logic of the inquiry. A method of determining rates, or divisions thereof, is unjust and unreasonable if the result reached does not afford a compensatory return. One cannot, as United and Carolina try to do, reverse the order of this proposition and preserve its logical validity. . . . ([F]allacy of affirming the consequent.)

[4] *See* Treusch, *supra* note 2, at 554.

Crouse-Hinds Co. v. InterNorth, Inc.
634 F.2d 690, 702-03 (2d Cir. 1980)

We find no basis in the present case for the district court's conclusion that Inter-North carried its burden of demonstrating self-interest or bad faith on the part of the Crouse Hinds directors. As his starting point, the district judge gave extended consideration to the decision in *Treadway,* in which we found that because the Treadway directors, other than the chairman, were not to remain in office after the merger, perpetuation of their control could hardly have been their motivation for actions in furtherance of the merger. . . . Unfortunately, the district judge inferred from this that a quite different proposition must also be true—*i.e.,* that if the directors *are* to remain on the board after the merger, perpetuation of their control *must be presumed* to be their motivation. This inference has not basis in either law or logic. [Note 20] The proposition that "A implies B" is not the equivalent of "non-A implies non-B," and neither proposition follows logically from the other. The process of inferring one from the other is known as *"the fallacy of denying the antecedent."* J. Cooley. *A Primer of Formal Logic* 7 (1942).

French v. Indiana
266 Ind. 276, 362 N.E.2d 834, 842-43 (1977)
(De Bruler, J. dissenting)

I likewise disagree with the majority's argument that the Fifth Amendment's due process clause recognizes the legitimacy of capital punishment as it is logically fallacious.

[FN.1] This argument commits the classical fallacy known as "denying the antecedent of a conditional statement." This fallacy is committed when a statement in the conditional form 'if P then Q' is taken to imply 'if not P, then not Q.' The relevant language of the due process clause is 'no person shall be . . . deprived of life . . . without due process of law.' . . . This language may be represented in conditional form as follows: If a person is denied due process (if P) then that person shall not be deprived of life (then Q). The majority seeks to infer from this statement that if a person is not denied due process (not P) then he may be deprived of life (then not Q). This violates the rules of deduction, as may be seen in this example: If Columbia University is in California, then it is in the United States. Columbia University is not in California. Therefore, Columbia University is not in the United States. W. Salmon, *Logic* 28 (2d ed. 1973).

FALLACIES IN DISJUNCTIVE SYLLOGISMS

A disjunctive proposition expresses an either-or, or an if, then-not relation between two or more component propositions. A disjunctive syllogism consists of a disjunctive proposition as the major premise, a minor premise categorically affirming or denying one of the alternative propositions, and a conclusion which categorically denies or affirms the other alternative. For example:

Either *A* or *B*   Either *A* or *B*
But *A*   But not *A*
Therefore, not *B*   Therefore, *B*

The indispensable prerequisite to a valid conclusion in the case of a disjunctive syllogism is that the major premise express a complete disjunction in the sense that its alternative terms be mutually exclusive and collectively exhaustive. They admit of no third possible alternative.

Jevons tells us that the disjunctive syllogism consists of (a) a disjunctive major premise (containing "or") and (b) a minor premise that is a categorical proposition, either affirmative or negative.[5] Copi explains that the disjunctive proposition does not categorically assert the truth of either of its disjuncts, but says that at least one of them is true,

[5] W. Jevons, *Elementary Lessons in Logic: Deductive and Inductive* 166 (1870).

LOGIC FOR LAWYERS

allowing for the possibility that both may be true. [6] Thus arise two moods. First is the mood which by affirming denies:

A is either B or C,
A is B,
Therefore, A is not C.

For this form of argument to be valid it must proceed on the supposition that if one alternative of a disjunctive proposition is true, the others cannot also be true. Thus it is correct to say "the time of year must be either spring, summer, autumn or winter, and if it be spring it cannot be summer, autumn or winter."

The other form of disjunctive syllogism, is the mood which by denying affirms:

A is either B or C,
A is not B,
Therefore, A is C.

If the time of year be not spring, it must be summer, autumn or winter; if it be not autumn nor winter, it must be either spring or summer; and so on. In short, if any alternatives are denied, the rest remain to be affirmed as before. Thus, the disjunctive syllogism is governed by totally different rules from the ordinary categorical syllogism because a negative premise gives an affirmative conclusion in the former, and a negative conclusion in the latter. [7]

It is, of course, a very simple matter to draw the conclusion from the premises in these illustrations. The real problem in law consists in creating proper premises, in discovering the relations enumerated in the major premise. Errors are most likely to arise in formulating the major premise. The disjunctive members must be exhaustively enumerated and exclude one another. In the law we all can slip into a fallacy when we do not include all the alternatives in the major premise.

[6] I. Copi, *supra* note 1, at 223.
[7] *See* W. Jevons, *supra* note 5 at 166-67.

164

In brief writing and in writing opinions, it is not always easy to discover all the possibilities of a case, or to formulate them in such a way as to render them mutually exclusive. If we say "he is either a saint or a crook," we omit the possibility of his being both to some extent.

A great many statements expressed in the form of disjunctive propositions are not true logical disjunctives. Thus we might say, "every student works either from love of learning, or from love of praise, or for the sake of some material reward." But the disjunctive does not answer the logical requirements; for it is possible that two or more of these motives may influence a student's conduct at the same time, and that other motives might be at work. These disjunctive members are neither exclusive nor completely enumerated.

A true disjunctive proposition, however, becomes an excellent tool in legal argument. It is an attempt, by thorough legal research, to determine the whole series of circumstances or conditions within which any fact or perception may fall; it is to state the conditions in such a way that their systematic relations are at once evident. Positive knowledge of all the relevant cases in the jurisdictions is an absolute necessity. Enumerating possibilities must be exhaustive— no cases may be overlooked, no circumstances left out of account. The members of the proposition must be exclusive of one another. We cannot combine disjunctively any terms we please, as "perhaps this" *or* "perhaps that." It is only when we understand the systematic connections of things in the case law that we are able to express these connections in the form, *either* B *or* C, and thus assert that the presence of one excludes the other.

To summarize: A categorical proposition expresses no condition. Hypothetical propositions present their conditions as hypotheses (if the conveyance of real estate is oral, it is invalid). Disjunctive propositions present their conditions as alternatives (the defendant will be found guilty or he will be acquitted). Fallacies arise in the failure to include all possibilities or alternatives in the major premise. Thus, "the jury will either acquit or convict him" is deficient; it does not contemplate the possibility of a hung jury. Thus, "either the verdict at trial will be for the defendant or the defendant must pay the plaintiff" is deficient because it fails to consider post-trial motions granting a new trial, or a judgment n.o.v., or an appeal to any appellate court. "All personal injury complaints for negligence must be brought within the two-year statute of limitations or the claim will be barred," fails to contemplate the tolling of the limitations period because of a late discovery that the injury has occurred.

Danzig v. Superior Court
87 Cal App. 3d 604, 151 Cal. Rptr. 185, 188-89
(1978)

The question in *Southern California Edison* was whether a defendant can depose unnamed members of the plaintiff class upon notice to counsel for the named plaintiffs, or whether such deponents must be subpoenaed. Section 2019, subdivision (a)(4) provides that service of a subpoena is not required in order to depose a party or a person for whose immediate benefit an action is prosecuted. In *Southern California Edison,* the court addressed the question of whether unnamed class members are "persons for whose immediate benefit an action or proceeding is prosecuted," and determined that unnamed class members are in that category. The court did not address the question of whether unnamed class members are "parties" within the meaning of section 2019, subdivision (a)(4), or in any other context. Petitioners argue that the court in *Southern California Edison* would not have devoted so much of that opinion to determining that unnamed class members are "persons for whose immediate benefit an action or proceeding is prosecuted" if such class members are also "parties." In effect, petitioners contend our high court impliedly held that unnamed class members are not parties.

The argument suffers from a logical fallacy. When a proposition is in the form of two alternatives, if one alternative is false, then the other alternative must be true. But, if one of the alternatives is true, nothing can be said about the truth or falsity of the other alternative except in the situation when the two alternatives are mutually exclusive.

In *Southern California Edison,* the Supreme Court holding that unnamed members of a class represented by the named plaintiffs were persons for whose benefit the action was being prosecuted tells us nothing as to whether unnamed members of a class in a class action are "parties" within the meaning of section 1019, subdivision *189 (a)(1), unless a "party" and "a person for whose immediate benefit an action or proceeding is prosecuted or defended" are mutually exclusive concepts. Since it appears obvious that the two concepts are not mutually exclusive, we conclude that *Southern California Edison* is not authority for the resolution of the issue at bar.

Georgia S. & Fla. Ry. v. Atlanta Coast Line R.R. 373 F.2d 493, 498-99 (5th Cir. 1967)

However, we feel it proper to say that the trial court's almost exclusive reliance on *Pennsylvania R. Co. v. Reading Co.* . . . is misplaced. That case used eight "tests," distilled from former cases construing § 1(22). These tests have no statutory basis, and were developed for a case different from the one before us. But the present case adopts those tests as an exclusive, controlling list of the relevant considerations. We think that the tests are, at most, helpful factors to be considered, and not fiats to be bound by. . . .

[FN.8] . . . "I have heard a thoughtful woman argue against gambling thus: There are four ways to obtain money, earning, finding, receiving a gift, stealing. Gambling is neither of the first three. Therefore, it is the fourth." Chafee, *Progress of the Law-Equitable Relief Against Torts,* 34 Harv. L. Rev. 388, 391-392 (1921).

CHAPTER 11

Material Fallacies

Material, or factual, fallacies do not result from violations of formal logic rules. They exist not in the form of an argument but in its factual content or matter, hence, the description "material" fallacies. It is difficult to condense into a single definition all that is encompassed by material fallacies, yet two basic tenets of logic provide keys to their understanding:

- Logical reasoning presupposes that the terms shall be clearly and unambiguously defined and, as used in the premises and the conclusion, signify a uniform, fixed and definite meaning throughout.
- Logic demands that the conclusion be not assumed, but derived from the premises. [1]

IRRELEVANT EVIDENCE

We begin with the fallacies of irrelevant evidence. Irrelevant arguments miss the central point at issue. Over the years I have often asked counsel at oral argument to discuss an issue framed by the court. Often, lawyers treat me with the response: "But that's not the point, your honor!" My rejoinder is: "You tell us what conclusion you want and we will frame the issue." How you come out in a case often depends on how you go in.

The fallacy of irrelevance—or ignoratio elenchi—is an argument asserted to establish a particular conclusion, that

[1] *See* J. Creighton, *An Introductory to Logic* 406 (5th ed. 1958).

logically leads to a different conclusion or no conclusion at all. [2] It occurs whenever we advance as an argument something that has nothing to do with the point at issue. The method can make appeals to emotions, but not every case of *ignoratio elenchi* involves such an appeal. An argument may be stated in cold, antiseptic, neutral language and still commit the fallacy. [3] It also arises in what is sometimes called the fallacy of the strawman—erecting a strawman posed as an opponent's argument and then proceeding to demolish it.

Not every argument of irrelevant evidence is premeditated or deliberate. It may be the result of involuntary confusion on the part of an attorney or judge. But it also may be consciously adopted as a strategem to deceive an adversary or the court. When so used it is usually intended to conceal the weakness of a position by diverting attention from the real point at issue. It is my experience that willful perversions or confusions are the exception; more often than not, the instances of irrelevancy are unintentional. Many examples abide in the cases.

United States v. Standefer
610 F.2d 1079, 1106 (3d Cir. 1979)
(Aldisert, J., concurring and dissenting)

[The majority opinion outlined problems that might occur in other cases, referring to complex criminal cases with multiple defendants, great variations in available and admissible evidence, and other factors not present in the case at bar. The dissent responded.]

To consider consequences that might occur in other cases containing factual problems not before us is always legitimate, whether in a lawyer's brief or a judge's opinion, but it is just argument. The rules of logic inexorably limit permissible rhetoric; one risks committing the fallacy of division, erroneously reasoning that what holds true of a composite whole necessarily is true for each component part considered separately, or being seduced into the fallacy of *ignoratio*

[2] *See* I. Copi, *Introduction to Logic* 103 (7th ed. 1986).
[3] *Id.* at 104.

elenchi, irrelevant evidence, proving unrelated point B instead of point A, which is at issue, or disproving point D instead of point C.

Here, we are confronted with two short trials of two individual defendants on virtually identical indictments returned simultaneously by the same grand jury on essentially the same evidence involving a common set of facts [and having no resemblance to complex criminal trials with multiple defendants].

Soto v. Texas
681 S.W.2d 602, 611 (1984)
(Miller, J., dissenting)

One redeeming feature of the opinion is the tacit acknowledgment of its internal weakness; the form of that acknowledgment, however, constitutes still another problem with the opinion—by misinterpreting the issue presented as including whether the appellant's evidence establishes that Rosalinda Cervantes was a "law enforcement agent," the opinion interjects what logicians call the fallacy of the strawman. At no time has the State in the trial court, in the Court of Appeals, or in this Court ever disputed or contested the issue that Cervantes was acting as a law enforcement agent. If this was an issue raised by the appellant, the majority would have (and has on numerous occasions) summarily dismissed this contention by citing the well-worn and well-established rule that there was "no objection at trial, thus nothing is presented for review." For some unexplained reason the majority fails to apply that same rule of law to the State, in its appeal before this Court.

Schiaffo v. Helstoski
492 F.2d 413, 436 (3d Cir. 1974),
(Aldisert, J., concurring and dissenting)

While it may be true, as the majority states that there is "no evidence in the legislative history [of §§ 3210-3212] suggesting that Congress specifically considered the enforcement problem," this proves nothing. Enforcement is allocated to other statutes, to those statutes covering the Postal Service. The majority attempts to disprove point B (legislative history of enforcement of franking laws), instead of disproving point A (Postal Service enforcement), which is the real issue at stake. Logicians call this technique the fallacy of irrelevance, *ignoratio elenchi.*

EEOC v. Franklin and Marshall College
775 F.2d 110, 119 (3d Cir. 1985)
(Aldisert, J., dissenting)

The cited legislative history convincingly demonstrates that Congress intended Title VII to apply to universities and colleges. No one can argue to the contrary. The majority nonetheless rest their *ratio decidendi* entirely upon an analysis of the 1972 amendment to Title VII that eliminated the exemption for academic institutions. We are thus treated to a classic fallacy of irrelevance, or *ignoratio elenchi.* The error is made by attempting to prove something that has not been denied, to-wit that the 1972 amendment to Title VII took in institutions of higher learning. The question under consideration, however, is not whether Title VII was so amended but whether, on the strength of a mere conclusory allegation of discrimination, the EEOC is permitted the kind of intrusion into the tenure review process it seeks here.

United States v. Jannotti
673 F.2d 578, 622 (3d Cir. 1982)
(Aldisert, J., dissenting)

The majority's clever approach to this very sensitive problem is a tribute to the skilled advocate's art. . . . [I]t is an unrelenting exhortation of major and minor premises that has an uncanny resemblance to mechanical justice. I do not fault its syllogistic structure; I quarrel only with the choice of major premises. I fault the majority's refusal to take as a beginning point the critical issue in any case where, as here, there is evidence of government inducement: Did the prosecution make out a *prima facie* case of *predisposition* on the part of the defendants beyond a reasonable doubt so as to merit submitting the entrapment question to the jury?

Instead, the majority have turned our American criminal justice system upon its head and reversed the burden of proof: Instead of requiring the government to prove that the issue was properly submitted to the jury, they demand proof from the defendants that it should not have been. Thus, the majority's approach, ringing and singing, is a classic example of the fallacy of *ignoratio elenchi,* or irrelevance. Instead of proving point A, the defendants' predisposition, their argument proves unrelated point B, a rebuttal of factors which the district court considered in setting aside the verdict. In the scholastic rhetorical sense, the majority's obligation was to present a *confirmatio* of the government's proof, not a *refutatio* of isolated contrary contentions.

The United States Supreme Court is not immune to involuntarily falling into this trap. In *Saint Francis College v. Majid Ghaidan Al-Khazraji,* [4] the Court was required to interpret the phrases "all persons" and "white citizens" in 42 U.S.C. § 1981, which provides:

> All persons within the jurisdiction of the United States shall have the same right in every State and Territory to make and enforce contracts, to sue, be parties, give evidence, and to the full and equal benefit of all laws and proceedings for the security of persons and property as is enjoyed by white citizens, and shall be subject to like punishment, pains, penalties, taxes, licenses, and exactions of every kind, and to no other. [5]

Stripped to its basics, the statute was designed to give "all persons" the same rights as those enjoyed by "white citizens." Homer nodded, and a unanimous decision reasoned

[4] 55 U.S.L.W. 4626 (1987).
[5] *Id.* at 4628.

as follows: "Although § 1981 does not itself use the word 'race,' the court has construed the section to forbid all 'racial' discrimination in the making of private as well as public contracts." [6] The Court then proceeded to interpret the word "race," which was not in issue because it was not in the statute, instead of "all persons" and "white citizens," which were in issue because these terms are the statutory language up for interpretation. The opinion referred to nineteenth century dictionaries that equated "race" to ancestral origin and described the following as "races:" Finns, Gypsies, Basques, Arabs, Hebrews, Swedes, Norwegians, Germans, Greeks, Spaniards, Russians, Mongolians, Jews, Hungarians. Thus, reasoned the Court, the plaintiff, an Arab (and, in *Shaare Tefila Congregation,* [7] the plaintiffs, Jews) although members of the caucasian race, may sue and have the same privileges of white persons because they were members of specific races. Thus the holding, paraphrased, is: "All white citizens should have the same rights as are enjoyed by white citizens." [8] By falling into the trap of the fallacy of irrelevance, the Court also became guilty of a classic reductio ad absurdum.

Shapiro v. Merrill Lynch, Pierce, Fenner & Smith, Inc.
353 F. Supp. 264 (S.D.N.Y. 1972)

. . . Defendants' argument does, however, contain a defect of a more substantial nature.

This defect is contained in the basic premise of defendants' argument: that regardless of whether defendants traded or abstained from trading, plaintiffs would still have purchased the Douglas stock. As an abstract proposition that statement is undoubtedly true. Plaintiffs had no knowledge of defendants' transactions and it logically follows that plaintiffs' decision to purchase Douglas stock would have been unaffected had defendants' abstained from any transactions. But therein lies the fallacy of defendants' reasoning: it is

[6] *Id.*
[7] Shaare Tefila Congregation v. Cobb, 55 U.S.L.W. 4629 (1987).
[8] *Saint Francis College, supra* note 4, at 4628.

not the act of trading which causes plaintiffs' injury, *it is the act of trading without disclosing material inside information which causes plaintiffs' injury.* Had Merrill Lynch and the individual defendants refrained from divulging the earnings information to the selling defendants, or had the selling defendants decided not to trade, there would have been no liability for plaintiffs' injury due to the eventual public disclosure of Douglas' poor financial position. But defendants did not choose to follow that course of action, and by trading in Douglas stock on a national securities exchange they assumed the duty to disclose the information to all potential buyers. It is the breach of this duty which gives rise to defendants' liability.

Kobell v. Suburban Lines, Inc.
731 F.2d 1076, 1100 (3d Cir. 1984)
(Aldisert, J., concurring)

To suggest that the district court found "anti-union animus" or "improper behavior" are conclusions artificially and self-constructed by the majority. At the very best, the technique is known as the fallacy of irrelevance, often referred to as irrelevant conclusion or *ignoratio elenchi:* the material fallacy of attacking something that has not been asserted. In the vernacular, this is known as erecting a strawman and then striking it down.

United States v. Berrigan
482 F.2d 171, 183 (3d Cir. 1973)

It hardly deserves extended discussion to observe that appellants' syllogism strains to a conclusion which is invalid and illicit. At issue is not the right of a prisoner to send or receive mail; rather, it is the right of a warden to establish an authorized channel of communications for the sending or receipt of this mail. Assuming, without deciding, that a prisoner has an unqualified right to send and receive all mail, there is no allegation that prisoner Berrigan's right to send or receive mail was denied him.

FALLACIES OF DISTRACTION

Some material fallacies are substantive. They shift attention from reasoned argument to other things that are always irrelevant, always irrational, and often emotional. They are ploys, but ploys that are used everyday, everywhere. They are used in advertising and political campaigning, by essay writers, columnists, editorial writers, and television commentators. For our purposes we will call them "fallacies of distraction."

We will discuss a few of these fallacies that appear in the legal profession. We will not discuss others: appeals ad envidium (to envy), ad mitum (to the few), ad modum (to due measure or proportion), ad edum (to hatred), ad superbium (to snobbery or pride) and ad superstitionem (to credulity). Others exist as well.

Argumentum Ad Misericordium
(Appeal to Pity)

The appeal to pity is familiar in many jury trials, civil and criminal. This fallacy evades the pertinent issue and makes a purely emotional appeal. It's an appeal for sympathy. Pity is appealed to in order to reach a desired conclusion. Defending the youth on trial for killing his parents, counsel tells the jury: "In your hearts, consider that this young man is an orphan." In a civil case, we hear, "My client, although not entirely without fault (in running the red light while under the influence), is the family breadwinner. His wife and children are here. And arrayed against them is the gigantic, multi-national corporation, General Motors, who designed a faulty rear seat in the car. Sure, no one was in the rear seat at the time of the collision, but these little innocent children could have been."

I must confess that in my salad days when I was an active member of the criminal court bar, I resorted to this fallacy often in my closing speech to the jury, probably hearkening to the adage: "When the law is against you, argue the facts; when the facts are against you, appeal to anything that will convince a jury." But I venture that none of us surpassed the eloquence of Clarence Darrow, the celebrated trial lawyer who was the master of this device. In defending Thomas Kidd, a union official on trial for criminal conspiracy, he closed to the jury:

> I appeal to you not for Thomas Kidd, but I appeal to you for the long line—the long, long line reaching back through the ages and forward to the years to come—the long line of despoiled and downtrodden people of the earth. I appeal to you for those men who rise in the morning before daylight comes and who go home at night when the light has faded from the sky and give their life, their strength, their toil to make others rich and great. I appeal to you in the name of those women who are offering up their lives to this modern god of gold, and I appeal to you in the name of those little children, the living and the unborn. [9]

Another "considerably more subtle example of argumentum ad misericordiam" is found in Plato's *Apology,* which purports to be a record of Socrates' defense of himself during his trial.

> Perhaps there may be someone who is offended at me, when he calls to mind how he himself on a similar, or even a less serious occasion, prayed and entreated the judges with many tears, and how he produced his children in court, which was a moving spectacle, together with a host of relations and friends; whereas I, who am probably in danger of my life, will do none of these things. The contrast may occur to his mind, and he may be set against me, and vote in anger because he is displeased by me on this account. Now if there be such a person among you,—mind, I do not say that there is,—to him I may fairly reply: My friend, I am a man, and like other men, a creature of flesh and blood, and not "of wood or stone," as Homer says; and I have a family, yes, and sons, O Athenians, three in number, one almost a man, and two others who are still young; and yet I will not bring any of them hither in order to petition you for acquittal. [10]

[9] I. Copi, *supra* note 2, at 95 (quoting I. Stone, *Clarence Darrow for the Defense* (1941)).
[10] *Id.* at 96.

California v. Sonleitner
185 Cal. App. 2d 350, 8 Cal. Rptr. 528, 540-41
(1960)

Throughout defendant's briefs runs the recurring contention that because the court found that he was financially unable on a given date to deposit the security fixed by the board as a condition to a hearing for redetermination, he should be excused from exhausting his administrative remedies and be permitted to contest the tax in the action brought by the State on the jeopardy determination. Defendant phrases this contention in his statement of "Issues" as follows: "Can the Legislature and the Board of Equalization compel courts to restrict due process in tax cases to the wealthy?" This, logicians refer to as "argumentum ad misericordiam," an appeal to pity. This is of course a contention which could be made against any tax and can have no relevancy here. A similar contention was [previously] advanced and thus answered: "It would be strange indeed if this court were to sanction a practice whereby a taxpayer could regularly refrain from paying taxes, the obligation of which he disputes, and then urge that, by reason of his large delinquency, the ordinary remedies provided for reviewing his liability are inadequate in his particular case."

Marsh v. Scott
2 N.J. Super. 240, 63 A.2d 275, 278-79 (1949)

It would be unthinkable that this court be powerless to grant support to a minor child in need of funds within the control of the court, of which the income belongs to the father and the corpus will ultimately belong to the child. The answer is found in the expression of Judge Cardozo, which has been quoted with approval by the courts of this state: "There is no undeviating principle that equity shall [be] . . . unmoved by an appeal *ad misericordiam,* however urgent or affecting. The development of the jurisdiction of the chancery is lined with historic monuments that point another course.... Equity follows the law, but not slavishly nor always.... If it did, there could never be occasion for the enforcement of equitable doctrine.... Let the hardship be strong enough, and equity will find a way, though many a formula of inaction may seem to bar the path."

The will under which the trust in the instant case is created contains a spend-thrift clause, prohibiting payment to creditors of the cestui, and it is urged that this provision bars the application. The obligation of a parent for the support of his child does not arise from a creditor-debtor relationship. It is not a debt within the contemplation of the testatrix or the interpretation of the clause.

The needs of both the incompetent and the minor are to be considered.

Argumentum Ad Verecundiam
(Appeal to Prestige)

This fallacy makes an appeal to authority, respect, or prestige instead of to pertinent data, to win assent to a conclusion. This appeal equates prestige with reasoned argument or evidence and attempts to gain support for legal argument by associating it with highly respected individuals or hallowed institutions. It is, of course, appropriate to set forth an argument, with a formal or informal syllogism, and then attribute the contention to a renowned legal scholar or treatise author. But I do not think it appropriate to ever by-pass the reasons for the argument, offer only a conclusion, and then say it's true by citing an authority. Emphasis on a publication from a famous institution does not in itself have a stronger bite simply because of the reputation of the institution.

Common and subtle forms of argument ad verecundiam may be found in the paraphernalia of pedantry:

- Use of pedantic words and phrases
- Use of references
- Use of quotations
- Use of length

- Use of detail and specificity

What Professor Fischer has said about historians may also be applicable to law students, lawyers, and judges:

> The first of these forms of error is committed by scholars who never use a little word when a big one will do. Historians take a certain pride in their alleged immunity from this fallacy—in their freedom from jargon and academic affectation. But their conceit is not correct; indeed, it is growing increasingly inaccurate as an understanding of contemporary historiographical language. Ordinary everyday words like "simple" are replaced by monstrosities such as "simplistic" without any refinement of meaning. Special fields of historical inquiry are building pedantic vocabularies at an appalling rate. Urban historians, for instance, speak endlessly of "urbitecture," "areal differentiation," "ecosystems," "nodal points," "metropolitan matrices," "ruralization," "subareal mosaics," "conurbation," and other such neologisms, which are in some cases useful for their precision and defensible for their utility. But these terms are also used for purposes of legitimization, as ritual incantations which serve to camouflage doubt, confusion, illogic, imprecision, and ignorance. [11]

Cresap v. Pacific Inland Navigation Co.
78 Wash. 2d 563, 478 P.2d 223, 228 (1970)
(Neill, J., dissenting)

Moreover, I am reluctant to accept as harmless the additions of source references where the statute, rule or regulation has no dispositive effect, as in this case. There is danger inherent in the very nature of such additions. When the source of the law is not significant per se, the only effect of citation is rhetorical. In formal logic the device is known as *Argumentum ad verecundiam,* playing upon the prestige of the source. At best, its use in instructions needlessly injects a misleading element into the legal search for truth. At worst, the balance of images created by such additions may be unduly prejudicial to one of the parties. Further, there is the potential danger that the refusal of

[11] D. Fischer, *Historians' Fallacies* 285 (1970).

a trial court to cite some sources while naming others may amount to a comment on the evidence.

Argumentum Ad Hominen
(Appeal to Ridicule)

This fallacy shifts an argument from the point being discussed (ad rem) to irrelevant personal characteristics of an opponent (ad hominen). It shifts attention from the argument to the arguer; instead of disproving the substance of what is asserted, the argument attacks the person who made the assertion. It may take several forms. First, drawn from the negative campaigning of office seekers, and very common in the law, is what we might call the abusive argumentum ad hominem. The argument attacks the assertion based on the adversary's reputation, personality, or some personal shortcoming. X's statement must be wrong because X is a communist. The argument rests not upon the merits of the case, but on the character or position of those engaged in it.

The abusive ad hominem argument tries to shift the burden of proof. It's a would-you-buy-a-used-car-from-this-man? type of question. Unfortunately, too many lawyers degenerate into this practice during the heat of a trial: "My opponent is cheating and committing fraud upon the court!" "The lawyer for the government deliberately withheld information from me, and is continuing the treachery that began with the first pre-trial conference. He has been misrepresenting from the start and now is trying to pull a fast one on the court." "Continuing her tactics, that I can only describe as sleazy, my opponent is not telling the truth, and my total experience with her is that this is the way she does business." The classic ad hominem argument, often repeated, is the note passed from one defense lawyer to another: "No case, abuse plaintiff's attorney."

The second form of argumentum ad hominem is the circumstantial variety. The argument is that an opponent's circumstances are such that a given result is dictated. [12] If A accuses B of illegally dumping waste in Lake Erie, a coun-

[12] I. Copi, *supra* note 2, at 93.

terattack by *B* that *A* is *B*'s largest competitor or that *A* dumps hazardous wastes in Lake Ontario, therefore *A*'s accusation cannot be true, is an example of argumentum ad hominem.

For examples of both types of ad hominen argumentum, tune in to television and movie courtroom dramas and you get the impression that this goes on in every case. Fortunately, it does not.

Crook v. Alabama
42 Ala. App. 270, 160 So. 2d 884, 886-87 (1963)

We consider the trial judge erred in not sustaining the objections. The solicitor's counter argument was not directed to the irrationality or inconsistency of the defense argument. Rather it partook of the fallacy of the "argumentum ad hominem" condemned by logicians as appealing to the passions and prejudices of the hearers as distinguished from "ad rem," an argument directed to the matter at hand.

Here the expression "ad hominem" has another meaning since the argument is directed to the person of Crook's counsel.

The symbolic identification of the accused in the personality of his champion is one of the significant drawbacks of the adversary system of our common law. To make the system work fairly, a contestant should have to defend but one cause—the issue against his principal. For a lawyer to have to prove his heart is pure as well as his client's is to make him fight a two front war.

In *Taylor v. State,* we find: 'In the closing argument the solicitor stated: "They (defense counsel) are laying like vultures to take this case to the Supreme Court." '

The opinion commented: This remark was undignified, highly improper, and had no place upon the trial of this case. It was contumely in all that the word implies and tended to place counsel for defendant in an improper light and disrepute before the jury; this, in the absence of any improper or illegal conduct upon the part of defendant's counsel, who, as shown by the record, were ably and earnestly undertaking to defend their client and to protect him in his legal rights, in accordance with the solemn oath which every attorney at law is required to take before he shall be permitted to practice in this state.

Another argument deriding defense counsel was the cause of reversal in [another case]. There Bricken, P. J., said: * * * the solicitor in addressing the jury * * * stated: Counsel for the defendant are trying to make monkeys out of this jury, and they are laughing up their sleeves at you.

It clearly appears that the above quoted statement by the solicitor was wholly unwarranted as not being based upon any fact, incident, or testimony, in the case. Its effect necessarily was harmful and prejudicial. The statement cast opprobrium upon the three reputable members of the bar who were, as the law requires, defending their client to the best of their ability, and in an orderly manner, and tended to place them and their client in a very unfavorable light before the jury. This of itself would necessitate a reversal of the judgment of conviction.

The office of solicitor is of the highest importance; he is the representative of the state, and as a result of the important functions devolving upon him as such officer necessarily holds and wields great power and influence, and as a consequence erroneous insistences and prejudicial conduct upon his part tend to unduly prejudice and bias the jury against the defendant.

Patterson v. Board of Supervisors
202 Cal. App. 3d 22, 248 Cal. Rptr. 253, 260 (1988)

Appellant Geary contends that the deleted ballot arguments, characterized by the city attorney as "idle scandal-mongering (*sic*)" and "base personal attacks" inconsistent with the purposes of the limited public forum, were neither misleading nor inconsistent. Having reviewed the deleted materials . . . we explain our reasons upholding the rulings below.

The personal attacks concerning Hagan's marital problems and Callinan's financial circumstances bore no relationship, certainly none which could be considered reasonable, to the question whether the Poly High School property should be rezoned, the only subject before the voters. Hagan's name had been mentioned in connection with possible development of the Balboa property, the property proposed for rezoning under Proposition B.

The statements concerning Callinan's financial status were totally unrelated to the proposed rezoning. Since there was no specific development project or potential developer before the voters, they could have been easily misled by the statements into believing that they were also voting to approve or disapprove specific individuals.

The statements deleted from the second argument were similarly misleading and inconsistent with the singular purpose of providing relevant information supporting or opposing specific ballot propositions. The Balboa property was not the subject of Proposition A. And no information was presented concerning the relative merits of the proposed rezoning or any other problems associated with the proposed zoning change. Appellant's remedy for any election fraud or improper interference with the right to petition was through conventional legal channels and not the voter's pamphlet.

The *ad hominem* attack on the two city officials reflected in the third argument again had no relationship to the ballot proposition to rezone the Poly High School property. In fact, the statement is an apparent reference to a frivolous lawsuit filed after the June 1986 election accusing the officials of impropriety in connection with an earlier proposal regarding development of the Balboa site.

Brice v. Maryland
71 Md. App. 563, 526 A.2d 647, 652-53 (1987)

The officer in this case did what the statute and *State v. Werkheiser* indicate he was obligated to do.

Under the circumstances, we cannot agree with the appellant that "the conduct of the trooper was repugnant to generally accepted standards of fair behavior, even police behavior." The appellant's case in this regard reduces itself to little more than innuendo. He does not claim to have been in a life-threatening situation; he simply makes the *ad hominem* argument that "so far as the trooper knew, this might well have been a life-threatening situation." With no support in the evidence, the appellant goes on to insinuate, "The trooper apparently believed nevertheless that it was his duty to use any means in order to make (or fake?) a case against the appellant." As the case law discussed earlier makes clear, Society imposes upon the trooper the obligation to move with all possible diligence against drunken drivers. The appellant's final insinuation goes only to the credibility of the trooper and is, therefore, beyond our concern: "That he endeavored to prosecute at all in the context of this case casts suspicion upon all such reported timings and on the animus of the trooper." The blood alcohol content of 0.24 percent indicates that the trooper did precisely what Society expects him to do.

Brock v. Ward
28 Utah 2d 305, 501 P.2d 1207, 1211-12 (1972)
(Crockett, J., dissenting)

It is appreciated that an *ad hominem* argument, based on the number of persons who believe a proposition, may ordinarily seem to have little weight as a matter of logic, because many people can be and often are in error. Yet in an admittedly close case such as this, where a consideration underlying the issue of law is what reasonable minds might believe that reasonable persons might do, it seems proper to give at least some attention to what other presumably reasonable minds have thought about the problem. This is particularly so in this case where the critical question is in the final analysis not really a question of law, but a question of fact as to the care of ordinary persons.

On that question the jurors, being people from various walks of life, and having different points of view, have a special advantage and should be just as competent to judge such a matter of everyday conduct as any lawyer, judge, or justice. If we indulge the presumption, as we should, that the trial judges and jurors performed their duties honestly and conscientiously, it does not seem amiss to regard their collective judgment as lending support to plaintiff's argument that it is not proved that her conduct was wholly outside what an ordinary, reasonable and prudent person might have done under the particular circumstances.

[Author's note: Was this *ad hominem* or *ad populum?*]

Argumentum Ad Populum
(Appeal to the Masses)

This is the political candidate's dream: "I'm for the working man, the underprivileged, the poor, the homeless, and the senior citizens." This argument departs from the question under discussion and attempts to win assent to a proposition by making an appeal to the feelings and prejudices of the multitude. The arguments are calculated to excite the feelings of the masses and prevent them from forming a dispassionate judgment on the matter at hand. During an Ohio Senatorial race, Senator Robert A. Taft's opponent ridiculed him and said "I'm from the common people; I wasn't born with a silver spoon in my mouth." Martha Taft, the senator's wife, sallied forth with a brave rebuttal: "My husband is being accused of not being a common man. That's true. He's not common. He was first in his class in college; first in his class in law school; and first in the U.S. Senate. You don't want a senator who is common. You want someone who is outstanding. And that's my husband!"

Kobell v. Suburban Lines, Inc.
731 F.2d 1076, 1100 n.6 (3d Cir. 1984)
(Aldisert, J., concurring)

The majority, for example, unnecessarily and gra-
tuitously injects into its analysis an inflammatory hypothetical—not present or suggested in this case:
"Posting a sign, for example, that reads 'No Blacks
Need Apply' or that reads 'No Union Members Need
Apply' and that succeeds in its objectives is just as effective (and just as offending) a method of discrimination as a point-blank refusal to hire. . . ." This, of course,
is the classic material fallacy of *Argumentum ad
Populum,* an appeal to strong feelings of the multitude.

Argumentum Ad Antiquitam
(Appeal to the Ages)

Based on the notion that "we love all truths," this is the
fallacy that holds that determinations and customs of our
fathers and forebears must not be changed. We see this in
the constant debate on the original intent of the Constitution's drafters, and quotations from Washington, Madison,
Monroe, Jefferson, Franklin, and John Marshall. It always
presents the question of bowing down before propositions
inherited from our ancestors. The appeal to the ages is
based on the adage that age is wiser than youth. Yet we can
and do learn from the experience of others, and there is a
collective experience which we call history.

Not surprisingly, there exists the counter-fallacy of argumentum ad novitam, or an appeal to novelty, modernity,
current mores, or youth. We saw this demonstrated in force
in the later sixties and early seventies in the oft-repeated
phrase, "Don't trust anybody over thirty."

Argumentum Ad Terrorem
(Appeal to Terror)

This argument makes an appeal to fear of exaggerated
consequences in the event an adversary's argument pre-

vails. In the sixties and seventies, when the federal courts were enforcing the Bill of Rights through the fourteenth amendment in habeas corpus cases reviewing state court convictions, we heard almost daily the refrain: "If the defendant prevails here, the jails will be emptied of criminals turned loose upon an innocent public."

These arguments appear in many personal injury cases. "If the plaintiff prevails, insurance rates will go up all over." The physician's attorney in the malpractice case argues that lawsuits are requiring emergency rooms to shut down and hospitals to close obstetric wards. The city attorney argues "You know, of course, if we do not have immunity, municipal taxes will rise sky high." The district attorney complains that the *Miranda* rule has handcuffed the effectiveness of the police and crime will run rampant. The appellate advocate pleads: "If your honors sustain this appeal and reverse the trial court, your dockets will be hopelessly clogged with frivolous appeals."

County of Lake v. Mac Neal
24 Ill. 2d 253, 181 N.E.2d 85, 90 (1962)

Plaintiff argues that any refusal to extend the *Bright* rule to defending property owners will be an invitation to the unscrupulous to violate zoning regulations. However, such an *ad terrorem* appeal does not withstand either logical or historical examination. The alleged violation of the zoning ordinance in this case primarily involves a use of open land for recreation purposes. Most zoning litigation, to the contrary, involves proposed substantial investments in and improvements to real estate. In view of the judicial power to preserve the integrity of a zoning ordinance, by mandatory injunction if necessary, we do not foresee that money will be invested or properties substantially altered without first legally testing the zoning ordinance. We conclude that the court below correctly determined that the *Bright* rule did not extend to the defendants in this case.

Cunningham v. MacNeal Memorial Hosp.
47 Ill. 2d 443, 266 N.E.2d 897, 904 (1970)

Defendant implicitly raises the *Ad terrorem* argument that allowing a strict tort liability theory to obtain in this case will "open the flood gates" to disastrous litigation which will ultimately thwart the fulfillment of the hospitals' worthy mission by drainage of their funds for purposes other than those intended. Our answer to this contention is that (paraphrasing what we observed [before]) we do not believe in this present day and age, when the operation of eleemosynary hospitals constitutes one of the biggest businesses in this country, that hospital immunity can be justified on the protection-of-the-funds theory. The concept of strict liability in tort logically, and we think, reasonably, dictates that an entity which distributes a defective product for human consumption, whether for profit or not, should legally bear the consequences of injury caused thereby, rather than allowing such loss to fall upon the individual consumer who is entirely without fault.

Baker v. Carr
369 U.S. 186, 267 (1962)
(Frankfurter, J., dissenting)

Disregard of inherent limits in the effective exercise of the Court's "judicial power" not only presages the futility of judicial intervention in the essentially political conflict of forces by which the relation between population and representation has time out of mind been and now is determined. It may well impair the Court's position as the ultimate organ of "the supreme Law of the Land" in that vast range of legal problems, often strongly entangled in popular feeling, on which this Court must pronounce.

Webster v. Doe
56 U.S.L.W. 4568, 4576 (June 15, 1988)
(Scalia, J., dissenting)

Today's result, however, will have ramifications far beyond creation of the world's only secret intelligence agency that must litigate the dismissal of its agents. If constitutional claims can be raised in this highly sensitive context, it is hard to imagine where they cannot. The assumption that there are any executive decisions that cannot be hauled into the courts may no longer be valid. Also obsolete may be the assumption that we are capable of preserving a sensible common law of judicial review.

MISCELLANEOUS MATERIAL FALLACIES

These fallacies are not readily subject to classification. They have one characteristic in common: as in all material fallacies, what constitutes the fallacies are the contents of the premises and not logical form.

Dicto Simpliciter
(Fallacy of Accident)

This fallacy occurs when a general rule is applied to exceptional circumstances. It is the error that a proposition generally true is always true in exactly the same way, even though special conditions are present.

Jevons gives this classic example: "He who thrusts a knife into another person should be punished; a surgeon in operating does so; therefore he should be punished." [13] The maxim "the exception proves the rule" is relevant here. We run into this fallacy in arguments of the prosecution. "The Bible says, 'Thou shalt not kill.' The deliberate taking of life is murder; the defendant aimed and shot the intruder after the intruder knifed his wife and with bloody knife in hand

[13] W. Jevons, *Elementary Lessons in Logic: Deductive and Inductive* 177 (1870).

approached the defendant trapped in a corner; therefore, the defendant is a murderer."

If there is anything in the law that requires you to meticulously check the quotations in your opponent's brief, it is the possibility of a lurking fallacy of accident when a brief writer (or opinion writer) sets forth a quotation declaring a general rule, but omitting the central conditional clause: "Except for circumstances *A, B,* and *C,* the general rule is . . . ."

Carrier Corp. v. NLRB
311 F.2d 135, 147-48 (2d Cir. 1962)

It is clear that where a union engages in traditional picketing activities on the premises of the employer with whom it has a dispute, its actions may lawfully have the effect of encouraging employees of neutral suppliers or customers not to enter the premises. The cases have uniformly held, however, that such attempts to influence neutral employees are lawful only if incidental to the independently legitimate objective of publicizing the union's dispute with the primary employer to the employees of that employer. After all, the language found in a statute is not wholly irrelevant to its proper construction. Because a harm may be permitted in one instance only because incidental to lawful activities, it is fallacious reasoning to hold that the same harm must be permitted in another instance where it is independently pursued. Neither logic nor the sense of the different economic situations indicates that such a result is justified.

Converse Fallacy of Accident
(Hasty Generalization)

This fallacy is the bugaboo of inductive reasoning. It appears all too often in the cases and in the classroom. Also called the fallacy of selected instances, it results from enumerating instances without obtaining a representative number of instances in order to prove an inductive generalization. It occurs when one or two decisions, as the sole ingredient, are used to make a quantum leap to a conclusion that these decisions form a rule with general application. The error lies in failing to obtain a fair number of instances. Moreover, if only exceptional or "accidental circumstance" cases are considered, you may generalize to a rule that fits the exception alone, and thereby commit the converse fallacy of accident.

A special form of this problem is known as the fallacy of statistical simplicity. The probability of a sampling error tends to diminish as the size of the sample increases. But size alone is no protection.

> The classic example was a massive effort by the *Literary Digest* to forecast the presidential election of 1936. More than 10,000,000 ballots were sent out. Something like 2,367,523 came back, mostly marked for Alf Landon. The poll predicted 370 electoral votes for the Republican candidate, and 161 for Roosevelt. In the real election, Roosevelt won 523 votes, Landon 8. What went wrong? The *Digest,* it seems, sent ballots to addresses collected from the subscription lists of magazines, and also from telephone directories, and automobile registration lists. But magazines, telephones, and automobiles were not randomly distributed among the American population in 1936. [14]

The poll was such a disaster that it forced the *Literary Digest,* a distinguished popular magazine, to go out of business. The magazine's name was the butt of jokes for years. This experience should be kept in mind when making general predictions based solely on the use of statistics.

United States v. Gabriner
571 F.2d 48, 50-51 (1st Cir. 1978)

The fact that Reeves designated Broker as someone to whom his passport might be mailed indicates something about her relationship to Reeves, but nothing about her relationship to appellant or about appellant's relationship to Reeves. That Broker knew his true name indicates no more than that one person "with whom he was friendly knew his true name." The inference the court drew—that therefore all persons

---

[14] *See* D. Fischer, *supra* note 11, at 106-07.

with whom he was friendly had the same knowledge—is not permissible because it is based on a logical fallacy. The court's syllogism is: Broker is a friend of Reeves—Broker knew Reeves' true name; therefore, all friends of Reeves knew his true name. This is an obvious over-generalization.

Brennan v. United Steelworkers of America
554 F.2d 586, 613 (3d Cir. 1977)
(Aldisert, J., dissenting)

The majority has done what the Supreme Court refused to do in *Alyeska:* they have fashioned a far-reaching exception to the American Rule. Whatever precepts of statutory construction I apply—the Mischief Rule, the Golden Rule, the Literal Rule, the Plain Meaning Rule, or interpretations based on the legislative history—I cannot interpret Title IV as allowing such a result. The majority's reading, in my view, is reminiscent of *dicto simpliciter,* the fallacy of accident. It has not misapplied the general rule to an exceptional case, but has misapplied a limited exception to that which fits the general rule. The exception begins to take on the potency of the general rule. I am as unwilling to engage in such an inversion of the law as I am disinclined to join in the majority's adventure into the legislative cosmos.

Post Hoc Ergo Propter Hoc
(False Cause)

In the law, the fallacy of false cause takes at least two forms. In one form it is to mistake what is not the cause of a given effect as the real cause (non causa pro causa). In the other, more prevalent form, is the suggested inference that one event is the cause of another merely because the first occurs earlier than the other (post hoc ergo propter hoc) (after this, therefore in consequence of this). The post hoc fallacy consists of reasoning from sequence to consequence. It is reasoning from what happened in sequence to the assumption of a causal connection. We commit this fallacy

whenever we argue that because a certain event was preceded by another event, the preceding event was the cause of
the latter. The fact that *A* precedes *B* does not necessarily
make *A* the cause of *B*. An example is provided by the story
of a woman passenger on board the Italian liner Andrea
Doria. On the fatal night of the Andrea Doria's collision
with the Swedish ship Gripsholm, off Nantucket in 1956,
she retired to her cabin and flicked a light switch. Suddenly
there was a great crash, and the sound of grinding metal,
and passengers and crew ran screaming through the pas-
sageways. The lady burst from her cabin and explained to
the first person in sight that she must have set the ship's
emergency brake. [15] Many examples of this fallacy appear
in the cases.

Brennan v. United Steelworkers of America
554 F.2d 586, 614 (3d Cir. 1977)
(Aldisert, J., dissenting)

The particulars from which the majority's universals are drawn seem centered around two factual complexes: (1) tellers of *Local 1066* had been guilty of vote
fraud, and (2) Sadlowski's opponent, Samuel Evett, was
supported by the international union's "official family." I find the sweeping conclusions drawn from these
instances to be striking examples of the fallacy of composition and the fallacy of *post hoc ergo propter hoc*. To
conclude that, because *local* tellers ran a fraudulent
election the *international* union was responsible, is the
fallacious error of reasoning that what is true of a part
is necessarily true of the whole. To conclude that because international officers supported Sadlowski's opponent in a fraudulent election, the international was
therefore responsible for the fraud, is the classic *post
hoc* fallacy. The mere chronological sequence of events
does not establish a casual connection.

[15] A. Morrow, *Collision Course* 85 (1959).

194

Edward J. Sweeney & Sons, Inc. v. Texaco, Inc.
637 F.2d 105, 116-17 (3d Cir. 1980)

Logicians describe one process of reaching an ultimate fact from insufficient basic facts as the *false cause* or *post hoc* fallacy. The fallacy consists of reasoning from sequence to consequence, that is, assuming a casual connection between two events merely because one follows the other. For this reason the fallacy is often referred to as that of *post hoc ergo propter hoc* (after this and therefore in consequence of this), an expression which itself explains the nature of the error.

Here, the district court properly concluded that the basic facts adduced at trial were insufficient to allow the jury to find for appellants. The basic record facts were that some of Sweeney's competitors complained that Sweeney's stations undersold them by one to three cents per gallon, that Rodden did not know but "guessed" Texaco acted to terminate Sweeney because of these complaints, that Murray surmised Texaco was evaluating Sweeney's ability to get long hauling allowances for short deliveries, and that certain consequences of Sweeney's marketing strategy not directly related to Sweeney's competitive position figured into Doherty's decision to terminate Sweeney. Faced with this scanty record, the district court properly removed the issue of concerted action from the jury. It determined that insufficient narrative or historical evidence had been submitted to permit the conclusion that Texaco's decision was a reaction to the specific complaints received. Moreover, the record was devoid of proof of concerted action among Sweeney's competitors and Texaco. The court concluded that the jury could not infer this ultimate fact from the basic facts in evidence without engaging in pure *post hoc* guesswork. We will not fault the court for these determinations.

Dawson v. Hillsborough County
322 F. Supp. 286, 302 (M.D. Fla. 1971)

The school board's figures suffer from a basic fallacy in logic. There is no correlation of long hair with under-achievement. The board first advances statistics purporting to show that long-haired students have better than average abilities. The board then tries to show that these students' grades are less than average and are not up to their abilities. The board then proposes that the reason for this under-achievement is the length of the students' hair.

Sunward Corp. v. Dunn & Bradstreet, Inc. 811 F.2d 511, 521-22 (10th Cir. 1987)

In this case, we are not confronted with difficult line-drawing determinations. Inferences that the reports were understood as defamatory and that they caused or contributed to Sunward's financial difficulties are here supported only by speculation and conjecture. The record is devoid of evidence that anyone ever understood the credit reports in the defamatory manner inferred by the plaintiff. The only evidence offered was a chronological rendition of events which, among other things, indicated that the first inaccurate Dunn & Bradstreet report preceded Sunward's financial downturn, rumors of difficulty, and associated problems. Sunward's argument based on this evidence consists of "reasoning from sequence to consequence, that is, assuming a causal connection between two events merely because one follows the other."[8] The inferences required to establish proof of defamation in this case do not follow from the evidence and must be rejected.

[FN.8] This form of reasoning represents a logical fallacy known as the *post hoc ergo propter hoc* (after this and therefore because of this) fallacy. Other courts have held that a conclusion based upon such reasoning is not a reasonable inference but is mere speculation and conjecture. *See, e.g., Loesch v. United States,* 645 F.2d 905, 914-15, 227 Ct. Cl. 34 (rejecting an inference of a taking based upon evidence that erosion of plaintiffs' riverbanks was not a problem until after the government constructed certain dams and locks on the river) . . .; *Edward J. Sweeney & Sons, Inc. v. Texaco,*

Inc., 637 F.2d 105, 115-17 (3d Cir. 1980) (evidence that competitors' complaints to supplier preceded supplier's termination of agreement with plaintiff was insufficient evidence to permit a reasonable inference that defendant terminated plaintiff's distributor agreement because of competitor's complaints); *Dodge Motor Trucks, Inc. v. First National Bank*, 519 F.2d 578, 584 (8th Cir. 1975) (evidence that a seller, in selling a car to a buyer who later went bankrupt, had relied on a letter (allegedly a guaranty of credit) written by the defendant bank was insufficient to hold the bank liable; "merely because the letter preceded the injury and the injury followed hard on the heels of the letter does not establish the relation of cause and effect" (quoting *Ligget v. Levy*, 233 Mo. 590, 136 S.W. 299, 303 (1911))).

Gainey v. Folkman
114 F. Supp. 231, 237 (D. Ariz. 1953)

So the concrete question around which the determination of this case turns is, as stated in substance by me during the trial: Did the "dusting" actually damage the plaintiff?

This, in turn, depends upon the answer to another question: Did enough chemicals from the dusting or spraying in 1952 drift over to the plaintiff's field so that, when ingested or absorbed by the cattle directly and impregnated in the alfalfa pastured by or fed to the cattle, they caused their unthriftiness.

As already stated, no deleterious consequences to human beings or warm-blooded animals were discerned following the 1951 dustings. The testimony of many of the plaintiff's own lay witnesses, including the ranch manager's wife, may be dismissed as being an expression of that fallacy which is referred to in logic as *post hoc ergo propter hoc.* Translated into English, it means the fallacy of assuming that, because an event follows another, it is necessarily caused by it. The only testimony in this respect which showed any direct effect is that of witnesses who testified that when near the dusting, the drift of some of the chemicals made their eyes smart. But every person giving such testimony readily admitted that the discomfort was temporary and disappeared quickly.

Del Pilar v. Eastern Airlines, Inc.
172 F. Supp. 158, 160 (S.D.N.Y. 1959)

The Court is unable to find any causal connection between the condition of the seat and the condition of which plaintiff complains. Plaintiff has failed to meet his burden of establishing this causal connection by a fair preponderance of the evidence. He has relied upon the old logical fallacy of *post hoc propter hoc,* i.e., that because he felt pain after he had sat in the seat, therefore the condition of the seat was the cause of his pain, without offering competent proof to establish this causal connection.

Allegheny Corp. v. Kirby
218 F. Supp. 164, 181-82 (S.D.N.Y. 1963)

The Court concludes that the plaintiff has failed to establish that there was any secret understanding between Kirby and Ireland and Phillips whereby Phillips was to gain a position of status and compensation in return for assisting in securing a settlement satisfactory to Kirby. The evidence was all completely to the contrary. The inferences which plaintiff seeks to draw from the fact that Phillips after the withdrawal became a director of IDS do not warrant the conclusion that this was pursuant to a pre-existing agreement. Plaintiff's position is a typical example of the logical fallacy of *post hoc ergo propter hoc.*

Non Sequitur
(It Does Not Follow)

The non sequitur or the fallacy of the consequent is the best-known fallacy in the law. It consists of accepting a conclusion which does not follow logically from given premises or from any antecedent statements. Indeed, it often is an assertion of a conclusion that has no connection whatever with the premises. A non sequitur argument always exhibits this lack of a logical connection. The difference between the post hoc and the non sequitur fallacies is that the post hoc fallacy lacks a causal connection; the non sequitur fallacy lacks a logical connection. A non sequitur argument should also be distinguished from the fallacy of irrelevance, in which, as we have seen, the statement being made pertains to a question other than the one up for discussion. In a non sequitur argument the statements may all be relevant, but the relationships posited are logically disconnected.

Goldwater v. Carter
617 F.2d 697, 736-37 (D.C. Cir. 1979)
(Wright & Tamm, JJ., concurring)

The linchpin in the President's argument, and it is completely fallacious, is that he must be recognized as having the power, acting alone, to terminate the treaty because the position of the Mainland Chinese Government was that "termination of the Defense Treaty with Taiwan was a prerequisite to [normalization]" of relations between that government and the United States. But it is a logical *non sequitur* to conclude from the premise that because the *People's Republic* requires termination of the Taiwan Treaty that therefore the President must be recognized under our Constitution as having the *absolute power alone* to terminate that treaty. Such a conclusion is completely unjustified by the premise.

United States v. Williams
561 F.2d 859, 869 (D.C. Cir. 1977)
(Mackinnon, J., dissenting)

The great lengths to which the majority opinion goes in its attempt to dredge up evidence to strengthen the completely impeached testimony of the alibi witnesses is reflected in the following statement: Their recollection [that of the alibi witnesses] was corroborated by the introduction into evidence of *Nathaniel's birth certificate. . . .*

The reasoning of the majority opinion in this respect proceeds as follows:

1. Witnesses who testified that Williams was with them on November 19, 1974, recalled that the occasion was a birthday party for Nathaniel.

2. Nathaniel's birthday, as proved by his birth certificate, was November 19th.

3. Therefore, the birth certificate supports the witnesses' recollection that they were at a party with Williams on November 19th.

The logical fallacy in this syllogistic presentation is that of *non sequitur* because the conclusion does not really follow from the premises by which it is supposed to be supported. The introduction of the birth certificate only proves that Nathaniel had a birthday on the same day as the bank robbery. It might, at the most, furnish a reason as to why the witness might remember the day, but that does not corroborate that they correctly recall that Williams was present—the critical point—or even that they were present at a party. The logic behind the statement of the majority opinion in this respect is the same as that of the robber who testified he could not have been at the bank when it was robbed because at that time he remembered he was four miles away riding a white horse, and here is the white horse to prove it. Defense lawyers occasionally make this illogical argument to juries but this is the first instance to my knowledge of its acceptance by an appellate court.

Compound Questions

This is also known as the fallacy of multiple questions. It occurs when an argument is phrased as a single question, rather than the two or more separate questions actually at issue. Several questions are combined in such a manner as to place the opponent in a self-incriminating position. This fallacy arises when: (1) two or more questions are asked at once, and a single answer is required; (2) a question is phrased as to beg another question; (3) the question makes a false presumption, or (4) the assertion frames a complex question but demands a simple answer. [16] Unfortunately, it is used in cross-examination by real lawyers as well as by the Hollywood and television versions. The classic example is the question, "Have you stopped beating your wife?" where a yes or no answer is insisted upon. When I preside at court trials and a yes or no answer is demanded by counsel, I instruct the witness "You may answer the question and then take your time and explain what you mean." Eaton quotes Aristotle's definition: "Those fallacies that depend upon the making of two questions into one." [17] Eaton also refers to Joseph who offers as a common example the limitations on the President's veto because he has no line item veto power. "It is therefore not uncommon for the legislature to tack on a bill which the President feels bound to let pass a clause containing a measure to which it is known that he objects; so that if he assents, he allows what he disapproves of, and if he dissents, he disallows what he approves." [18]

Petitio Principii
(Begging the Question)

This fallacy is really a first-class rascal because it sneaks up on us so often. It is a species of question-begging that assumes as true what is to be proved. The rascal bears many names, petitio principii, arguing in a circle, circular reasoning, putting the bunny in the hat, failing to prove the original proposition asserted, and using the original premise as proof of itself. In order to prove that A is true, B is used as proof, but since B requires support, C is used in defense of B, but C also needs proof and is substantiated by A, the proposition which was to be proved in the first place. Thus, that what was to be proved in the first place is affirmed ultimately in defense of itself. In law we see this fallacy often. A conclusion, or some proposition that follows from the conclu-

[16] D. Fischer, *supra* note 11, at 8.

[17] R. Eaton, *General Logic* 354 (1931).

[18] H. Joseph, *An Introduction to Logic* 557 (1st ed. 1906), *quoted in,* R. Eaton, *supra* note 17, at 354.

LOGIC FOR LAWYERS

sion alone, appears tacitly or explicitly among the
supporting premises. It is essentially a fallacy of proof, rather than logical form.

In entertainment, this was used as the basic ingredient
in the long-running George Burns and Gracie Allen radio
show:

> Gracie: Gentlemen prefer blondes.
> George: How do you know that?
> Gracie: A gentleman told me so.
> George: How did you know he was a gentleman?
> Gracie: Because he preferred blondes.

The question is begged in the simplest form when we
proceed in a single step, by the use of synonyms to the conclusion already stated in the premises. We may put the fact
that we want to prove, or its equivalent, under another
name. For example, I define a sleeping pill as "a medicine
that has a soporific effect." Or Yogi Berra's, "It isn't over
until its over." Or, "You know you can see a lot by merely
looking." Where the inference takes several steps, the fallacy is called circular reasoning, or arguing in a circle.

**Thomas Walter Swan, *Hand*,
57 Yale L.J. 107, 170 (1947)**

Learned Hand would remind us "not to be misled
into assuming the conclusion in the minor premise—
not to beg the question. I can think of no single fault
that has done more to confuse the law and to dissemi-
nate litigation. One would suppose that so transparent
a logical vice would be easily detected: but the offend-
ers pass in troops before our eyes, bearing great names
and distinguished titles. The truth is that we are all
sinners; nobody's record is clean; and indeed it is only
fair to say that much of the very texture of the law invites us to sin, for it so often holds out to us, as though
they were objective standards, terms like 'reasonable
care,' 'due notice,' 'reasonable restraint,' which are no
more than signals that the dispute is to be decided with
moderation and without disregard of any of the inter-

ests at stake. So inveterate is the disposition to eschew all deduction in such cases, that some ironist might argue that, given the average judicial capacity for self-scrutiny, it is safer not to expose the springs of decision, because the chances of a right result are greater than that its support will endure disclosure. Perhaps so: maybe, for the ingenuous and the artless to beg the question is nature's self-protective artifice."

Gitlow v. New York
268 U.S. 652, 666 (1925)

For present purposes we may and do assume that freedom of speech and of the press—which are protected by the First Amendment from abridgement by Congress—are among the fundamental personal rights and "liberties" protected by the due process clause of the Fourteenth Amendment from impairment by the States. We do not regard the incidental statement in *Prudential Ins. Co. v. Cheek,* 259 U.S. 530, 543, that the Fourteenth Amendment imposes no restrictions on the States concerning freedom of speech, as determinative of this question.

United States v. Jannotti
673 F.2d 578, 626 (3d Cir. 1981)
(Aldisert, J., dissenting)

The essential flaw in the majority's opinion is its failure to appreciate the jurisdictional nature of the commerce element in a Hobbs Act case. The majority interweaves its jurisdictional argument with the argument that factual impossibility of completing a substantive offense does not bar a conviction of conspiracy. They confuse *proof* of the crime of conspiracy with the jurisdictional *power* to punish the crime. The presence of subject matter jurisdiction is a discrete and primary issue in each case presented to a federal court, unlike a state court. The effect on commerce is both jurisdictional and substantive in a Hobbs Act prosecution, but the two inquiries are separate and distinct. The majority have accepted the government's strawman argument that impossibility is no defense to crime of conspiracy. Even if I could in the exercise of judicial patience, tolerate a litigant's aggrandizement of irrelevancies, I must object to the majority's agreement to join the government in demolishing the strawman.

I can imagine "the persons of the dialogue," in the form of Socrates and Crito:

Soc.:   Is there federal jurisdiction?
Cr.:   Yes, there is federal jurisdiction.
Soc.:   How is there federal jurisdiction?
Cr.:   There is federal jurisdiction because the factual impossibility of performing a conspiracy is no defense to a charge of conspiracy which may be brought when there is federal jurisdiction.

In terms of formal logic, how does one analyze this synthesis of the government's argument, which, nodding like Homer, the majority have accepted? To borrow from Lord Devlin, "I confess that I approach the investigation of this legal proposition with a prejudice in favor of the idea that there may be a flaw in the argument somewhere."

Two such flaws quickly leap to the surface. Obviously, it is a *non sequitur.* More unfortunately, the reasoning "cooks the books," to use Professor Neil MacCormick's phrase, or more popularly, it puts the bunny in the hat by begging the question in a classic *petitio principii:* Instead of *proving* the conclusion (presence of federal jurisdiction), the argument *assumes* it and then argues substantive law: factual impossibility as a defense to the conspiracy charge. The fundamental issue of this court's jurisdiction deserves a more serious, rational analysis.

Ungar v. Dunkin' Donuts of America, Inc.
531 F.2d 1211, 1225 (3d Cir. 1976)

As an alternative to proving a policy to persuade, the district court would allow illegal use of economic power to be inferred from proof of "acceptance by large numbers of buyers of a burdensome or uneconomic tie." This test, in our view, has the same pragmatic drawback as the policy to persuade test. Assuming that what is "economic" from a franchiser's point of view is "uneconomic" from a franchisee's, this test would render prima facie illegal virtually every franchise system involving "large numbers" of franchisees.

But there is another, equally serious, problem with the district court's alternative theory. Whether we call it "*petitio principii*" or "arguing in a circle" or "begging the question," the brute fact is that this test is based on circular reasoning. Obviously, if the question is whether there is a "tie," proof that large numbers of buyers accepted a burdensome or uneconomic "tie" is not helpful. The "proof" assumes the answer rather than proving it. We understand the argument that proof of acceptance of a burdensome or uneconomic offer of a secondary ("tied") product is some evidence of coercion. We cannot, however, accept the proposition that such proof, alone, would suffice to establish, prima facie, the coercion element of an illegal tie-in claim. Establishing that buyers purchase products A and B from the seller does not establish that the seller ties the sale of product A to the purchase of product B. It merely establishes that buyers purchase products A and B from the seller.

Adams v. Gould, Inc.
687 F.2d 27, 30-31 (3d Cir. 1982)

[W]e believe that in its application of [the cited case], the district court embraced the fallacy of *petitio principii* by assuming the conclusion that sum certain financial rights under the pension plan already had vested in the plaintiffs. The clear words of the pension plan militate against this assumption, for its schedule of priorities for distribution upon plan termination provides that "to the extent that such assets are sufficient," they are to be distributed first to retirees, then to participants with vested interests "in full if the remaining assets be sufficient, otherwise on a proportional basis." Thus, the agreement was drafted in contemplation of a circumstance where there might not be enough money to go around, and the employees' "vested" right was only a right to participate in whatever distribution there might be.

United States v. Torres
583 F. Supp 86, 104-05 (N.D. Ill. 1984)

[A]s to the All Writs Act, its "provision does not enlarge or expand the jurisdiction of the courts but merely confers ancillary jurisdiction where jurisdiction is otherwise granted and already lodged in the court." [T]he statute presupposes existing complete jurisdiction "and does not contain a new grant of judicial power." The government's argument on this point consists of that common fallacy in logic: begging the question, because it assumes that Title III gives a federal judge the authority to issue an order for visual surveillance when it does not.

Lowe v. SEC
472 U.S. 181, 226-27 (1985)
(White, J., concurring)

The Court reasons that given these decisions, which forbade certain forms of prior restraints on speech, the 76th Congress could not have intended to enact a licensing provision for investment advisers that would include persons whose advisory activities were limited to publishing. The implication is that the application of the Act's penalties to unregistered publishers would violate the principles of *Lovell* and *Near;* and because Congress is assumed to know the law, the Court concludes that it must not have intended that result.

This reasoning begs the question. What we have been called on to decide in this case is precisely whether restraints on petitioner's publication *are* unconstitutional in light of such decisions as *Near* and *Lovell.* While purporting not to decide the question, the Court bases its statutory holding in large measure on the assumption that Congress already knew the answer to it when the statute was enacted. The Court thus attributes to the 76th Congress a clairvoyance the Solicitor General and the Second Circuit apparently lack—that is, the ability to predict our constitutional holdings 45 years in advance of our declining to reach them.

Tu Quoque
(You Yourself Do It)

The Sahakians list as a material fallacy circumstances under which an individual who is being criticized will defend his actions by accusing his or her critic of doing the same thing himself. They call it tu quoque, or you yourself do it. [19] But what is sauce for the goose in the law, may not always be sauce for the gander. "Son, I want you never to smoke a cigarette." "But, Dad, you smoke."

Yet, in the law, this tu quoque argument can sometimes be used as an effective defense. Tu quoque is a valid defense in matters of provocation. If lawyer A moves the court for sanctions against lawyer B for delay in responding to interrogatories, it is a good defense for B to show that A is constantly derelict in responding to B's request for answers to other sets of interrogatories. Moreover, under the common law, if the plaintiff in a negligence action was negligent at all, the defendant, if negligent, could in effect say "tu quoque" and thus have a complete defense. Most states now have a comparative negligence law where, if the plaintiff's negligence is below 50 percent, a recovery can be granted and the award adjusted accordingly.

The equitable defense of in pari delicto, which literally means "in equal fault," is rooted in the common law notion that a plaintiff's recovery may be barred by his own wrongful conduct. Traditionally, the defense was limited to situations where the plaintiff bore "at least substantially equal responsibility for his injury," and where the parties' culpability arose out of the same illegal act. Contemporary courts

[19] W. Sahakian & M. Sahakian, *Ideas of the Great Philosophers* 21 (1966).

have expanded the defense's application to situations more closely analogous to those encompassed by the "unclean hands" doctrine, where the plaintiff has participated "in some of the same sort of wrongdoing" as the defendant and is denied recovery.

La Porta v. Leonard
88 N.J.L. 663, 97 A. 251, 252-53 (1916)

The plaintiff alleges that during a proceeding in the recorder's court of the city of Hoboken the defendant, a lawyer of many years standing, remonstrated with him, a colaborer at the bar, in the following manner: 'You are a vermin. You are a disgrace to the bar, and are starting out in the wrong way as a young lawyer. This will give you a black eye. You and your client committed perjury. Your suborned your client.'

This language resulted in a suit at law for slander, in which the plaintiff alleged serious injury to his reputation and standing in the community, and demanded substantial damages by way of reparation. To this demand defendant replied that he did not utter the language, and that, if he did, he was protected in so doing by the legal privilege peculiar to counsel, which, as he conceived, hedges him about in absolute security, so long as his utterances are honestly conceived, to conduce to the advantage of his client.

. . .

. . . [T]he testimony of the defendant shows that the plaintiff at the same hearing expressed himself of and concerning the defendant and his legal modus operandi as follows: 'Mr. Leonard and Mr. S., being shrewd lawyers, so manipulated and coaxed their client that he committed perjury and obtained his judgment by fraud.'

Therefore the defendant upon this trial insisted that, while the remarks which are the basis of this action may not be entitled to receive recognition in any logical compendium of the retort courteous, they may without question be properly classified under the classic appellation of a *tu quoque*. And, if to this to be answered that in a court of law his legal status thus acquired is no answer to the plaintiff's claim for damages, his insistence is nevertheless that the jury should have had the opportunity to consider the offense in question, in conjunction with the serious accusation which provoked it, and that in the light of this provocation the offense charged to him might appear to be but the natural and indignant ebullition of a learned advocate, whose ripe experience in the trials of the forum had reached the didactic stage of the seer and yellow leaf, which entitled him to paternally admonish a neophytic junior, whose practical vision of a legal career is usually circumscribed by the buoyant and unstable perspective of the radiant hues of incipient morn. Concededly in such a status experentia docet. Such an exalted state of mind upon the part of the defendant might be said to exclude any semblance of malice, as an animating motive, and may have supplied raison d'etre upon which a jury might base an argument in mitigation of damages. The trial court declined to so view the case, and, ignoring that contention, charged that the damages to which the plaintiff might be entitled, if they accepted his view of the case, were sufficiently comprehensive to include damages of a punitive or exemplary character, dependent upon their finding the existence of actual malice. In consonance with that view the learned trial court declined to charge the request alluded to, which was as follows: 'If you believe the story of the plaintiff, La Porta, and you find from the testimony that the utterances of the defendant, Leonard, then you may consider this in mitigation for damages.'

The refusal to charge this request, obviously eliminated from the case all consideration by the jury of the question of provocation to which we have adverted, and which was properly a subject for their consideration, as a basis for mitigation of damages. The doctrine which requires the court to submit to the jury the question of provocation, in cases where the complaining party insists upon punitive or exemplary damages, is settled beyond controversy by the great trend of adjudication in this country.

SFM Corp. v. Sundstrand Corp.
102 F.R.D. 555, 559 (N.D. Ill. 1984)

One purely collateral issue merits some discussion, albeit in the nature of dictum as to Sundstrand's Rule 11 motion. SFM's responsive submission to that motion repeatedly implies this Court did not issue findings of fact even though Rule 56(d) required it to do so in the circumstances. That is really beside the mark, for this Court's compliance or non-compliance with Rule 56(d) is irrelevant to SFM's (or its counsel's) liability under Rule 11.

LINGUISTIC FALLACIES

Categorical syllogism Rule 1 insists that the argument contain exactly three terms, each of which is used in the same sense throughout the argument. When different senses are utilized, linguistic fallacies are present.

Equivocation

Equivocation is the fallacy of ambiguity. It refers to the use of terms which are ill-defined, vague, and signify a variety of ideas, none of which can be made clear or precise either by definition or by the context. When we confuse the different meanings a single word or phrase may have, or use a word or phrase in different senses in the same context, we are using it equivocally. The fallacy is committed whenever we allow the meaning of a term to shift between the premises of our argument and our conclusion. The fallacy is especially to be condemned when we give the impression that a term is being used to express only one and the same meaning throughout the argument. Sometimes, this is willful quibbling:

All criminal actions ought to be punished.
Prosecutions for theft are criminal actions.
Therefore, prosecutions for theft ought to be punished.

Any of the three terms of the syllogism may be subject to a shift in meaning, but it is usually the middle term which is used in one sense in one premise and in another sense in the other. Sometimes, this is called the *fallacy of the ambiguous middle.* Avoidance of this fallacy is critical. It is important to keep in mind rule one of the categorical syllogism:

> A valid categorical syllogism must contain exactly three terms, each of which is used *in the same sense* throughout the argument.

Another kind of ambiguity exists in the use of an old term in a new way. Be careful of using abstract buzz words—democracy, the American ideal, equality, etc.—without an *ad hoc* definition of what is meant in the context. In examining legislative history, be careful to understand the meaning of a phrase used by a member of Congress: "This bill is designed to bring peace and order to the marketplace." What did the legislator mean by "peace," "order," "the marketplace"?

Sir Lewis Namier provides an amusing example of a Victorian lady who complained that she did not like a house because it was "*very romantic.*" Her correspondent responded, "I don't understand why you should wish it not to be *very romantic.*" The Victorian lady replied, "When I said romantic I meant damp." [20]

Also to be avoided is a special sub-species of the fallacy of equivocation, what the logicians call *litotes,* double or multiple negatives. Consider Harold Laski's simply delicious statement (reminiscent of some briefs I have read):

> I am not, indeed, sure whether it is not true to say that the Milton who once seemed not unlike a seventeenth-century Shelley had not become, out of an experience ever more bitter each year, more alien [sic] to the founder of that in Jesuit sect which nothing could induce him to tolerate. [21]

[20] L. Namier, "History and Political Culture" in *Varieties of History* 386 (F. Stern ed. 1956).
[21] Discussed by George Orwell, *Politics and the English Language* 156-57 (1953).

United States v. Brawner
471 F.2d 969, 988 (D.C. Cir. 1972) (in banc)

There may be a tug of appeal in the suggestion that law is a means to justice and the jury is an appropriate tribunal to ascertain justice. This is a simplistic syllogism that harbors the logical fallacy of equivocation, and fails to take account of the different facets and dimensions of the concept of justice. We must not be beguiled by a play on words. The thrust of a rule that in essence invites the jury to ponder the evidence on impairment of defendant's capacity and appreciation, and then do what to them seems just, is to focus on what seems "just" as to the particular individual.

United States v. Gil
604 F.2d 546, 548-49 (7th Cir. 1979)

The defendant next argues that since one member of the alleged joint venture has established that his conduct was not criminal, applying the substantive law of conspiracy to the effect that it is impossible to have a conspiracy involving only one person, as a matter of law there is no conspiracy to supply the necessary predicate to admission of Villegas's statements pursuant to rule 801(d)(2)(E). Therefore, he contends, the statements were improperly admitted, and he has been convicted in substantial part because of the out-of-court hearsay statements of a declarant who was not under oath and has not been subjected to cross-examination.

The logical structure of this argument falls, however, because of at least one internal fallacy. It equates "conspiracy" as a concept of substantive criminal law, governing who may be punished for which acts, with "conspiracy" as part of an evidentiary principle, and burdens the latter with all of the theoretical limitations and formal requirements of the former. The two are not the same, though it is likely that any provable criminal conspiracy will satisfy the requirements of the evidentiary rule. Nor have the cases in which the issue has been presented treated them as the same.

City of Amsterdam v. Helsby
371 N.Y.S.2d 404, 417-18, 37 N.Y.2d 19, 332 N.E.2d 290, 300 (1975)

More troublesome would be the fact that the statute beforeus specifies that the arbitrators' award shall be "final and binding" and makes no express provision for review, were it not for accommodations to due process standards arising out of the involuntary quality of compulsory arbitration.

So, we [have previously] said: "At the inception it should be observed that the essence of arbitration, as traditionally used and understood, is that it be voluntary and on consent. The introduction of compulsion to submit to this informal tribunal is to change its essence. It is very easy to transfer, quite fallaciously, notions and principles applicable to voluntary arbitration to 'compulsory' arbitration, because, by doubtful logic but irresistible usage, both systems carry the descriptive noun 'arbitration' in their names. The simple and ineradicable fact is that voluntary arbitration and compulsory arbitration are fundamentally different if only because one may, under our system, consent to almost any restriction upon or deprivation of right, but similar restrictions or deprivations, if compelled by government, must accord with procedural and substantive due process."

Fallacy of Amphibology

The fallacy of amphibology occurs in arguing from premises whose formulations are ambiguous because of their grammatical construction. The double meaning lies not in a term but in the syntax or grammatical construction of a sentence or sentences. Professor Brennan furnishes an excellent example: "I give and bequeath the sum of $5,000 to may cousins Ruth Henning and Sylvia Woodbury." [22] You know that counsel for the beneficiaries are going to

[22] J. Brennan, *A Handbook of Logic* 190 (1957).

claim that each is entitled to $5,000; the estate lawyer will argue that the total sum is not $10,000 but $5,000.

A statement is amphibolous when its meaning is unclear because of the loose or awkward way in which its words are combined. An amphibolous statement may be true on one interpretation and false on another. When it is stated as a premise with the interpretation which makes it true, and a conclusion is drawn from it on the interpretation which makes it false, then the fallacy of amphibology has been committed. [23]

Amphibology differs from equivocation in two important respects: (1) amphibology pertains to the entire argument, whereas equivocation is limited to single terms; (2) the entire argument is susceptible to a two-fold interpretation due to its structure, not to any misuse on the part of the debater.

Amphibologies arise in an argument where meaning is muddled by slovenly syntax—bad grammer, poor punctuation, dangling participles, misplaced modifiers. At the trial of a drunken driver, the arresting officer's testimony was summarized. "When the officer arrested the driver, the officer said he did not know what he was doing." This is an example of amphibology deriving from a relative pronoun with more than one referent. Logicians uniformly cite the classic example: "He said, 'Saddle me the ass.' And they saddled him." [24]

Amphibologies are often attributable to the use of misplaced modifiers: Anthropology is defined as "the science of man embracing woman." Or they are the result of an ellyptical construction: In World War II, we had posters urging all to "Save Soap and Waste Paper." [25]

Thus, amphibologies come in all shapes and forms:

- "Richly carved Chippendale furniture was produced by colonial craftsmen with curved legs and claw feet."
- "Many Americans were outraged when President Theodore Roosevelt had a Negro for dinner."

23 I. Copi, *supra* note 2, at 75.
24 *See* D. Fischer, *supra* note 11, at 267.
25 *Id.*

- "The measures of the New Deal were understandably popular, for many men received jobs, and women also."
- "The ship was christened by Mrs. Coolidge. The lines of her bottom were admired by an enthusiastic crowd." [26]

Some interesting ones might appear as newspaper headlines:

- POLICE CAN'T STOP GAMBLING.
- CARRIBEAN ISLANDS DRIFT TO THE LEFT.
- SUSPECT HELD IN KILLING OF REPORTER FOR VARIETY.
- GREEKS FINE HOOKERS.

Fallacy of Composition

"The fallacy of composition consists of reasoning improperly from a property of a member of a group to a property of the group itself." [27] It is to argue that something is true of a whole which can safely be said of its parts taken separately. [28] The confusion is in an inference that proceeds from the specific to the general. "The defendant in this case is a very wealthy man. He owns a Jaguar." "There are muggings all over Philadelphia. I read about three that happened on Market Street." It also results from the generalization of a universal and collective term. "That cop lied on the stand. All cops are liars." We experience this often in daily life. For example, you visit Chicago for an overnight stopover. The taxi driver is surly; the room clerk is a snob; the waitress at breakfast is impatient. You leave Chicago, return home, and say, "That Chicago is a terrible town. All the people are horrid!"

Stereotypical images also are improperly formed by this fallacy. "Members of the Mafia break the law; therefore, all Americans of Italian origin are law breakers." The Ameri-

[26] *Id.* at 267-68.
[27] *Id.* at 219.
[28] J. Brennan, *supra* note 22, at 190.

can South is often represented as a homogenous unit. A custom in a rural town in South Carolina is attributed to the entire South, although there are many sub-groups in the southern states, extremely different from one another: the Northern Virginia South (suburbs of Washington, D.C), the modern Atlanta-Miami-Houston-Dallas South, the tidewater-Chesapeake South, the Appalachian South, the Carolina low-country South, the Kentucky bluegrass South, the Mississippi levee-and-delta South, the Alabama-Georgia blackbelt South, the Texas cow-country South, the Ozark South, and several distinct Floridian Souths.

In re Dailey
357 F.2d 669, 673 (C.C.P.A. 1966)
(Smith, J., dissenting)

The majority opinion stands without support as to either the facts upon which it predicates the opinion or the law which it applies thereto. Its logic is the fallacious logic which leads to the conclusion that since each of the words in Lincoln's "Gettysburg Address" were individually old and well known at the time he used them, it would have been obvious for anyone of ordinary skill with a dictionary before him, to have written it. It is this logic which supports the conclusion of the majority here from which we may assume that today with "The Gettysburg Address" before him, it would be obvious for any school boy to select the same words and place them in the same order.

Brennan v. United Steelworkers of America
554 F.2d 586, 614 (3d Cir. 1977)
(Aldisert, J., dissenting)

The particulars from which the majority's universals are drawn seem centered around two factual complexes: (1) tellers of *Local 1066* had been guilty of vote fraud; and (2) Sadlowski's opponent, Samuel Evett, was supported by the international union's "official family." I find the sweeping conclusions drawn from these instances to be striking examples of the fallacy of composition and the fallacy of *post hoc ergo propter hoc*. To conclude that, because *local* tellers ran a fraudulent election the *international* union was responsible, is the fallacious error of reasoning that what is true of a part is necessarily true of the whole. To conclude that because international officers supported Sadlowski's opponent in a fraudulent election, the international was therefore responsible for the fraud, is the classic *post hoc* fallacy. The mere chronological sequence of events does not establish a causal connection.

Fallacy of Division

The fallacy of division is the converse of the fallacy of composition. It occurs when you reason falsely from a quality of a group to a quality of a member of the group. We take separately what we ought to take jointly. The same confusion is present as in composition, but this time the inference proceeds in the opposite direction, from the whole to its parts. It argues that what is true of the whole must be true of its parts.

"The Pittsburgh Symphony is the best in the country; therefore, the concertmaster is the best violinist in the land." "Italy has the best pasta in the world. Therefore, if you eat pasta at Giovanni's in Rome you will eat the best dish of pasta in the world." "The Minnesota Twins is the best team in baseball. Thus, the guy who plays second is the best second baseman in baseball."

In re Dailey
357 F.2d 669, 673 (C.C.P.A. 1966)
(Smith, J., dissenting)

As a preliminary observation it is to be noted that all the appealed claims are drawn to a *combination* of elements which separately may be old. This, however, does not warrant the majority in treating the claims as claims to the *individually old elements*. It is the new *combination* of these elements which is claimed.

United States v. Standefer
610 F.2d 1076, 1106 (3d Cir. 1979)
(Aldisert, J., concurring and dissenting)

To consider consequences that might occur in other cases containing factual problems not before us is always legitimate, whether in a lawyer's brief or a judge's opinion, but it is just argument. The rules of logic inexorably limit permissible rhetoric; one risks committing the fallacy of division, erroneously reasoning that what holds true of a composite whole necessarily is true for each component part considered separately, or being seduced into the fallacy of *ignoratio elenchii,* irrelevant evidence, proving unrelated point B instead of point A, which is at issue, or disproving point D instead of point C.

Fallacy of Vicious Abstraction

The removal of a statement from its context, thereby changing the meaning of an argument, is known as the fallacy of vicious abstraction. Statements may be easily and critically altered merely by dropping something out of context. We see this where a general rule is confidently stated, for example, that no deviations will be permitted from a discovery order, although excuse from the rule is contained in an exception clause: "Except where approved by the court or motion made and served in the adversary, no deviations will be permitted from the discovery order."

The Sahakians illustrate this fallacy with four examples, each followed by the correct, complete statement:

> St. Paul said, 'Money is the root of all evil.' ("The *love* of money is the root of all evil.") "Ralph Waldo Emerson said: 'Consistency is the hobgoblin of little minds.' " ("*Foolish* consistency is the hobgoblin of little minds.") "Alexander Pope said, 'Learning is a dangerous thing.' " ("A *little* learning is a dangerous thing; drink deep, or taste not the Pierian spring. There shallow draughts intoxicate the brain, and drinking largely sobers us again.") Francis Bacon said, 'Philosophy inclineth man's mind to atheism.' ("A *little* philoso-

phy inclineth man's mind to atheism, but depth in philosophy bringeth men's minds about to religion.")[29]

Allegheny Gen. Hosp. v. NLRB
608 F.2d 965, 967-68 (3d Cir. 1979)

The Board's initial contention is that, although this court has disagreed with it on the issues of comity and appropriate hospital bargaining units, we must nevertheless enforce the Board order because it is a "reasonably defensible" construction of the National Labor Relations Act. We reject this attempt to emasculate judicial review of NLRB orders by a resort to an isolated phrase taken out of its context in the Supreme Court's opinion—a "fallacy of vicious abstraction."

We conclude, therefore, that the standard of review advanced by the Board is too narrow. The construction put on a statute by the agency charged with administering it is entitled to deference by the courts, and ordinarily that construction will be affirmed if it has a "reasonable basis in law," but "[t]he deference owed to an expert tribunal cannot be allowed to slip into a judicial inertia which results in the unauthorized assumption by an agency of major policy decisions properly made by Congress."

Borough of Lansdale v. Philadelphia Elec. Co.
692 F.2d 307, 311-312 (3d Cir. 1982)

Central to Lansdale's contention that the geographic market should have been determined as a matter of law is its reliance on a single sentence from *Otter Tail Power Co. v. United States:* "The aggregate of towns in Otter Tail's service area is the geographic market in which Otter Tail competes for the right to serve the towns at retail." From this single sentence Lansdale concludes that the relevant geographic market is identical to the service area.

It has been recognized that in [Sherman Act] § 2 cases identification of the relevant geographic market

---

[29] W. Sahakian & M. Sahakian, *supra* note 19, at 15-16.

is a matter of analyzing competition. "The geographic market encompasses the area in which the defendant effectively competes with other . . . businesses for the distribution of the relevant product," it is "defined in terms of where buyers can turn for alternative sources of supply." The definition of the relevant geographic market, therefore, is a question of fact to be determined in the context of each case in acknowledgement of the commercial realities of the industry under consideration. . . .

By dipping into the *Otter Tail* opinion and picking out a single sentence, Lansdale is guilty of the common fallacy of vicious abstraction—the removal of a statement from its context, thereby changing its intended meaning. What was before the Supreme Court in *Otter Tail* is not the issue presently before us: whether determination of the relevant geographic market was for the court or for the jury. Although in *Otter Tail* the relevant geographic market coincided with the aggregate of the towns in the defendant's service area, there is in that opinion no indication that its definition was achieved as a matter of law. Lansdale purports to represent as a decision of the Supreme Court only one line in its *ratio decidendi*. Although the Supreme Court's opinion reduces the definition of geographic market to one sentence, it is clear that it did so only upon determining that the district court had analyzed the extent and sources of competition to the defendant. Thus, we reject Lansdale's contention that the geographic market issue should be resolved as a matter of law.

Argumentum Ad Nauseum

Finally, we just had to include this one—a fallacy that is more understandable than explainable. It is more than an unnecessarily long brief or an exhausting oral argument where the advocate seeks to sustain his position by repetition rather than by reasoned proof or logical development.

We see it everyday in life—brought to us by television commercials, advertising executives, public relations specialists, and political consultants. Is it not obnoxious to look at a television news program every night of the week and see the identical commercial displayed every night? Or to watch a football game and be treated to the same commercial four times in four hours? I am not convinced that such repetition encourages critical consumer existence.

Lewis Carroll's bellman said it all in the *Hunting of the Snark:*

> "Just the place for a Snark!" the Bellman cried,
> As he landed his crew with care;
> Supporting each man on the top of the tide
> By a finger entwined in his hair.

> "Just the place for a Snark! I have said it twice:
> That alone should encourage the crew.
> Just the place for a Snark! I have said it thrice:
> What I tell you three times is true." [30]

SUMMARY

Our purpose in emphasizing the importance of straight thinking by concentrating heavily on formal and informal fallacies is to illuminate pitfalls that you must avoid. Yet, you must not go too far. You must not commit the *fallacist's fallacy.* This means seeing a fallacy pop up behind every bush, under every tree, and around every corner. The advice a noted historian has given to those who chronicle history should help you avoid the fallacist's fallacy:

- *Don't* conclude that an argument which is structurally fallacious in one particular is therefore structurally fallacious in all respects.
- *Don't* conclude that an argument which is structurally false in some respect, or even in all its premises, is therefore substantially false in its conclusion.
- *Don't* conclude that the appearance of a fallacy in an argument is an external sign of its authors' deliberately evil intention.
- *Don't* conclude that an argument devoid of fallacies is, ipso facto, a sound or correct one. [31]

[30] L. Carroll, *The Complete Works of Lewis Carroll* 757 (1936).
[31] D. Fischer, *supra* note 11, at 305.

Our understanding of fallacies can be honed and sharpened in our daily lives. Read editorials and newspaper columns and the digest of news in weekly magazines and put the reasoning to the tests that you have learned. Are the authors guilty of erecting strawmen and knocking them down in the fallacy of irrelevant conclusions? Do they beat their breasts over an answer expressed in a news conference by the President or governor or mayor when the question was loaded with three or four compound parts? Does the content of the editorial, column, or account truly follow logical form? Does it appear as a categorical, hypothetical, or disjunctive syllogism? Do you see ad hominems (appeals to ridicule)?

Pay attention to television correspondents in their thirty-to-sixty-second bites following news accounts. Are they guilty of the fallacy of hasty generalization by prophesizing broad consequences from one single event in a fast breaking story. Do you detect any fallacies of distraction? Appeals to pity or to the masses? Are they guilty of dicto simpliciter, attempting to project a general rule from that which obviously is an exception to the rule? For the apogee of political science fiction, analyze carefully the television comments of Senators and Congresspersons who blithely offer comments on sudden events without a whit of understanding of the underlying factual premises.

Or at the friendly corner tavern, listen to the loud defense of conclusions on church, school, family, religion, and politics. Without entering the discussion yourself (don't ever try to use logical reasoning in a bar), attempt to identify the premises employed by the discussants. Are there any premises? Listen to conclusions that they draw from current facts. Are these permissible inferences, that is, inferences that would reasonably follow in logical sequence based on past human experience, or are they sheer speculation? How about: "I know the game was fixed! How could a team lose three in a row to the Mets when they beat them six times straight?" In the tavern or the cocktail lounge, take an end seat and drink deeply of non sequiturs and post hocs.

But don't get smug. All of us commit fallacies every day in reaching judgments—all of us, and that includes judges, lawyers, professors, preachers, and authors of books. We do this because our thinking is not always reflective. We are "thinking" every waking moment of the day. At any time, there is always a penny for our thoughts. We have day-dreams and reveries. We build castles in the air. We conjure up mental pictures and random recollections. We some-times "think" and "conclude" because we want a certain conclusion. We think that wishing will make it so.

Sometimes, we unwittingly insert a note of invention and add it to a faithful record of observation. We simply want to believe something. We are certain our kids did not smoke pot or mess around. We are totally convinced that our best friends did not say what others reported that they said. We are constantly influenced by emotions, beliefs, and social wants and demands. We are humans; we are not com-puters.

So, sometimes we do draw conclusions by a process that lies somewhere between a flight of fancy and a dispassion-ate weighing of the relevant considerations that should be employed to reach a reasoned conclusion. We must all con-fess to this. But by now you have learned that what is de-sired is reflective thinking and that this involves more than a sequence of ideas. To do our jobs as members of the legal profession, and of community and family units, and to earn the respect of those who know us, and the accolade that we are clear thinkers, we have an obligation. That obligation is to employ reflective thinking when called upon to solve a problem, any problem whether at home, school, church, office, business, or in our social relations. We must respect the canons of reflective thinking, what John Dewey called "a *con*-sequence—a consecutive ordering in such a way that each determines the next as its proper outcome, while each outcome in turn leans back on or refers to, its predeces-sors." [32]

What Professor Dewey said over three-quarters of a cen-tury ago is important and should be our watchword:

> The successive portions of a reflective thought grow out of one another and support one another; they do not come and go in a medley. Each phase is a step from something to some-

[32] J. Dewey, *How We Think* 4 (1933).

thing. . . . The stream or flow becomes a train or chain. There are in any reflective thought definite units that are linked together to a common end. [33]

If we follow these watchwords we will go a long way in avoiding the pitfalls of fallacy.

[33] *Id.* at 4-5.

CHAPTER 12

Conclusion

It is now possible to pull together the varying concepts we have discussed and reach some conclusions about clear legal thinking. In so doing, of course, I am using inductive reasoning to draw certain generalizations from instances I have enumerated.

To offset any criticism that I have unduly emphasized formal inductive and deductive reasoning in the law, and that the legal process involves far more than adherence to logical form, I repeat now what I have tried to emphasize— there is much subjectivity in the value judgments inherent in the legal process. We see this in the galaxy of cases where an appellate court reverses a court inferior in the hierarchy. We also see it in the many cases where dissents are filed. A good example is seen in the majority and dissenting opinions in *MacPherson v. Buick,* referred to in Chapter 5, to illustrate our discussion of syllogisms.

Clearly, value judgments affect the resolution of the three flashpoints of legal conflicts: choosing between or among competing legal precepts to formulate the major premise, interpreting the precept as chosen, and applying the chosen and interpreted precept to facts found by the fact finder.

Involved here is an interrelationship between two terms that sound alike, but whose meanings diverge in the decisional process: "reasonable" and "reasoning." A judge's decision on the choice, interpretation, and application of a legal precept involves a value judgment justifiable in his or her mind because the decision is "reasonable," in the sense that it is fair, just, sound, and sensible. One judge may believe that it is "reasonable" to maintain the law in harmony with existing circumstances and precedents, and accede to the magnetic appeal of consistency in the law; another may assert that the issue should be considered pragmatically, and will respond only to its practical consequences.

What is "reasonable" in given circumstances may permit endless differences of opinion. And this is how it should be. The inevitably varying views found in multi-judge courts is one of the most vitalizing traditions animating the growth of common law. So is the balance between respect for and ongoing reexamination of precedents. In today's jurisprudence, precedents are subject to constant scrutiny. We are all influenced by the tradition of the Holmes-Pound-Cardozo philosophy: The great aim of the law is to improve the welfare of society. We seek to achieve this aim by reaching decisions that are "reasonable."

Determining what is "reasonable," however, is closely related to the overarching process we call "reasoning," or solving a problem by pondering a given set of facts to perceive their relationship and reach a logical conclusion. The application of "reasonableness" to "reason" is an ever-recurring scenario: If A has been found to be liable in set of circumstances B, we have to decide, often without an exact precedent to guide us, whether A is also liable if B obtains plus or minus circumstance C. To do this we must determine which facts are material. Given the situation that A is liable if set of circumstances B applies, we must decide if plus or minus circumstance C is material or immaterial.

Two famous cases dramatically illustrate this. In *Rylands v. Fletcher* [1] the defendant employed an independent contractor to make a reservoir on his land. Because of the contractor's negligence in not filling up some unused mine shafts, water escaped and flooded the plaintiff's mine. The case could have been decided solely on the theory of the contractor's negligence, but the court chose to decide it on the theory of strict liability; it determined that the negligence of the contractor was immaterial. Compare the actual facts of the case with the facts deemed material by the court:

[1] L.R. 3 H.L. 330 (1868).

Actual Facts

D had a reservoir built on his land.
Through the negligence of the contractor
(Our plus circumstance *C*)
Water escaped and injured *P.*
Conclusion: *D* is liable to *P.*

Material Facts as Seen by the Court

D had a reservoir built on his land.
Water escaped and injured *P.*
Conclusion: *D* is liable to *P.*

Thus by the determination that circumstance *C* was immaterial, the doctrine of absolute liability was established in 1868 and is still alive and kicking today.

In *Brown v. Board of Education,* [2] the Court addressed circumstance *B,* black children in segregated schools. It decided that under the doctrine of "separate but equal," no black school could be considered "equal." In *Mayor of Baltimore v. Dawson,* [3] the Court was again presented with a segregation issue—this time minus circumstance *C* (i.e., not in the context of segregated schools). The Court affirmed the Fourth Circuit's ruling that the *Brown* decision would nevertheless apply to end segregation in public beaches and bathhouses. Segregation minus circumstance *C* led to the same result in *Holmes v. Atlanta* [4] (municipal golf course) and *Gayle v. Browder* [5] (buses). When *Browder* came down, it was recognized that, as a matter of law, the entire doctrine of separate but equal was overruled without being limited to the reasons stated in *Brown:* the special and particular problems of segregated education. Changing social and judicial perspectives had rendered that circumstance immaterial.

From this, we can learn something about the process of analogy, which lies at the heart of the system of evaluating precedents. In analogizing, it is mandatory to determine which facts in the previous case are to be deemed material.

[2] 347 U.S. 483 (1954).
[3] 350 U.S. 877 (1955).
[4] 350 U.S. 879 (1955).
[5] 352 U.S. 903 (1956).

227

The decision in a subsequent case depends as much on the exclusion of "immaterial" facts as it does on the inclusion of "material" ones.

I have purposely waited until now—until we have had a full discussion of the methods of deductive and inductive reasoning and an examination of formal and material fallacies—to offer some guidelines in determining what are the positive analogies (resemblances) and negative analogies (differences) to be taken into consideration in applying a putative precedent to a given case. Whether stated facts will serve to provide a true resemblance or a difference is strictly dependent upon whether a court deems those facts to be material. To one judge the added or subtracted circumstances may be immaterial, so that the new case is simply a new instance of a fact scenario governed by a prior case; to another judge they may appear so entirely new as to constitute a material difference, thus, the new case does not fall within the holding of the putative precedent.

The analytical process comes down to this. First, we establish the holding of the case claimed to be a precedent to learn the legal consequence attached to a specific state of facts and exclude any dictum, i.e., suggested legal consequences to hypothetical facts not found in the record. The next step is to determine whether that holding is a binding precedent for a succeeding case in which the facts are prima facie similar. This involves a double analysis. We must first state the material facts in the putative precedent and then attempt to find those which are material in the compared case. If these are identical, then the first case is a binding precedent for the second, and the court should reach the same conclusion as it did in the first one. If the first case lacks any fact deemed material in the second case, or contains any material facts not found in the second, then it is not a direct precedent.

Here are some guidelines to help determine which facts are material and which are immaterial in the process of analogy. [6] I suggest these with some trepidation and advance them not as truths, not even as probabilities, but only

[6] *See* Goodhart, "Determining the Ratio Decidendi of a Case," 40 Yale L.J. 161, 169-79 (1930).

as, to use the most weaselly of terms, "possible possibilities:"

— All facts which the court specifically stated to be material must be considered material.
— All facts which the court specifically stated to be immaterial must be considered immaterial.
— All facts which the court impliedly treats as immaterial must be considered immaterial.
— All facts of person, time, place, kind and amount are immaterial unless stated to be material.
— If the opinion omits a fact that appears in the record this may be due to (a) oversight, or (b) an implied finding that the fact is immaterial. Option (b) will be assumed to be the case in the absence of other evidence.
— If the opinion does not distinguish between material and immaterial facts then all the facts set forth must be considered material.
— A conclusion based on a hypothetical set of facts is a dictum.

The law then, is reduced in the case of the judge, to the art of drawing distinctions, and in the case of the lawyer, to the art of anticipating the distinctions the judge is likely to draw. To be sure, "in a system bound by precedent, such distinctions may often be in the nature of hair-splitting, this being the only instrument at hand for avoiding the consequence of an earlier decision which the court now considers unreasonable or as laying down a principle which is not to be extended." [7]

Let us now pause and place this process in proper perspective. The agony of examining a host of earlier decisions to determine the materiality or immateriality of facts is forced upon us in the practice of law in only a relatively small number of cases. Based on my own judicial experience of almost thirty years, I suggest that 90 percent of the cases appearing before a court of general trial jurisdiction or general appellate jurisdiction fall within two categories: Where the law and its application alike are certain, or where the

[7] *See* Lloyd, "Reason and Logic in the Common Law," 64 L.Q. Rev. 468, 482 (1948).

law is certain and the only question concerns its application to the facts before it, judges are bound by much settled legal doctrine and a great number of statutory rules. [8] The common-law tradition has been followed for over two centuries in this country, and when we began here we had already absorbed centuries of the English common-law experience, recorded at least since the time of Sir Edward Coke and Sir William Blackstone. The oldest appellate court in the United States, the Pennsylvania Supreme Court, has been handing down recorded decisions since 1686.

Justice William O. Douglas has noted the reserves of conceptual grounds for decisions in the hard cases: "There are usually plenty of precedents to go around; and with the accumulation of decisions, it is no great problem for the lawyer to find legal authority for most propositions." [9] The tradition of stare decisis places the judge under an obligation to follow prior judicial decisions unless exceptional circumstances are present. [10] (Here, of course, I beg the question because the presence of such circumstances requires a judicial decision.)

But here we must distinguish between the experience of studying law, where each new case in the textbook is a new adventure, and the experience of lawyers who already have gone through the process of assimilating the complexities of substantive law. Clearly, the student has a long up-

---

[8] My estimate is shared by Judge Cardozo's experience on the New York Court of Appeals and that of Judge Henry J. Friendly on the Court of Appeals for the Second Circuit. "Nine-tenths, perhaps more, of the cases that come before a court are predetermined—predetermined in the sense that they are predestined—their fate preestablished by inevitable laws that follow them from birth to death." B. Cardozo, *The Growth of the Law* 60 (1924). In 1961, Judge Henry Friendly wrote: "Indeed, Cardozo's nine-tenths estimate probably should be read as referring to the first category alone. Thus reading it, Professor Harry W. Jones finds it 'surprising' on the high side. . . . So would I. If it includes both categories, I would not." Friendly, "Reactions of a Lawyer—Newly Become Judge," 71 Yale L.J. 218, 222 n.23 (1961) (quoting Jones, "Law and Morality in the Perspective of Legal Realism," 61 Colum. L. Rev. 799, 803 n.16 (1961)).

[9] Douglas, "Stare Decisis," 49 Colum. L. Rev. 735, 736 (1949).

[10] In a small percentage of cases, no legal principles exist for guidance. These cases require the court to examine some justificatory principle of morality, justice, and social policy. How these abstractions are defined and applied is beyond the scope of this work. I refer you to my earlier book, *The Judicial Process: Readings, Materials and Cases* (West 1976).

hill struggle to arrive at the plateau now inhabited by the lawyers. What may be considered by a lawyer as an "easy" case may be a jaw-breaking one to a student only one-third of the way through a course. Yet "hard" or "easy," I reassert my endorsement of the Pound/Jones test to measure a good decision: not in terms of the correctness or incorrectness of the courts' application of precedents, and not in terms of the result, for this may simply be congruent with one's personal philosophy or inclination, but in terms of (1) how thoughtfully and disinterestedly the court weighed the conflicting interests involved in the case, and (2) how fair and durable its adjustment of the interest-conflict promises to be. The first goes to the "reasonableness" of the court's decision; the second to the logical validity of its reasoning.

Both the study and practice of law consist of problem solving. Because of the doctrine of stare decisis, however, the solving of problems cannot be done on an ad hoc basis. We must respect the overarching consideration that like cases be decided alike. But the beckoning question is always to decide what is a like case. All problems originate in a confused and often complicated setting. To solve a problem fairly and justly we must employ techniques of reflective thinking. That is what this book is all about. The function of reflective thought is to face a situation where there is obscurity, doubt, and conflict, and to transform that situation to one that is clear, coherent, and harmonious with what has gone before and what may occur again. It is a constant effort to suggest, search, and compare, and then suggest, search, and compare again and again.

As the preceding pages have indicated, logical reflective thinking is critically important. It is the cement that binds the determination of "reasonableness" with the statement of "reasons," the explanation or justification of an act. Judges and lawyers give "reasons" to prove that their conclusion is "reasonable." "Reasons" are the how in the process; "reasonableness" is the why. "Reasons" are the logical premises that imply the desired conclusion of "reasonableness." What is used to coalesce "reasons" and "reasonableness" is "reasoning," which we know as a logical process. It has been to the reasoning process that our efforts have been directed in this book.

Logical order in the law is an instrumentality, not an end. John Dewey has told us that "[i]t is a means of improving, facilitating, clarifying the inquiry that leads up to concrete decisions; primarily that particular inquiry which has just been engaged in, but secondarily, and of greater ultimate importance, other inquiries directed at making other decisions in similar fields." [11]

We have emphasized that, unlike in mathematics and science, there are few immutable major premises in the law. Holmes was certainly right when he said that, "[t]he actual life of the law has not been logic; it has been experience. The felt necessities of the times, the prevalent moral and political theories, intuitions of public policy, avowed or unconscious, even the prejudices which judges share with their fellow-men, have had good deal more to do than the syllogism in determining the rules by which men should be governed." [12] But, as we have explained, Holmes was speaking here only of a type of *deductive* logic that has fixed premises. By now it should be clear that by *inductive* logic we witness the drama of developing law to meet felt necessities of the times, current moral and political theories, intuitions of public policy, and the hopes, dreams, and aspirations of an informed society.

Certainly in the reasoning process of the law, we do not intend that the guidelines to materiality, the rules of the syllogism, and the idiosyncrasies of formal and material fallacies be only a "ballet of bloodless categories." [13] Instead, they are vibrant tools of analytic thought used to give force, power, sinew, and respect to a process that adjudicates claims, demands, and defenses asserted by live litigants in very live cases and controversies. They are society's sword and shield to fend off, in Frankfurter's felicitous phrase, "[t]he tyranny of mere will and the cruelty of unbridled, unprincipled, undisciplined feelings." [14]

Our use of logical processes in the law is not perfect. Inductive reasoning does not purport to reach truths; its aim

[11] J. Dewey, *How We Think* 19 (1933).
[12] O. Holmes, *The Common Law* 1 (1881).
[13] Lloyd, *supra* note 7, at 483.
[14] As quoted in the New York Herald Tribune, August 30, 1962, on the occasion of his retirement as a Supreme Court Justice.

is to produce a result that is more probably true than not. Rules of deductive reasoning go further. Properly applied, they present an argument based on the theory that if the premises are true, the conclusion must be true. But the genius of the common law is that these premises are not fixed in cement. In the popular idiom they are always up for grabs to meet changes in our social, political, philosophical, and economic climate. When invention is active, when industry, commerce, and transportation bring about new forms of human relations, and when community relations change because of the extension of ethical and moral ideas, the law is able to keep pace with the variety and subtlety of social change. "Old" new law may sometimes give way to "new" new law.

We know by now that court decisions are not necessarily a precise barometer of the beliefs and demands of society. Always present are the jurisprudential idiosyncracies of the men and women in black robes who sit on our tribunals. Some prize stability and are hesitant to depart from precedent; others, using Justice Walter V. Schaefer's phrase, "view the court as an instrument of society designed to reflect in its decisions the morality of the community, [and] will be more likely [than not] to look precedent in the teeth and to measure it against the ideals and the aspirations of [the] time." [15] Whatever be the judge's view of his or her court, whether as a passive institution or a force for change, the judge must adhere to the canons of logical order to present a reasonable, and therefore, acceptable, "performative utterance."

We end as we began. Our thesis has been straightforward. We do not say that knowledge of these materials is absolutely essential to studying or practicing law. A person may reason correctly without knowing a single rule of the syllogism; conversely, a person may know all the details of logic and not be able to discover truths that are necessary in the law. A guide to logical reasoning, or logic in the law, is tautologically speaking, simply a guide.

But what we do suggest is that an understanding of what we have said here should assist you:

[15] Schaefer, "Precedent and Policy," 34 U. Chi. L. Rev. 3, 23 (1966).

- To develop clarity and consistency in your approach to law.
- To avoid error in analyzing reported judicial opinions.
- To avoid error in preparing and presenting a written or oral argument.
- To detect error in the reasoning process mounted by your adversary.
- To think and reason about difficult matters.
- To avoid the pitfalls of both formal and informal fallacies.
- And most importantly, to develop and improve the specific mental discipline which the study and practice of law demands and requires.

The importance of this mental discipline, commonly called "learning to think like a lawyer," was well summarized by Nicholas F. Lucas, who as a law student in the year that I was born, observed:

> It is by this mental training rather than by the explicit, positive knowledge of its technical rules, that logic gives us the power and habit of thinking clearly. Probably more than any other science, a careful study trains and develops the reasoning powers, not merely the power of thinking consistently, but the power of discovering the truth. [16]

A final word. Logical reasoning and avoidance of fallacies does not always guarantee a solution. There is still the dilemma and counter-dilemma, one of which, "Litigiosus," kept ancient Greek logicians busy for many years:

Protagoras, the Sophist, is said to have agreed to train a certain Euathlus in the art of pleading. Half of the fee was to be paid when the course was completed; the remaining half when Euathlus should win his first case in court. Euathlus delayed undertaking any suit, and Protagoras eventually sued his pupil for the other half of the agreed fee, urging the following dilemma:

> If this case is decided in my favor, Euathlus must pay me by judgment of the court; and if it is decided in his favor, he must pay me by the terms of our contract.

[16] Comment, "Logic and Law," 3 Marq. L. Rev. 203, 204 (1919).

But it must be decided either in my favor or in his.

Therefore, he is in any case obligated to pay.

Euathlus urged the following rebuttal:

If this case is decided in his favor, I am free by the terms of our contract; and if it is decided in my favor, I am free by the judgment of the court.

But it must be decided in his favor or in mine.

Therefore, I am in any case freed of the obligation. [17]

Take your time to work this out. (A couple of years will do.) Happy thinking!

[17] *Id.* at 210.

Bibliography

References are to chapters and footnotes

Aldisert, R.J., *The Judicial Process* (1976), ch.3 n.20; ch.12 n.10

Amsterdam, "Perspectives of the Fourth Amendment," 58 Minn. L. Rev. 349 (1974), ch.2 n.8

Austin, J., *Philosophical Papers* (1961), ch.5 n.3

Brand, N. & White, J., *Legal Writing: The Strategy of Persuasion* (1976), ch.1 n.2

Brennan, J., *A Handbook of Logic* (1957), ch.1 n.8; ch.3 n.7, n.9; ch.4 n.6; ch.9 n.1; ch.11 n.22, n.28

Burton, S., *An Introduction to Law and Legal Reasoning* (1985), ch.1 n.1

Cardozo, B., *The Growth of the Law* (1924), ch.12 n.8

Cardozo, B., *The Nature of the Judicial Process* (1921), ch.2 n.14, n.26, n.34; ch.5 n.4; ch.6 n.12

Carroll, L., *The Complete Works of Lewis Carroll* (1936), ch.11 n.30

Comment, "Logic and Law," 3 Marq. L. Rev. 203 (1919), ch.1 n.4; ch.12 n.16

Complete Works of Lewis Carroll, Modern Library ed. (New York, n.d.), ch.10 n.3

Cooley, J., *A Primer of Formal Logic* (1942), ch.1 n.8; ch.3 n.8; ch.4 n.5

Copi, I., *Introduction to Logic* (7th ed. 1986), ch.1 n.8; ch.3 n.1, n.15; ch.4 n.5, n.6; ch.6 n.3; ch.10 n.1, n.6; ch.11 n.2, n.9, n.12, n.23

Creighton, J., *An Introductory Logic* (1898), ch.1 n.8; ch.4 n.5; ch.9 n.2; ch.11 n.1

Cross, R., *Precedent in English Law* (1968), ch.2 n.29

de Morgan, A., *Formal Logic* (1847), ch.9 n.6

"De Sophisticis Elenchis," in *The Works of Aristotle,* W.D. Ross trans. (1928), ch.9 n.4

Dewey, J., *How We Think* (2d ed. 1933), ch.3 n.4, n.16; ch.4 n.1; ch.5 n.10; ch.6 n.7, n.10, ch.11 n.32; ch.12 n.11

Dewey, "Logical Method and Law," 10 Cornell L.Q. 17 (1924), ch.2 n.9, n.10

Douglas, "Stare Decisis," 49 Colum. L. Rev. 735 (1949), ch.12 n.9

Eaton, R., *General Logic, An Introductory Survey* (1931), ch.1 n.8; ch.4 n.5; ch.9 n.3; ch.11 n.17

Ely, "The Supreme Court, 1977 Term—Foreword: On Discovering Fundamental Values," 92 Harv. L. Rev. 5 (1978), ch.2 n.8

Fischer, D., *Historians' Fallacies* (1970), ch.10 n.11, n.14, n.16, n.24

Freund, "Social Justice and the Law," in *Social Justice* (R. Brandt ed. 1962), ch.2 n.36

Friendly, "Reactions of a Lawyer—Newly Become Judge," 71 Yale L.J. 218 (1961), ch.12 n.8

Fuller, "The Forms and Limits of Adjudication," 92 Harv. L. Rev. 353 (1978), ch.2 n.6

Golding, M., *Legal Resoning* (1984), ch.2 n.33; ch.5 n.11

Goodhart, "Determining the Ratio Decidendi of a Case," 40 Yale L.J. 161 (1930), ch.6 n.11; ch.12 n.6

Holmes, "Codes and the Arrangement of the Law," 5 Am. L. Rev. 1 (1870), *reprinted in* "Early Writings of O.W. Holmes, Jr.," 44 Harv. L. Rev. 725 (1931), ch.2 n.8

Holmes, O. *The Common Law* (1881), ch.2 n.17, n.24; ch.12 n.12

Holmes, "The Path of the Law," 10 Harv. L. Rev. 457 (1897), ch.2 n.1

Hughes, "Rules, Policy, and Decision Making," 77 Yale L.J. 411 (1968), ch.2 n.4

Hutcheson, "The Judgment Intuitive: The Function of the 'Hunch' in Judicial Decisions," 14 Cornell L.Q. 274 (1929), ch.3 n.2

Jevons, W., *Elementary Lessons in Logic: Deductive and Inductive* (1870), ch.1 n.8; ch.4, n.5; ch.5 n.1; ch.6 n.8; ch.10 n.5, n.7; ch.11 n.13

Jones, "An Invitation to Jurisprudence," 74 Colum. L. Rev. 1023 (1974), ch.1 n.6; ch.2 n.18, n.27

Jones, "Law and Morality in the Perspective of Legal Realism," 61 Colum. L. Rev. 799 (1961), ch.12 n.8

Joseph, H., *An Introduction to Logic* (1st ed. 1906), *quoted in* Eaton, *General Logic* (1931), ch.11 n.18

Landau, "Logic for Lawyers," 13 Pac. L.J. 59 (1981), ch.1 n.2, n.3, n.7; ch.9 n.5

Levi, "An Introduction to Legal Reasoning," 15 U. Chi. L. Rev. 501 (1948), ch.2 n.31; ch.3 n.14; ch.6 n.2

Lloyd, "Reason and Logic in the Common Law," 64 L.Q. Rev. 468 (1948), ch.12 n.7

McCall, R., *Basic Logic* (2d ed. 1952), ch.1 n.8

Mill, J. S., *A System of Logic Ratiocinative and Inductive* (8th ed. 1916), ch.3 n.10; ch.4 n.7; ch.6 n.6

Morrow, A., *Collision Course* (1959), ch.11 n.15

Murphy, "Law Logic," 77 *Ethics* (1966), ch.3 n.11; ch.6 n.9

Namier, L., "History and Political Culture" in *Varieties of History* (F. Stern ed. 1956), ch.11 n.20

Orwell, G., *Politics and the English Language* (1953), ch.11 n.21

Plato, *The Republic and Other Works* (B. Jowett trans.), ch.8 n.1

Pound, "The Causes of Popular Dissatisfaction with the Administration of Justice," address *printed in* 40 Am. L. Rev. 729 (1906), *reprinted in* 8 Baylor L. Rev. 1 (1956), ch.2 n.20

Pound, "Hierarchy of Sources and Forms in Different Systems of Law," 7 Tul. L. Rev. 475 (1933), ch.2 n.3

Pound, "Mechanical Jurisprudence," 8 Colum. L. Rev. 605 (1908), ch.2 n.22

Pound, "Survey of Conference Problems," 14 U. Cin. L. Rev. 324 (1940), ch.2 n.16

Sahakian, W. & Sahakian, M., *Ideas of the Great Philosophers* (1966), ch.1 n.8; ch.9 n.7; ch.11 n.19, n.29

Schaefer, "Precedent and Policy," 34 U. Chi. L. Rev. 3 (1966), ch.12 n.15

Smith, M., *Jurisprudence* (1909), ch.2 n.5, n.7; ch.6 n.16

Stebbing, L., *A Modern Introduction to Logic* (6th ed. 1948), ch.1 n.8; ch.3 n.6; ch.4 n.2, n.3, n.4, n.5

Stone, "The Common Law in the United States," 50 Harv. L. Rev. 4 (1936), ch.2 n.11, n.12, n.13

Stone, "Man and Machine in the Search for Justice," 16 Stan. L. Rev. 515 (1964), ch.2 n.37

Summers, "Two Types of Substantive Reasons: The Core of a Theory of Common-Law Justification," 63 Cornell L. Rev. 707 (1978), ch.2 n.35

Traynor, "Reasoning in a Circle of Law," 56 Va. L. Rev. 739 (1970), ch.2 n.39

Truesch, "The Syllogism," in *Readings in Jurisprudence* (Hall ed. 1938), ch.10 n.2, n.4

Von Jhering, R., *Der Geist Des Rominischen Rechts* (1877), ch.2 n.19

Weber, "Value Judgments in Social Science," in *Weber Selections* (W. Runciman, ed. 1987), ch.2 n.38

Whitehead, A., *Adventure of Ideas* (1956), ch.2 n.2

Wigmore, J., *Wigmore's Code of the Rules of Evidence in Trials at Law* (3d ed. 1942), ch.6 n.13

Wisdom, J., *Philosophy and Psycho-Analysis* (1953), ch.5 n.9

Index

References are to pages

A

Accident
Converse fallacy, *see* **Hasty generalization fallacy**
Fallacy of (dicto simpliciter), 143, 190-91

Adams, John Quincy, 35

Adams v. Gould, Inc., 205-06

Adams v. New Jersey Steamboat Co., 103-04

Adjudication
Of specific cases in common-law tradition, 8, 9, 10

Affirmative statement
Proposition as, 57, 58

Affirming the antecedent
Fallacy of, 143, 160-61

Affirming the consequent
Fallacy of, 142, 143, 198-200, 204

Ages
Fallacy of appeal to the (argumentum ad antiquitam), 143, 187

Allegheny Corp. v. Kirby, 198

Allegheny Gen. Hosp. v. NLRB, 12, 18, 219

Allen, Gracie, 202

Ambiguity (equivocation)
Fallacy of, 143, 210-13

Amphibology
Fallacy of, 143, 213-15

Amusement Equipment, Inc. v. Mordelt, 149-50

Analogy
Criteria for argument by, 95-99
Defined, 89
And enumeration compared, 49-50
Example of process of, 50-51
Function of, 39-40
And inductive generalization compared, 89
New precept, forming, by, 100-06
In paradigmatic common-law case, 115, 119-21

Brown v. Board of
Education, 35, 78-79,
227
Burns, George, 202
Burton, Steven I., 2

C

California v. Gardner,
138-39
California v. Sonleitner, 178
Cardozo, B., 11, 15-19, 40,
55-58, 63-64, 95-99,
178-79
Carroll, Lewis, 157, 221
Case law, *see* **Common law**
Case method
Defined, 25
Purpose of, 25
Categorical syllogism
Defined, 44-47
Disjunctive compared with,
164, 165
Fallacies in, 141, 145-59,
210
Inductive reasoning in, 47
Rules for, 46-47
Terms of, in rules, 46
Circular reasoning
Fallacy of, 202
City of Amsterdam v.
Helsby, 213
Civil law
And common law,
distinguished, 11
Clark v. Burns, 103
Coke, Edward, 230
Common law (and
common-law
tradition), 7-24

Common law (*cont.*)
Basic concept behind, 27-28
As case law, 11
Categories of cases in,
229-30
Decisional process in, 10-11
Dedutive reasoning in, 9-10
Defined, 7
Growth of, 7-8
Inductive generalization in,
90-91
Inductive reasoning in, 8-9
Major premise in, 35
Paradigmatic case in,
113-22
Precedent in, 12-13, 88; *see*
also **Precedent**
Recapitulation of
conclusions on, 23-24
Role of logic in, 5-6, 13-18
Statutes compared, 14
Value judgments in, 18-23;
see also **Value**
judgments
Community standards, *see*
Social conditions
Composition
Fallacy of, 143, 215-17
Compound (multiple)
questions
Fallacy of, 143, 200-01
Conclusions
In analyzing deductive
reasoning, 53
Of argument, 36-37
In categorical syllogism, 45,
46
In deductive reasoning, 30,
43-44, 56
In disjunctive syllogism, 163
Fallacist's fallacy in, 221

245

Conclusions *(cont.)*
Grounds for, 27
By induction and deduction, 30
Inductive generalization in, 90
In irrelevance fallacy, 169-70
With negative premises, 157
Non sequitur, 199
In relation with premises, 28-30, 37, 38, 60-62, 66
Truth of, 37
Constitution (U.S.), 21, 35, 72
Continental Group v. Coppage, 30-31
Cooley, J., 6, 29-30, 162
Copi, I., 6, 26, 36, 46, 89, 148, 149, 163-64, 177, 181
County of Lake v. MacNeal, 188
Cresap v. Pacific Inland Navigation Co., 180-81
Crito, 125-32
Crook v. Alabama, 182-83
Cross, R., 16
Crouse-Hinds Co. v. InterNorth, Inc., 162
Cunningham v. MacNeal Memorial Hosp., 189
Curtis, Justice, 75

D

Dailey, In re, 216, 217
Danzig v. Superior Court, 166-67
D'Arcy v. Prison Commissioners, 121

Darrow, Clarence, 176-77
Dawson v. Hillsborough County, 195-96
Decisions
Process of, in common law, 10-11
Process of court, as source of precepts, 14
Test of good, 4-5
Deductive reasoning, 43-47, 53-85
Analyzing, 53-85
Categorical syllogism, in, *see* **Categorical syllogism**
In common law, 9-10
Conclusions from, 30, 43-44, 56
Inductive compared with, 47-48
Syllogisms and, *see* **Syllogisms**
Usefulness of, 232
Value judgments in choice of premises in, 63-85
Del Pilar v. Eastern Airlines, Inc., 198
De Morgan, Augustus, 140
Denying the antecedent
Fallacy of, 142, 161-63
Denying the consequent
Fallacy of, 142, 160-61
Devlin, Lord, 114, 204
Dewey, John, 9-10, 27, 37, 39, 44, 65, 223-24, 232
Dicto simpliciter (fallacy of accident), 143, 190-91
Diplock, Lord, 47, 90, 113-22
Disjunctive syllogism
Categorical compared with, 164, 165

F

Facts
Material and immaterial, 227-29
Factual fallacies, *see* **Material fallacies**
Fallacies, 137-224
Case examples of, 137-39
Defined, 37, 139-40
Formal (logical), defined, 47, 140-42; *see also* **Formal fallacies**
Material (informal), defined, 140-44; *see also* **Material fallacies**
Fallacist's fallacy, 221
False cause
Fallacy of (post hoc ergo propter hoc), 143, 193-99, 216-17
False disjunction (opposition)
Fallacy of, 159
Fischer, D., 180, 192
Formal fallacies
Defined, 47, 140-42
Disjunctive syllogism, fallacy of, 142, 163-67
Four terms, fallacy of, 142, 146-47
Hypothetical syllogism, fallacy of, 142, 159-63
Illicit process of the major term, fallacy of, 141, 154-56
Illicit process of the minor term, fallacy of, 141, 156

Formal fallacies *(cont.)*
Negative premises, fallacy of, 141, 156-59
Undistributed middle, fallacy of, 142, 149-56
Frank, Jerome, 21
Frankfurter, Felix, 4, 232
Franklin, Benjamin, 187
French v. Indiana, 162-63
Freund, Paul, 20

G

Gainey v. Folkman, 197-98
Gayle v. Browder, 227
Generalization
Hasty, *see* **Hasty generalization fallacy**
Inductive, *see* **Inductive generalization**
In mathematics, 87
Georgia S. & Fla. Ry. v. Atlanta Coast Line R.R., 167
Gitlow v. New York, 203
Gluck v. Baltimore, 16
Golding, M., 18
Goldwater v. Carter, 199
Goodell, In re, 109-11
Goodhart, Arthur L., 95
Greenman v. Yuba Power Products, Inc., 101-02
Griswold v. Connecticut, 79-80, 83

H

Hand, Learned, 202-03

Harris case, 67
Hasty generalization
Fallacy of, in inductive
reasoning, 48, 143,
191-93
Principle from, 12-13
Hatcher v. Jackson, 68
Hedley Byrne & Co. Ltd. v.
Heller & Partners
Ltd., 120
Hixson v. Arkansas, 104-06
Hogan v. Florida, 66-67
Holmes, Oliver Wendell, Jr.,
7, 14-16, 20, 40, 64,
232
Holmes v. Atlanta, 227
Hughes, G., 8
Hunching
Defined, 26
Hutcheson, Joseph C., Jr.,
26
Hynes v. New York Central
Railway Co., 16
Hypothetical syllogism
Fallacies in, 142, 159-63

I

Ignoratio elenchi (fallacy of
irrelevant evidence),
142-43, 169-75, 199,
218
Illicit process
Of major term, fallacy of,
142, 154-56
Of minor term, fallacy of,
142, 156-58
Imperfect disjunctive, 142

Implication
And inference
distinguished, 29-30
Induction
Conclusions by, 30
In legal logic, 35-36
Inductive generalization
Analogy compared with, 89
Common law development
through, 90-91
Defined, 48, 49, 88
Enumeration in, 88, 91-93,
99; see also
Enumeration
Precedent (stare decisis),
87-88
Truth in, 88, 93
Universal proposition by,
56-58
Uses of, 88-89
Inductive reasoning, 47-51,
87-112
By analogy, see **Analogy**
In common law, 8-9; see also
Common law
Deductive compared with,
47-48
Hasty generalization fallacy
in, see **Hasty**
generalization
fallacy
Inductive generalization in,
see **Inductive**
generalization
Truth in, 35, 232-33
Inference
Agreement needed to
proceed with, 157
Defined, 29
Of factual conclusions,
31-32

LOGIC FOR LAWYERS

Material (factual) fallacies (*cont.*)
Linguistic fallacies, *see* **Linguistic fallacies**
Non sequitur, fallacy of, 142, 143, 161, 198-200, 204
Tu quoque, fallacy of, 143, 207-10
Mayor of Baltimore v. Dawson, 227
McCall, R., 6
McCulloch v. Maryland, 72-73
Menora v. Illinois High School Assocs., 150
Middle term, 29
In categorical syllogism, 45, 46
Defined, 45, 53, 54
Mill, John Stuart, 33, 50, 91
Miller, Charles A., 39
Minor premise
Defined, 44
In disjunctive syllogism, 163
Examples of, 37, 38, 56-58
Inductive reasoning in, 47
Minor term in, 45, 46
Minor term, 29
In categorical syllogism, 45, 46
Defined, 45, 53, 54
Fallacies of illicit process of, 141, 156
Monroe, James, 187
Multiple (compound) questions
Fallacy of, 143, 200-01
Murdoch v. Pennsylvania, 38
Murphy, Jeffrey G., 35, 93

N

Namier, Lewis, 211
Near case, 206
Negative analogies
Defined, 50, 91-92, 227-29
Negative premises
Fallacy of, 141, 156-59
Negative statement
Proposition as, 57, 58
Negatives
Double or multiple, 211
Non sequitur (it does not follow) 142, 143, 198-200, 204
Novelty
Fallacy of appeal to (argumentum ad novitam), 187

O

Omitted premise, *See* **Enthymeme**
Otter Tail Power Co. v. United States, 219, 220
Particular proposition
Defined, 56-58
Patterson v. Board of Supervisors, 183-84
Pennsylvania R.R. Co. v. Reading Co., 167
Performative utterance, 63
Persuasion, 37
Argument and, 39
Scrutiny of legal reasoning in, 69-71

252

Petitio principii
Fallacy of
(begging-the-question),
143, 201-07
Philosophy
Jural, *see* **Value
judgments**
Pity
Fallacy of appeal to
(argumentum ad
misericordiam), 143,
176-79
Plessy v. Ferguson, 12, 78,
79
Plato, 125, 177
Pope, Alexander, 218
Positive analogies, 50
Post hoc ergo propter hoc
(false cause, fallacy
of), 143, 193-99, 216-17
Pound, Roscoe, 4-5, 8, 12-16,
70
Precedent (stare decisis)
Concept of, 11
Defined, 12-13, 88
And gathering principle
from specific instance,
13
Inductive reasoning behind,
87-88
As major premise, 63
Precepts, legal
Analogy in the forming of
new, 100-06
Evolution of, 43, 99-100
Inductive generalization
and, 49
In legal analysis, 65
In paradigmatic
common-law case, 114
Principles as, 9, 10

Precepts *(cont.)*
As rules of law, 8; *see also*
Rules of law
Source of, 14
Value judgments in, 19-23
Value judgments, legal
reasoning and, 70
Premises
Of argument, 36
Fallacies in, 141
Omitted, *see* Enthymeme
In relation to conclusion,
28-30, 37, 38, 60-62, 66
In rules of categorical
syllogism, 46
Value judgments as source
of, 63-65
See also **Propositions**
Prestige
Fallacy of appeal to
(argumentum ad
verecundiam), 143,
179-81
Principles
In common law, 11
From hasty generalizaton,
12-13
As precepts, 9, 10
And rules, distinguished, 12
From rules of decision, 8
Rules of law as, 13
Social conditions and, 14-17
Value judgments in, 19-23
Propositions
Argument as group of, 36
Authority for most, 230
Conclusion and, 37
Defined, 28
Evolution of, 35-36
Major, defined, 35
Sources of, 29

253

Propositions *(cont.)*
Term and, 28-29
Universal, 56-58
See also **Premises**
Prosyllogism
Defined, 60-62
Protagoras, 234-35
Prudential Ins. Co. v.
Cheek, 203

Q

Quaternio terminorum
(fallacy of four terms),
146-47

R

Reasoning
Defined, 36
Socratic method of, *see*
Socratic method
See also **Deductive**
reasoning; Inductive
reasoning; Legal
reasoning
Reasons
Defined, 36-37
Reflective thinking
Defined, 25-28
Importance of, 231
Rehnquist, William H., 81
Resemblances
In analogy, 50-51, 91-93,
116-17
Rhetoric, 37

Ridicule
Fallacy of appeal to
(argumentum ad
hominem), 143, 181-86
Roe v. Wade, 38, 80-82
Royer v. Florida, 152-53
Roosevelt, Franklin D., 192
Rostow, Dean, 21
Rule
Precedent as narrow, 12; *see*
also **Precedent**
Rules of law
Altering content of, 64-65
Analogy and change in, 18
Development of, 102
Precepts as, 8; *see also*
Precepts
As principles; 13; *see also*
Principles
Social conditions and, 14-17
Universal proposition from,
see **Inductive**
generalization
Value judgments in, 19; *see*
also **Value**
judgments
Russell, Bertrand, 34
Rylands v. Fletcher, 55, 226

S

Sahakian, Mabel and
William, 6, 142, 207,
218-19
Saint Francis College v.
Majid Ghaiden
Al-Kazraji, 173-74
Saint Paul, 218
Salmon, W., 156, 163
Schaefer, Walter V., 233

Schiaffo v. Helstoski, 137-38,
171-72
*Scott v. Commanding
Officer,* 34
*SFM Corp. v. Sundstrand
Corp.,* 210
*Shaare Tefila Congregation
v. Cobb,* 174
*Shapiro v. Merrill Lynch,
Pierce, Fenner, &
Smith, Inc.,* 174-75
Sheward v. Virtue, 101
Smith, Munroe, 5, 8, 100
Smith v. Leurs, 117
Social conditions
Analogy influenced by,
106-12
Good decisions and, 4-5
The law and, 14-17, 232,
233
Major premises in light of,
63-65
See also **Value judgments**
Social justice
As organon of law, 64
Socrates, 124-32, 146, 177
Socratic method, 123-35
Daily use of, 123
And hypothetical
syllogisms, 159
In law school, 124-25 132-35
Learning logic by, 25-26, 28
And reasoning by analogy,
95
In Socrates/Crito dialogue,
125-32
Soto v. Texas, 171
Spencer v. Texas, 148-49
Stanley v. Georgia, 84-85
Stare decisis, *see* **Precedent**
State v. Werkheiser, 184

State v. Zespy, 155-56
Statutes
Major premise in, 35
As source of precepts, 14
Stebbing, L., 6, 29, 44
Stone, Harlan Fiske, 10, 11
Stone, Julius, 21-22
Stewart, J. P., 82
Strawman fallacy (irrelevant
evidence fallacy),
142-43, 169-75, 199,
218
Summers, Robert S., 20
*Sunward Corp. v. Dunn &
Bradstreet, Inc.,*
196-97
Syllogisms
Analyzing, 53-59
Canons of, 53-54
Criticizing, in criticizing
legal reasoning, 69-71
Defined, 44
In *Dorset Yacht Co. v. Home
Office,* 116, 117
Episyllogism and
prosyllogism, 60-62
Examples of, 37, 38, 44
Fallacies in, *see* **Fallacies**
Formal fallacies in, *see*
formal fallacies
Term of, 28-29; *see also*
Terms
Validity and truth of,
distinguished, 65-66
*See also specific types of
syllogisms; for
example;* **Categorical
syllogism**

255

T

Taft, Martha, 186
Taft, Robert A., 186
Taney, Roger, 73
Taylor v. State, 182
Terms
Fallacies in, 141
Of logic, 28-39; *see also*
**Major term; Middle
term; Minor term**
Proper content of, 65-66
Of the syllogism, 53-54
Terror
Fallacy of appeal to
(argumentum ad
terrorem), 143, 187-90
Thomas v. Winchester, 96,
97
**Thomas Walter Swan,
Hand,** 202-03
*Tose v. First Pennsylvania
Bank, N.A.,* 31
Traynor, Roger J., 22,
100-02, 106
Traynor v. Turnage, 91
*Tri-Boro Bagel Co. v.
Bakery Drivers
Union Local 802,* 159
Truth
Of conclusion, 37
Of inductive generalization,
88, 93
Inductive reasoning, 35,
232-33
Reasoning as logical
relation between more
than one, 26, 27
Validity and, of syllogism,
distinguished, 65-66

Tu quoque
Fallacy of (you yourself do
it), 143, 207-210

U

Undistributed middle
Fallacy of, 141, 147-54
Undistributed proposition
Defined, 56-58
Undistributed subject term
Defined, 46
*Ungar v. Dunkin' Donuts of
America, Inc.,* 204-05
United States v. Berrigan,
147, 175
United States v. Brawner,
212
United States v. Gabriner,
192-93
United States v. Gil, 212
United States v. Jannotti,
172-73, 203-04
United States v. Menke, 67
United States v. Standefer,
20, 39, 170-71, 218
United States v. Torres, 206
United States v. Williams,
199-200
*United Telephone Co. of
the Carolinas, Inc. v.
FCC,* 161
Universal proposition
Defined, 56-58

V

Value judgments
In choice of premises, 63-85

About Clark Boardman Company

Clark Boardman Company, Ltd. has been a leading publisher of landmark reference works for the legal community for over seventy years. Founded in 1916, and a member of the International Thomson Organisation Limited since 1980, the company today enjoys both a national and international reputation for publishing and servicing quality legal treatises, handbooks, and newsletters in diverse specialities. Among its acclaimed publications are the Securities Law Series, Criminal Law Series, Environmental Law Series, Federal Practice Series, Intellectual Property Law Library, and the Immigration Law Library.

Clark Boardman is constantly strengthening its tradition of excellence by defining emerging legal trends and publishing them in authoritative, cutting-edge reference tools that set the highest standards of coverage. And our products are updated with the same scholarship and care that went into the original volumes. So whether it's an ongoing or special legal reference need, Clark Boardman has the resources everyone needs—resources that are today's cutting-edge publications and tomorrow's classics.

Examination copies of books under consideration for class adoption are available upon request. For a copy of Clark Boardman's current catalog of publications, please write to:

Marketing Department
Clark Boardman Company, Ltd.
435 Hudson Street
New York, NY 10014

Or order by calling toll-free: 1-800-221-9428 (in N.Y.S. call collect: 0-212-645-0215). If you prefer, you may also fax your order by calling 212-924-0460.